The Written Dead

D1523162

CONTRIBUTIONS TO ZOMBIE STUDIES

White Zombie: *Anatomy of a Horror Film*. Gary D. Rhodes. 2001

The Zombie Movie Encyclopedia. Peter Dendle. 2001

*American Zombie Gothic: The Rise and Fall (and Rise)
of the Walking Dead in Popular Culture*. Kyle William Bishop. 2010

*Back from the Dead: Remakes of the Romero
Zombie Films as Markers of Their Times*. Kevin J. Wetmore, Jr. 2011

*Generation Zombie: Essays on the Living Dead
in Modern Culture*. Edited by Stephanie Boluk and Wylie Lenz. 2011

*Race, Oppression and the Zombie: Essays on Cross-Cultural Appropriations
of the Caribbean Tradition*. Edited by Christopher M. Moreman
and Cory James Rushton. 2011

Zombies Are Us: Essays on the Humanity of the Walking Dead.
Edited by Christopher M. Moreman and Cory James Rushton. 2011

The Zombie Movie Encyclopedia, Volume 2: 2000–2010. Peter Dendle. 2012

Great Zombies in History. Edited by Joe Sergi. 2013 (graphic novel)

Unraveling Resident Evil: *Essays on the Complex Universe
of the Games and Films*. Edited by Nadine Farghaly. 2014

"We're All Infected": Essays on AMC's The Walking Dead
and the Fate of the Human. Edited by Dawn Keetley. 2014

Zombies and Sexuality: Essays on Desire and the Living Dead.
Edited by Shaka McGlotten and Steve Jones. 2014

…But If a Zombie Apocalypse Did *Occur: Essays on Medical,
Military, Governmental, Ethical, Economic and Other Implications*.
Edited by Amy L. Thompson and Antonio S. Thompson. 2015

*How Zombies Conquered Popular Culture: The Multifarious Walking
Dead in the 21st Century*. Kyle William Bishop. 2015

Zombifying a Nation: Race, Gender and the Haitian Loas on Screen.
Toni Pressley-Sanon. 2016

*Living with Zombies: Society in Apocalypse in Film, Literature
and Other Media*. Chase Pielak and Alexander H. Cohen. 2017

The Written Dead: Essays on the Literary Zombie.
Edited by Kyle William Bishop and Angela Tenga. 2017

The Written Dead

Essays on the Literary Zombie

Edited by
KYLE WILLIAM BISHOP *and*
ANGELA TENGA

Afterword by Robert G. Weiner

CONTRIBUTIONS TO ZOMBIE STUDIES

VAN PELT AND OPIE LIBRARY
Michigan Technological University
HOUGHTON, MICHIGAN

WITHDRAWN

McFarland & Company, Inc., Publishers
Jefferson, North Carolina

ISBN (print) 978-1-4766-6564-1
ISBN (ebook) 978-1-4766-2968-1

LIBRARY OF CONGRESS CATALOGUING DATA ARE AVAILABLE

BRITISH LIBRARY CATALOGUING DATA ARE AVAILABLE

© 2017 Kyle William Bishop and Angela Tenga. All rights reserved

*No part of this book may be reproduced or transmitted in any form
or by any means, electronic or mechanical, including photocopying
or recording, or by any information storage and retrieval system,
without permission in writing from the publisher.*

Front cover image: Shannon Eberhard, *Whistler's Mother
as a Zombie with Book* (ink/digital, 5" × 7") © 2017

Printed in the United States of America

*McFarland & Company, Inc., Publishers
Box 611, Jefferson, North Carolina 28640
www.mcfarlandpub.com*

Table of Contents

v

SEP 0 4 2018

SEP 0 4 2018

Preface

A Note from the Editors

Zombies have garnered considerable scholarly attention in recent years. Kyle William Bishop's *American Zombie Gothic*, Stephanie Boluk and Wylie Lenz's *Generation Zombie*, Deborah Christie and Sarah Juliet Lauro's *Better Off Dead*, Dawn Keetley's *"We're All Infected,"* Chase Pielak and Alexander H. Cohen's *Living with Zombies*, and Wayne Yuen's *The Walking Dead and Philosophy* are familiar titles to students of zombie culture. This volume not only features contributions from a number of those who have written or edited these volumes or otherwise contributed to this body of existing scholarship, but also represents the first scholarly effort to address the zombie as a specifically literary phenomenon.

In doing so, the essays featured in this collection necessarily participate in a process of selection and exclusion that might be considered a step toward establishing a canon of sorts. As editors and scholars, we consider the primary works addressed in this volume important in the realm of the written dead. However, we are also conscious of the limitations of our efforts. Because of practical and logistical considerations, some works have received less attention than we would have liked. We therefore wish to recognize, formally, that while we are aware of our role in defining a nascent canon of zombie literature, we do not wish to draw attention *only* to the works that are covered here. Rather, we hope that others will be inspired to study the literary zombie both more closely and more widely and to engage in an ongoing dialogue about the growing body of zombie literature.

We are grateful to the talented scholars who enthusiastically committed themselves to this project. We hope that their insights promote greater scrutiny of literary zombies and provide a resource for those who wish to deepen their appreciation of the written dead.

Introduction

The Rise of the Written Dead

Angela Tenga *and* Kyle William Bishop

For every filmgoer who has ever lamented, "It just wasn't as good as the book," the zombie narrative has traditionally offered a refreshing anomaly. Zombie films have rarely been the source of this sort of disappointment because, for most of the history of the zombie, there has been no print predecessor to which a film could be compared. Unlike many of the familiar monsters of our popular culture—especially the ubiquitous vampire—the zombie did not leap from folklore to page and then to stage and screen.[1] Instead, it passed from folklore to stage and screen with minimal print coverage and, for most of its existence as a popular narrative in Western culture, remained largely a screen phenomenon.

Until recently, that is.

Two of the most popular and highest-grossing zombie films in history, Marc Forster's *World War Z* (2013) and Jonathan Levine's *Warm Bodies* (2013), are, in fact, adaptations of literary works, drawing upon source novels by Max Brooks (2006) and Isaac Marion (2010), respectively. Clearly, we now find ourselves at an exciting point in the development of the zombie in popular culture. Zombies are increasingly the subject of all sorts of fictional treatments—not merely movies, comic books, or video games—from short stories to novels, and their gripping stories have been taken on by established writers of genre fiction, critically acclaimed authors, and emerging talents. It has taken an unusually long time, however, for the zombie to reach this point in its evolution, and this kind of "reverse adaptation" of the subgenre makes studying this literary phenomenon important. What took the zombie so long to infect literary fiction in the same way that it has come to dominate horror cinema? Why are we now seeing such a proliferation of zombie-themed short stories, novels, and even poetry?

2

The Origins of Zombie Literature

The matter of where and how zombie literary fiction began is open to debate. Certainly precedents exist around the world—from the oft-cited reference to the goddess Ishtar's threat to raise the dead from their graves to eat the living in the *Epic of Gilgamesh*, to Mary Shelley's flesh golem *Frankenstein*, to even the Christian New Testament's account of the raised Lazarus—but our study focuses primarily on the evolution of the literary zombie as a distinct phenomenon and especially on works that apply this specific label to the reanimated dead or the contagiously infected. While accounts of the raised dead, reanimated corpses, the resurrected, or the merely hypnotically mesmerized can be found throughout the history of oral and written fiction, the zombie as a bloodthirsty, mindless, and contagious threat—in the spirit of the cinematic tradition of George A. Romero or Danny Boyle—has only recently manifested in popular short stories and novels, such as Neil Gaiman's "Bitter Grounds" (2003), Sherman Alexie's "Ghost Dance" (2003), Stephen King's *Cell* (2006), Colson Whitehead's critically acclaimed *Zone One* (2011), and M.R. Carey's revisionist *The Girl with All the Gifts* (2014).

Nonetheless, we would be remiss if we overlooked certain works that contributed to the popularization of the figure of the reanimated corpse as monster. Certainly Shelley's *Frankenstein*, the tale of a lonely monster pieced together from dead body parts, brought to life, and abandoned by his maker, provides an important backdrop for the evolution of zombie fiction. In particular, it evokes the theme of irresponsible science—what Noël Carroll calls the "overreacher plot"[2]—a thread that is woven into the fabric of later zombie fiction. We can look, for example, to H.P. Lovecraft's tales of "Herbert West—Reanimator," published in serialized form in *Home Brew* in 1922. In Lovecraft's *Frankenstein* parody, in which a mad scientist develops a serum that can be injected into human cadavers to reanimate them, readers will easily recognize the influence of Shelley, yet they may also glimpse the approach of the more popular figure of the zombie.

Millennial zombie works continue to adapt and reshape this tradition in response to cultural forces. For example, in Brian Keene's *The Rising* (2003), villainous science plays its traditional role: particle physicists (whose real-life counterparts at CERN faced a lawsuit when the Large Hadron Collider was about to begin operations in 2008) are conducting secret experiments that bring about a zombie plague when an accelerator accident leads to demonic possession of the dead, who return to hunt and feed on the living. While Keene's zombies are reanimated through supernatural agency, the activities of the scientific community provide the interdimensional gateway that allows the demons to reanimate and control dead bodies. Keene's work is exceptional in that its zombies behave more like Victor Frankenstein's creature than most zombies do: they are articulate, thinking, planning creatures. Lia Habel's *Dearly, Departed* (2011) also imagines zombies that are fully conscious and still very human, but here it is only the intervention of science that allows them to function in this manner. Habel very consciously evokes Shelley's work through names and circumstances: protagonist Nora Dearly's father is Victor Dearly, a scientist who has lost his beloved wife, Elizabeth; his friend, Henry, whose home is in Shelley Falls, is killed because of him. The novel is set in postapocalyptic New Victoria, a technologically advanced society that has adopted cultural practices from Victorian England, and the link to Victorian monster literature is reinforced and extended in the names of Nora's love interest, Bram, and his friend, Renfield. Victor Dearly, however, is a new man of science who seeks a vaccine for the virus that causes the zombie transformation. Habel's work resonates deeply with the plight of the inheritors of the *Frankenstein* legacy, who are still fighting to master a nature that refuses to yield to their advances. The Romantic movement of Shelley's time challenged the supremacy of science, whereas today's undead voice the disillusionment of a generation that has largely accepted the sovereignty of science, only to find that science is not its savior; people must still age and die. Our resentment at this failure is figured as the massive return of the dead. In recognizing that human efforts to overcome the laws of nature inevitably fail, the zombie figure has thus evolved over time to reflect our changing relationship to science, embodiment, and mortality.

While zombie narratives such as these are clearly operating within *some* literary tradition, the more direct antecedent for the modern zombie tale must be sought in the milieu of folklore, first-person nonfiction accounts, and sensational travel narratives. As many readers will already be aware, the zombie is a mythological figure from Africa that migrated to the USA via Haiti and the slave trade. It was primarily brought to the attention of Americans in 1929 via William Seabrook's *The Magic Island*,[3] a travelogue that chronicles the author's adventures in Haiti, where he claims to have seen real zombies—that is, people who had been transformed into mindless slaves through sorcery. Under the tutelage of his local guide, Constant Polynice, Seabrook learned of the existence of this "living dead" creature, a monster similar to those found in Europe yet uniquely original and distinctly terrifying. Seabrook writes,

> As Polynice talked on, I reflected that these tales ran closely parallel not only with those of the negroes in Georgia and the Carolinas, but with the mediaeval folklore of white Europe. Werewolves, vampires, and demons were certainly no novelty. But I recalled one creature I had been hearing about in Haiti, which sounded exclusively local—the *zombie*.
>
> It seemed (or so I had been assured by negroes more credulous than Polynice) that while the *zombie* came from the grave, it was neither a ghost, nor yet a person who

had been raised like Lazarus from the dead. The *zombie*, they say, is a soulless human corpse, still dead, but taken from the grave and endowed by sorcery with a mechanical semblance of life—it is a dead body which is made to walk and act and move as if it were alive.[4]

In other words, the New World afforded its people a "New Monster," and, not surprisingly, this folkloric terror of the former slave nation of Haiti manifests primarily a fear of enslavement. These creatures were not allowed the natural rest of the dead but were instead forced to continue their existence, unnaturally, as slaves in this world, used for criminal purposes or simply as farm hands who labored ceaselessly in the sugarcane fields—forever.

Seabrook's scandalous account of this mythology, though now widely discredited, struck a chord in the popular imagination. In 1932, just a few years after the publication of *The Magic Island*, Kenneth S. Webb's *Zombie: A Drama of Startling Revelations* opened at the Biltmore Theatre in New York. Inspired by Seabrook's work, *Zombie* is set in Haiti and depicts the plight of the unfortunate dead who have been reanimated to serve as slaves to a prosperous planter. Though Webb's play did not meet with critical acclaim—offering, according to a *New York World-Telegram* review by William Boehnel, "more reasons for laughs than spinal chills"[5]—it inaugurated the early era of zombie productions. *Zombie* inspired Victor Halperin's *White Zombie* (1932), a film that also met with lukewarm critical reviews.[6] Yet the zombie, a monster perceptually original to the Americas rather than a recycled European creature,[7] continued to appear in the years that followed, especially on the silver screen, in films such as *Ouanga* (1935, directed by George Terwilliger), *King of the Zombies* (1941, directed by Jean Yarbrough), or the critically heralded *I Walked with a Zombie* (1943, directed by Jacques Tourneur).[8] It wouldn't take long for filmmakers such as Romero to take the zombie mythology in a more ferocious and frightening direction, a move that would pave the way for the "zombie renaissance" that we continue to enjoy today.

Seabrook's book was not the only literary account of zombies that would serve as thematic inspiration for aspiring and savvy filmmakers, nor does zombie literary fiction appear only in the wake of Halperin's landmark film. In fact, Halperin's scriptwriter on *White Zombie*, Garnett Weston, had published one of the earliest fictional zombie short stories the year *before* either Webb's play or Halperin's film was released. Published under the pen name of G.W. Hutter,[9] "Salt Is Not for Slaves" appeared in *Ghost Stories* magazine in August of 1931,[10] and it imagines an interview with an ancient Haitian woman who is intimately familiar with zombies. This Marie recounts for the unnamed narrator the legend of how salt, when ingested, overcomes the effects of enslavement, returning the "zombie" to its current, natural state— that is, death. Hutter's story, while original, nonetheless echoes a tale found in Seabrook's work: when a woman takes pity on her zombie "herd" and gives them a confection that, unbeknownst to her, contains salt, the zombies "knew that they were dead and made a dreadful outcry and arose and turned their faces toward the mountain."[11] Marie's account is similar, offering the following grisly description of her fellow workers after they had tasted of the forbidden mineral:

> "I stood in amazement looking at their bare feet. They seemed unaware of the glass [on the floor], unaware of everything. Great gashes were in their feet. As he lifted his feet ceaselessly across the floor, two of Tresaint's toes dangled like broken palm leaves. The wounds had a strange unnatural appearance. There was no sign of blood.
> "Horrified I looked in Tresaint's face. His eyes did not move, his nostrils and mouth gave no sign of breathing. And as I looked I saw his face set in rigidity, the flesh seemed to drop away leaving nothing but cheek bones and eyes. His ribs stood out through the torn shirt—bare.
> "I screamed in horror. He was dead! They were all dead! They were corpses treading a fantastic dance of death."[12]

Hutter's story vividly emphasizes the liminal status of zombies, creatures that are both living and dead, corpses that remain ambulatory yet lack consciousness or human agency. Furthermore, "Salt Is Not for Slaves"—not to mention Seabrook's account presented above—demonstrates how the uncanny horror of the zombie can be conveyed effectively through words alone.

The Zombie as Literary Figure

In 2006, when the contemporary zombie renaissance was getting into full swing, Kyle William Bishop claimed that the zombie genre failed to enjoy a rich literary tradition prior to the film age primarily because the monsters are essentially visual in nature.[13] While it is true that the traditional zombie is particularly well suited for visual media such as cinema, comic books, and video games—especially after Romero upped the ante on the visceral horror of the creature—skilled writers can nonetheless tap into their readers' imaginations to craft abject visions whose horror matches, if not surpasses, that of screen zombies. In addition to the literary examples already presented, more recent zombie works masterfully illustrate the power and potential of this kind of literature. For example, John Ajvide Lindqvist's *Handling the Undead*, published in Swedish in 2005, exploits the graphic nature of the risen dead. Lindqvist takes a particularly realistic approach to his reanimates, an approach that remains effective even when translated into English:

> [David's wife Eva's] arm jerked, hitting against his legs. She sat up without warning. David instinctively backed up. The blanket slid off her, there was a quiet clinking and … no, he had not realised the full extent of it at all.
> Her upper body was naked, the clothes had been cut away. The right side of her

chest was a gaping hole bordered by ragged skin and clotted blood. From it came a metallic clanking. For a moment, David could not see Eva, he only saw a monster and wanted to run away. But his legs would not carry him and after several seconds he came to his senses. He stepped up next to the bed again.

Now he saw what was making the sound. Clamps. A number of metal clamps suspended from broken veins inside her chest cavity. They swayed and hit against each other as she moved.[14]

Lindqvist's undead Eva is certainly horrifying, with her ragged skin and clotted blood, and fulfills much of a reader's generic expectations for the creature.[15] But she is also notably *pathetic*. Lindqvist's skills as a writer, coupled with the fundamental quality of written narratives, allow him to draw his reader's attention to small details that might go unnoticed or be dismissed as insignificant by a casual film viewer.

Literary zombie narratives have thus begun to demonstrate much untapped potential in this versatile creature—from beast to victim, from monster to slave, from antagonist to protagonist. Perhaps one of the most literary examples of the "new" zombie of the twenty-first century can be found in Whitehead's multilayered and complex *Zone One*. Early in the novel, when protagonist "Mark Spitz" encounters a trio of dead office workers long trapped in an abandoned skyscraper in New York, their tragic state and pathetic condition are described for readers with shocking detail:

After all this time, they were a thin membrane of meat stretched over bone. Their skirts were bunched on the floor, having slid off their shrunken hips long ago, and the dark jackets of their sensible dress suits were made darker still, and stiffened, by jagged arterial splashes and kernels of gore. Two of them had lost their high heels at some point during the long years of bumping around the room looking for an exit.[16]

For Whitehead, zombies are more than just supernatural monsters, more than just feeble slaves with blank faces and empty eyes. He presents readers with zombies that are the physical embodiment of death itself, animated corpses that show all the signs of death and decay without the normally prerequisite immobility. Yet, as with Lindqvist's undead, these "new" zombies are strikingly moving, victims of a fate *worse* than death, manifestations of a new kind of horror, one that seems foreign to Romero's canon yet hauntingly familiar to the original, Haitian versions of the walking dead.

The zombie's (d)evolution into a pathetic monster aligns neatly with contemporary trends in monster narratives. The representation of monsters as victims—another legacy of *Frankenstein*—has been fashionable since the last third or so of the twentieth century, when, as William Patrick Day has suggested, vampires became lonely, alienated protagonists, endowed with "artistic sensibility, wisdom, and insight" but cursed with a dark secret; this complex duality, Day argues, made the vampire a figure of "the apotheosis of the human."[17] Anne Rice's Vampire Chronicles (1976–) present the suffering of Louis de Pointe du Lac, a vampire who despises his monstrosity and avoids taking human lives. In the world of young adult fiction, Stephenie Meyer's Cullen vampires (from the Twilight series, 2005–2008) offer a similar model of the monster-victim, and they also eschew drinking human blood. Such reformed vampires paved the way for a surprisingly nuanced version of the zombie—one whose internal struggles were more readily expressed in words than in images. Influenced by its vampiric relatives, zombie-victims have come to perform as proxies for society's victim-turned-monster. In this respect, the zombie also responded to other trends in popular literature. For example, the protagonist of Jeff Lindsay's Dexter novels (2004–2015) is a likeable serial killer whose turn toward the monstrous is linked to a severe childhood trauma. It seems natural, then, that the zombie would participate in this movement toward a softening of the monstrous, an attitude of compassionate recognition or pity.

At the same time, and perhaps to offset the softening tendency, the zombie also has retained its monstrosity so that it can serve as a figure of threat. In the late twentieth and early twenty-first centuries, the zombie has been interpreted as a figure of many cultural anxieties—as a projection of rampant consumerism, a vector of infection, a slave of capitalism, and the contemporary individual drained of distinctive qualities and unique identity, among others. In the current context, however, one of the most interesting perspectives on how zombies mean comes from the view of the zombie as a figure of the posthuman. If the zombie has, as Sarah Juliet Lauro and Deborah Christie argue in the introduction to their collection *Better Off Dead: The Evolution of the Zombie as Post-Human*, "not just evolved within narratives … [but] in a way that transforms narrative,"[18] the zombie narrative's recent evolutionary leap into literature seems to signal an important interpretive opportunity and perhaps even a historic moment. In particular, if we find, as Lauro and Christie do, that the zombie has manifested "most recently as an expression of our own evolving relationship to new technologies,"[19] what does it mean that zombie narratives have "devolved" by going from screen to page rather than developing in the traditional page-to-screen direction? Why have zombies, after spreading from the big screen to the smaller screens of video games and television, now migrated to the page in an era that increasingly favors digital media and frequently questions the future of print culture?

Kiene Brillenburg Wurth has noted that "paper has long been implicated in the construction of humanness and subjectivity in Western culture [...] literature—and the novel in particular—has been a mediator of human identity and consciousness, and the construction of an individual, humanistic subjectivity in Western culture has often been associated with the reading of books."[20] If the evolution of the zombie *as a figure* has provided a channel for expressing uncertainty about the future of the human subject in a time of rapid technological advancement and radical shifts in the relationship between humans and machines, the evolution of zombie narrative has done the opposite. The literary zombie restores the role of the page as a locus of individual subjectivity in the digital age. The appearance of literary zombies challenges assumptions about the end of print culture and demonstrates that the screen has not supplanted the page. Despite the explosion of zombie narrative in films, video games, television shows, and webisodes, the invention of "the written dead" was not only inevitable, but also necessary.

The written dead are evolutionary masterpieces and exemplars of adaptation. Unlike their zombie subjects, who are driven by a need to devour that which they once were, the written dead do not seek to consume their digital counterparts. Instead, they celebrate intertextuality by borrowing from, building on, and referring freely to their screen antecedents. Adam-Troy Castro's "Dead Like Me," a short story featured in John Joseph Adams' *The Living Dead* anthology, is a prime example of this feature of written zombie narratives. Set in a postapocalyptic wasteland, it is structured as a set of survival tips offered by a narrator who, readers infer, is the younger brother of Ben from Romero's *Night of the Living Dead* (1968). This strategy breaks the border between film and literature by inviting readers to bring their knowledge of the cinematic history of the figure of the zombie to bear on a textual issue. The story stands on its own even if the reader does not possess this knowledge; however, the savvy reader enters a cross-medial space that bridges print and screen. Meaning is situated in the space between the cinematic past and the literary present.

The living dead creature is, in a sense, a fitting figure of the printed page. Forever frozen in a state from which it can no longer evolve, the zombie defies the ceaseless onslaught of progress in a world of feverishly paced technological advancement. The published page, too, is fixed, no longer subject to perpetual change like its digital successors. As more and more of our artistic productions are crafted in visual media, zombie literature reminds us of the viscerality of the page. The written dead are a logical material response to the zombie's insistent corporeality. They Gothicize the zombie by grounding it in a form that is increasingly associated with archaic practices of a past world that refuses to submit to the finality of the grave. This impulse is artfully rendered in Alden Bell's *The Reapers Are the Angels* (2010), which exploits the Southern Gothic style and its traditional concern with the persistence of the past to produce a tale that self-consciously merges the literary past with conventions of contemporary zombie apocalypse fiction. Bell's novel, perhaps more than any other, insists that the reader apprehend the zombie as a distinctly literary phenomenon. And those of us who continue to be fascinated by the zombie—as fans, scholars, or both—can no longer ignore this growing force, these "written dead."

Examining the Written Dead

While academic attention has been increasingly directed toward the zombie as a cultural figure, the majority of scholarly investigations focus on films, television serials, video games, and even comics. Key monographs such as Jamie Russell's *Book of the Dead: The Complete History of Zombie Cinema* (FAB Press, 2005), Kim Paffenroth's *Gospel of the Living Dead: George Romero's Visions of Hell on Earth* (Baylor University Press, 2006), and Bishop's *American Zombie Gothic: The Rise and Fall (and Rise) of the Walking Dead in Popular Culture* (McFarland, 2010) limit their critical investigations to cinematic manifestations of the zombie, and critical anthologies such as Shawn McIntosh and Marc Leverette's *Zombie Culture: Autopsies of the Living Dead* (Scarecrow Press, 2008) and Christopher M. Moreman and Cory James Rushton's *Zombies Are Us: Essays on the Humanity of the Walking Dead* (McFarland, 2011) have very limited engagement with literary zombies. While collections such as Stephanie Boluk and Wylie Lenz's *Generation Zombie: Essays on the Living Dead in Modern Culture* (McFarland, 2011) and Christie and Lauro's *Better Off Dead: The Evolution of the Zombie as Post-Human* (Fordham University Press, 2011) include some essays on the literary zombie—such as "Gray Is the New Black: Race, Class, and Zombies" by Aalya Ahmad and "'Off the page and into your brains!': New Millennium Zombies and the Scourge of Hopeful Apocalypses" by Margo Collins and Elson Bond—relatively few academic articles focus primarily on zombie literature, and no monograph or scholarly anthology is dedicated entirely to the written dead—until now.

The goal of this anthology is to provide an extensive collection of current academic essays that investigate the social, cultural, and literary significance and merit of a host of innovative and imaginative stories, novels, and narratives that push the boundaries of the zombie figure as both a traditional and nontraditional monster, as a supporting character, or even as a protagonist. This volume is divided into four sections that trace the "lifespan" of the literary zombie.

The first section, "Zombie Literature—First Words, Baby Steps," offers insight about both the origins of zombie literature and the innovations that have led to the current explosion of interest in the written dead. In the first essay, Kevin Alexander Boon tracks the transformation of early representations of the zombie as slave or drone to its later incarnation as flesh-eating menace. Boon pinpoints the 1980s as an important turning point: in the preceding decades, zombie fiction had been written largely in response to the popularity of the cinematic zombie, but zombie literature flourished in the 1980s, forging new paths that would later be followed by zombie films. In the next essay, Bernard Perron argues that since the early 2000s, literature has in fact surpassed film as the most important medium for zombie narrative.

Perron's essay examines how the written articulation of the zombie body, the names applied to the undead, and the sounds attributed to the living dead reflect innovations that are especially suited to print. In the third essay, Laura Hubner examines short fiction about zombies to explore how this particular form provides a special experience of some of the core questions of zombie narratives, such as the values that give meaning to human life. In particular, she argues that the short-fiction form adds urgency to the questions that frame the story's structure and its message.

The second section, "Max Brooks—Rite of Passage," focuses on the literary contribution of one of the most important innovators in zombie writing. *The Zombie Survival Guide* (2003) and *World War Z: An Oral History of the Zombie War* (2006) brought the written dead to the attention of readers around the world. Marcus Leaning reads the two works as exempla of the late-modern condition. Leaning argues that these works critique large-scale global capitalism and showcase the efficacy of individual and community actions that are explicitly noncapitalist. W. Scott Poole paints a more ambivalent picture of Brooks' work in his essay. Poole highlights the ambivalence of *World War Z*, which he views as ideologically confused—a confusion that he finds rooted in American uncertainty about geopolitics and the nature of war in an era in which the nation fears hordes of faceless enemies who must be contained or destroyed.

Having completed its rite of passage in section two, the literary zombie is ready to be approached as an "adult" literary form in section three, "The Zombie Novel—Coming of Age." The essays in this section explore the written dead's connection with artistic traditions and with their sociopolitical context. Cory James Rushton places Carrie Ryan's *The Forest of Hands and Teeth* series (2009–2011) within the Gothic tradition in his essay. Reading Ryan's series against Ann Radcliffe's *Romance of the Forest* (1791), Rushton demonstrates how Ryan's work draws not only on traditional Gothic elements like ruins and antiquity, but, importantly, also on the features of traditional Gothic heroines, who often struggle against oppression but need a strong male to save them. Wylie Lenz then argues that emphasizing the cinematic precedent of the literary zombie has led to widespread neglect of the zombie's important heritage in another literary tradition: the apocalyptic plague narrative. Lenz examines Colson Whitehead's *Zone One*—the novel widely considered the pinnacle of zombie literature—alongside Daniel Defoe's *A Journal of the Plague Year* (1722), placing the written dead in a more comprehensive literary context. Kelli Shermeyer's analysis of *Zone One* in her essay focuses on how the novel participates in discourse on the politics of diagnosis. She argues that Whitehead's version of the zombie apocalypse articulates institutional practices of coding and recoding "normality" that resonate with the current cultural moment.

The fourth section, "Revisionist Novels—Entering Maturity," addresses the diversity and complexity of the mature zombie novel—an instrument of social commentary, a mirror for the human condition, and a marvel of adaptation. Dawn Keetley examines how David Moody's Hater trilogy uses the unusual perspective of one of the infected to express a distinctly postmillennial anxiety. Keetley argues that the psychology of the enraged zombie subject in Moody's trilogy reflects a social-political-economic environment that is effectively producing enraged "zombie" subjects. In the next essay, Steven Holmes discusses another novel written from the point of view of a zombie subject: Marion's *Warm Bodies*. Holmes proposes that by situating his narrative within a system of allusion to Shakespeare's *Romeo and Juliet* and its theatrical legacy, Marion uses intertextual play as a means of modulating the novel's critique of the state of the individual subject within global consumerism. Next, Arnold T. Blumberg addresses Mira Grant's creation of a "virtual soapbox" in her Newsflesh series (2010–2012). Blumberg argues that Grant, speaking through the voices of blogger Georgina Mason and her colleagues, uses the zombie narrative as a tool for instructing readers about their reality. Kyle William Bishop looks at how Carey's *The Girl with All the Gifts* offers insight about the problems and possibilities of teaching. In this tale, Bishop finds a warning against objectifying, labeling, and stereotyping students in favor of an invested, student-centric pedagogy that promotes learning and growth. Jesse Stommel reads Cormac McCarthy's *The Road* (2006) as a novel that is zombic in both form and substance, a story of emptiness told in stark, blank prose without ornamentation or even chapter breaks. Empty people and their empty landscape are the zombies here, Stommel argues, in a desolate world where everyone is undead.

Collectively, these essays constitute the first focused scholarly effort to address the growing body of zombie literary fiction. The past decade has seen a veritable explosion of this specialized subgenre, and this rapid proliferation is a significant development within a wider popular cultural phenomenon. The rise of zombie novels, short stories, plays, and poetry both responds to and sustains the wider popularity of zombies in contemporary culture, whether in other forms of narrative—such as films, comic book serials, video games, and television programs—or consumable products—such as toys, tee shirts, bumper stickers, and lunchboxes. For so long the zombie was the epitome of visual horror; now, however, we are beginning to see what a powerful and prominent role that same creature can play in literature. Situated within traditions of print culture, psychological narrative, and horror literature, zombies teach us about our fears, our values, and our cultural moment. The new zombie literature is the evolved voice of the ravenous undead monster that has fascinated generations. We hope that this collection will encourage further attention to what the zombie, now more than ever, is telling us.

NOTES

1. Dendle, *Zombie Movie Encyclopedia*, 3.
2. Carroll, *Philosophy of Horror*, 118.
3. While undoubtedly the most famous and the most influential, Seabrook wasn't the first writer to present a version of the zombie creature to Western readers. As early as 1889, journalists and ethnographers such as Lafcadio Hearn were publishing their allegedly true encounters with the walking dead, establishing the scanty literary tradition that marks the foundation of our study. In "The Country of the Comers-Back" (1889), for example, Hearn recounts his experiences with myths and legends of the undead during his two-year stay on the island of Martinique (Haining, Introduction, 15).
4. Seabrook, *Magic Island*, 93.
5. Qtd. in Rhodes, *White Zombie*, 256.
6. For more on *White Zombie's* critical reception, see Gary D. Rhodes' thorough study *White Zombie: Anatomy of a Horror Film*, 121–24.
7. See Bishop, *American Zombie Gothic*, 38.
8. Note that Tourneur's film does have a literary tradition, although *I Walked with a Zombie* is primarily inspired by Charlotte Brontë's *Jane Eyre* (1847) rather than a novel or story about Haitian zombies.
9. Hutter was his wife's maiden name.
10. Haining, Introduction, 14.
11. Seabrook, *Magic Island*, 98.
12. Hutter, "Salt Is Not for Slaves," 47.
13. Bishop, "Raising the Dead," 197.
14. Lindqvist, *Handling the Undead*, 24.
15. Mark Seltzer's discussion of the consumption of serial killer narratives within American "wound culture" also provides insight about the role that images like Lindqvist's have played in the surge in popularity of zombie narratives. Wound culture, Seltzer argues, reflects "the public fascination with torn and open bodies and torn and opened persons, a collective gathering around shock, trauma, and the wound" (Seltzer, *Serial Killers*, 1).
16. Whitehead, *Zone One*, 14.
17. Day, *Vampire Legends*, 34.
18. Lauro and Christie, Introduction, 2.
19. *Ibid.*, 3.
20. Wurth, "Posthuman Selves, Assembled Textualities," 76.

Trailing the Zombie Through Modern and Contemporary Anglophone Literature

KEVIN ALEXANDER BOON

The beginning of zombie literature is more difficult to pin down than the beginning of zombie film. Most writers mark the start of zombie film in 1932 with RKO's release of *White Zombie* (directed by Victor Halperin), the first film to use the term "zombie." Those of us who contend that a zombie by any other name is still a zombie lean toward the 1920 release of *The Cabinet of Dr. Caligari* (directed by Robert Wiene) as the start of zombie film.[1] However, in Anglophone literature, the term "zombie" does not arrive fully formed. It emerges over a period of nearly two centuries, during which time its meaning undergoes radical transformations before coalescing into our conventional understanding and application of the term. Its journey through the lexicon, particularly in twentieth-century zombie literature, branches off into semantic tributaries, each variation resulting from cultural influences on the term's meaning and usage. Some paths trail off into obscurity while others lead to contemporary, mainstream representations of the zombie.

Ultimately, a pattern emerges in the relationship between zombie literature and zombie film. Zombie literature (which originally appropriated the zombie mythos from African oral traditions) begins to follow innovations in zombie film during the middle of the twentieth century, only to regain its place as the primary source of innovation in the late 1980s and 1990s.

Precursors

The term "zombie" (variously spelled—for example, "zombi," "Nzambi") finds its first reliable Anglophone appearance in the 1819 publication of the

15

third volume of Robert Southey's *History of Brazil*, where it is applied to the elected chief of a seventeenth-century community of escaped slaves who resided in the Palmares. The term reflects the esteem in which the population held their chief and summons the earliest known use of the word "zombi"—as a term referring to a god ("Nzambi") worshiped in the lower Congo region. This positive application of the term continues into the twentieth century; it appears in more modern works, such as John H. Weeks' *Among Congo Cannibals* (1913), where it refers to a "supreme being."[2] However, the zombie as we've come to know it in contemporary literature and film descends from a separate etymological path that branched off from the original line following the introduction of slavery to the West Indies in the sixteenth century. By the late eighteenth and early nineteenth centuries, the term "zombie" for many in the region had come to refer to a soulless corpse rather than a spirit god—a source of fear rather than a source of awe.[3]

The zombie initially finds its way into Western literature, film, and popular culture by way of the writings of cultural tourists from the West who visited the region in the late nineteenth and early twentieth centuries. These reports of island culture(s) are filtered through Western bias and ingrained racism. Works such as Spenser St. John's incendiary *Hayti or the Black Republic* (1884), for example, use zombie mythology as a means of denigrating the African population, linking such beliefs to childish superstitions in an attempt to characterize the people of the region as primitive, uncivilized, and incapable of effective self-government. St. John writes of the people's "superstition with regard to *zombis, revenants,* or *ghosts.*"[4] Lafcadio Hearn in *Two Years in the French West Indies* (1890) posits that the zombie myth might be based on "that form of nightmare in which familiar persons become slowly and hideously transformed into malevolent beings"[5] and claims that "the word ['zombi'] is perhaps full of mystery even for those who made it, [and that] the explanations of those who utter it most often are never quite lucid."[6] Hearn asserts that the zombie has come to represent vague, malignant, supernatural creatures, such as "ghosts"[7] and other dangerous beasts along the lines of "goblins."[8] We must be cautious to avoid accepting biased Western writing about non–Western cultures as accurate, but it is from these vagaries—which reflect the inability of Westerners to divine local island culture(s)—that Western notions of zombies in Anglophone literature arise.

Before Brains

The first period in zombie literature arises from Woodrow Wilson's invasion of Haiti in 1915, which is why the earliest zombies in literature are usually referred to as "Haitian" zombies. The U.S. occupation of the island from 1915–34 marks the beginning of zombie literature as a genre of literary fiction, as it is here that the term "zombie" finds its first homogenous incarnation as the Haitian zombie of voodoo lore, which falls into a classification of zombie to which I refer as the "zombie drone."[9] It is our first proper type of zombie and is founded on the writing of Americans who traveled to Haiti and other islands in the West Indies during the first part of the twentieth century. Some key works were Martha Warren Beckwith's *Black Roadways* (1929), John Houston Craige's *Black Bagdad* (1933), and W.B. Seabrook's highly influential *The Magic Island* (1929), which offers a seminal definition for the creature. Seabrook writes,

> It seemed ... that while the *zombie* came from the grave, it was neither a ghost, nor yet a person who had been raised like Lazarus from the dead. The *zombie*, they say, is a soulless human corpse, still dead, but taken from the grave and endowed by sorcery with a mechanical semblance of life—it is a dead body which is made to walk and act and move as if it were alive.[10]

This description defines the zombie, almost exclusively and with only slight alterations, through fifty years of zombie literature and about forty years of zombie film (until George A. Romero's *Night of the Living Dead* in 1968).

Inspired by Seabrook and others,[11] fictional works about zombies began to appear with regularity in the early 1930s. In 1932, *Zombie*, the play, opened at the Biltmore Theatre in New York City, and *White Zombie*, the film, hit theaters; the two works are credited to different writers despite striking similarities between them (*White Zombie* credits Hollywood writer Garnett Weston, while *Zombie* credits playwright Kenneth Webb). Neither work received critical acclaim, but both were popular. In 1933, Vivian Meik published a short story that was also titled "White Zombie." It is important to note that the subtext of these early works is largely racial and centers on the possibility of a *white* person becoming a zombie. The title "White Zombie" plays to racist, xenophobic fears prevalent among white, Western audiences in the same manner that precursory accounts of the West Indies do. All forty-eight U.S. states had laws against mixing of races in the 1930s, and the early focus on the possibility of "white" zombies suggests that much of the fear that zombies generated early on is attributable to an ingrained fear of miscegenation among white Americans. In contrast, the fear among citizens in the West Indies, we might theorize, was more likely informed by a fear of returning to a life of slavery and the inability to escape slavery even in death.

The first work of literary fiction to qualify as zombie literature is arguably H.P. Lovecraft's "Herbert West—Reanimator," which was serialized in *Home Brew* in 1922. Lovecraft's six-part story does not feature either a Haitian zombie or a variant of the zombie drone, nor does it use the word "zombie";

nevertheless, it is one of the most important early works of zombie fiction. The influence of Mary Shelley's *Frankenstein* (1818) is apparent in "Reanimator." Both deal with medical students who obsessively pursue the secrets of life and death. Both involve the procurement of dead tissue from graveyards. In both, attempts to resurrect the dead lead to horrific consequences. But there is a key difference. Frankenstein's monster is a new creature brought to life from dead tissue, one that develops into an articulate, rational being and is driven to violence only when confronted by the cruelty of the world. Herbert West's creatures are still dead, but are endowed with what Zora Neale Hurston calls "a mechanical semblance of life"[12] and are compelled to violence by their nature. While Victor Frankenstein's creature is more man than monster, Herbert West's creatures are more monster than man.

Lovecraft's use of the reanimated dead is prescient. The type of zombie he describes does not appear in film until Romero's *Night of the Living Dead,* forty-six years later, and does not appear in literature again for a decade after that. Lovecraft's "Reanimator" is the first work of literature to link the zombie to the ghoul and the eating of human flesh, an honor reserved exclusively for Romero among zombie film aficionados, but one that belongs more properly to zombie literature and Lovecraft.

> He [Herbert West] usually finished his experiments with a revolver, but a few times he had not been quick enough. There was that first specimen on whose rifled grave marks of clawing were later seen. There was also that Arkham professor's body which had done cannibal things before it had been captured and thrust unidentified into a madhouse cell at Sefton, where it beat the walls for sixteen years.[13]

Lovecraft is describing a zombie ghoul, a type of zombie that dominates virtually all tales of zombies in the twenty-first century.

With the notable exception of "Herbert West—Reanimator," emerging zombie fiction in the 30s and 40s dealt exclusively with the Haitian zombie— the shambling, soulless dead reanimated for mysterious and often nefarious purposes. These works appeared almost exclusively in pulp publications and cheap paperbacks and employed zombies of the type mentioned in Hurston's *Tell My Horse*. In a radio appearance on the Mary Margaret McBride show in 1943, Hurston echoes Seabrook's definition of a zombie: "A zombie is supposed to be the living dead. People who die and are resurrected, but without their souls. And they can take orders. And they're supposed to be ... never to be tired. And to do what the master says without cease."[14]

Most pulp zombie writing during the first phase of zombie literature was of questionable quality and written largely for its sensationalism, a point vividly evident in Richard E. Goddard's *The Whistling Ancestors*, a convoluted 1936 novel that involves an evil doctor intent on using his considerable knowledge of voodoo (among other talents) to conquer the world. The zombies in these works would be considered tame by conventional standards, mostly plot devices that add an element of mystery to otherwise conventional plots.

Pulp writer Theodore Roscoe's novel *A Grave Must Be Deep,* which was serialized in *Argosy* from 1934 to 1935, is a representative example of how the zombie was utilized in these early works. The plot follows an artist's model (Patricia Dale) who is named as potential heir to a large Haitian estate (Morne Noir[15]) after her uncle is presumed to have been murdered (he reappears later, reportedly as a "zombie"). She travels with her artist boyfriend (Cartershall) to the island and is exposed to the exotic region and its people. There is talk of zombies in the novel, but this talk, like the descriptions of the strange surroundings, is primarily designed to imbue the story with mood. Roscoe's *A Grave Must Be Deep* draws on the mystery genre as Lovecraft's "Reanimator" draws on Shelley's *Frankenstein,* and the novel is essentially a mystery novel set in an unfamiliar location. The caretaker and seven other possible heirs to the estate are brought to the island, and after the uncle's voodoo burial, the first seven on the list are murdered under curious circumstances until the heroine is the only remaining heir. She and her artist friend proceed to unmask the mystery, which ultimately involves an intricate rum-running business driven into financial ruin after the repeal of prohibition. As a mystery, *A Grave Must Be Deep* foreshadows Agatha Christie's *And Then There Were None,* which appeared four years later in 1939.

The use of the zombie and island voodoo as an exotic backdrop in *A Grave Must Be Deep* bears a striking resemblance to Peter Tremayne's *Zombie!* (1981). As in Roscoe's novel, *Zombie!* recounts the trials of a man and woman (a married couple, Steve and June Lambert) as they travel to the fictional Caribbean island of St. Maquelon.[16] June, like Patricia Dale in *A Grave Must Be Deep,* is heir to an island estate—this time after the death of a grandmother. *Zombie!* is also essentially a mystery. The Lamberts uncover a plot by a former dictator (Colonel Gum, fashioned after former Haitian president, Papa Doc Duvalier) to regain control of the region through voodoo. The significance of these and other striking similarities between Roscoe's *A Grave Must Be Deep* and Tremayne's *Zombie!* is that the two publications are separated by almost fifty years: *A Grave Must Be Deep* first saw print in 1934–35; *Zombie!* was first published in 1981. Thus, the two novels bookend the first phase of zombie fiction—a period that witnessed almost no change in the basic nature of the zombie myth.

The initial interest in zombie fiction in the 1930s continued into the 1940s, but began to wane by the 1950s and 1960s. Fewer works of zombie fiction were being published just as zombie movies were gaining ground and moving "beyond ... [the zombie's] stagnant, two-decade-old paradigm."[17] Part of the decline in zombie fiction during this time may be attributed to the growth of television. In the 1930s and 1940s, pulp magazines such as *Astounding Stories* and *Weird Tales* provided large audiences of young readers with a regular supply of strange and horrifying stories, but by the mid–1950s, pulp magazines had lost much of their audience and were forced out of business, leaving fewer potential markets for zombie fiction. The markets that remained had grown weary of the shambling zombie drone of Haitian lore. Innovation was needed, but zombie literature resisted change and continued to use the zombie as a tool to generate atmosphere long after the jungle noises, unblinking eyes, strange rituals, and dark, lumbering figures had lost their exoticism for Western audiences. One of the core problems with early zombies is that they lacked agency. They were always under the control of someone else and therefore not a direct source of danger. Without orders, they were nothing more than standing corpses, and once one became accustomed to the idea of a dead person moving around, there was little to fear from them. They were easy to defeat, too. To get rid of them, one had only to feed them salt, and they would meander back to their graves. The actual source of danger originated with the master who controlled the zombies. He was the focus of the narrative and the thing to be feared. By the 1950s and 60s, zombies in literature had largely become props.

Meanwhile, zombie cinema was experimenting with new directions for the zombie. The zombie drone that had captured the public's imagination with *White Zombie* in 1932 began to evolve after the initial flurry of interest. While literary works clung to the zombie's voodoo origins until the early 1980s, screen zombies, as Peter Dendle points out, "largely left their voodoo origins behind"[18] by the 1960s and 1970s. In 1968, *Night of the Living Dead* hit theaters, giving birth to the zombie ghoul in cinema and directing the course of future zombie films. When film zombies revitalized interest among audiences, publishers took notice and, in the 1970s, turned once again to zombie literary works, but fiction writers were slow to embrace the zombie ghoul and tended toward earlier depictions of the zombie as a reanimated worker-bee under someone else's control.[19] Zombie fiction of the 1970s adhered to tradition. As a consequence, it lacks the visceral terror of films from the same period. For example, Hugh B. Cave's *Legion of the Dead*, a novel whose use of voodoo and zombies varies little from the voodoo and zombies found in Roscoe's writing in the 1930s, was first published in 1979, around the same time Romero's *Dawn of the Dead* (1978) and Lucio Fulci's *Zombie* (1979) were released in theaters. Cave's ambling dead, who would have terrified audiences in the 1930s, were no match for the gory, flesh-eating creatures of the cinema.

After Brains

In the 1980s, writers finally abandoned the shambling, controlled, slavish, atmospheric zombie-prop crafted from West Indies mythology and, taking their lead from Romero's films, adopted a more dangerous zombie, one that did not obey orders, one with a taste for human flesh. If 1968–83 was "The Golden Age" for zombie film, as Dendle claims,[20] then the 1980s–1990s were surely a golden age for zombie literature.

Curt Selby's[21] *I, Zombie* (1982) marks the last hurrah of the zombie drone's reign. *I, Zombie*, a science fiction story told from the first-person point of view in a similar fashion to Isaac Marion's *Warm Bodies* (2010), recounts the story of a drowned woman who is outfitted with a control pack after her death and brought back as a tech zombie to labor in dangerous alien environments. The narrator retains her consciousness and identity and therefore doesn't quite qualify as an actual zombie (she is more akin to a zombie ghost),[22] but the other workers are typical zombie drones brought back from the dead to work as slave labor like the zombie of Haiti. *I, Zombie* is basically the Haitian zombie myth of the 1930s set in space.

Zombie fiction appearing after 1982 moved away from the zombie drone and focused on zombies more akin to those articulated by Romero's films. The occasional short story or novel still reached back to Haiti for its inspiration, particularly after Wade Davis published *The Serpent and the Rainbow* in 1985, recounting his personal investigation of zombies on the island, but in general, zombies from 1982 on became increasingly brutal and dangerous. Romero's fusing of the zombie with the ghoul (and the frequent repetition of that trope in the work of others) gave the zombie agency. Not only did zombies no longer need controlling, but they also could no longer be controlled. Their drive to eat flesh was primal and instinctual. Their motivations were mindless and amoral. They went from being corpses with the appearance of life to the incarnation of death and entered the realm of the symbolic, echoing the oppositional binary between life and death. They were active. They had agency. And they were after the living, who were entrenched in a futile struggle to keep going as long as possible with the existential understanding that eventually death catches everyone. In this period, the zombie became a monster on par with vampires and werewolves, and this transformation is one of the main reasons that zombie fiction burgeoned into a significant genre from the mid–1980s on.

Zombie novels became commonplace among horror titles, with works such as Lucius Shepard's *Green Eyes* (1984), Candace Caponegro's *The Breeze Horror* (1988), Gary Brandner's *The Brain Eaters* (1985) and *Carrion* (1986), and Philip Nutman's *Wet Work* (1993). Zombie short stories were also once again in high demand, and a number of significant collections found their way into print. The first and most significant collection was *Zombie: Stories of the Walking Dead* (1985), edited by Peter Haining. The collection provides an excellent preface to the zombie prior to the adoption of the zombie ghoul, and it includes a dozen stories from the early days of zombie fiction, including an excerpt from Seabrook's *The Magic Island* titled "Dead Men Working in the Cane Fields," G.W. Hutter's "Salt Is Not for Slaves," originally published in 1931, and Meik's "White Zombie." However, the jewel of the collection is Haining's introduction, which provides readers with the first overview of early zombie fiction.

Haining's introductory anthology was followed by a number of significant collections. In 1989, John Skipp and Craig Spector came out with a collection of new zombie fiction that includes stories by some of the best-known writers of horror and zombie fiction, such as Richard Laymon, Ramsey Campbell, Stephen King, Robert R. McCammon, and Joe R. Lansdale, many of whom have published zombie novels. Skipp and Spector's collection is not for the squeamish. Gone are the mild-mannered zombies of Haitian superstition. In their place are grotesque ghouls and flesh-hungry beasts. The collection is in line with the hard-core graphic direction that horror had taken among paperback aficionados, but it is ahead of its time for zombie cinema and includes morally uncomfortable works, such as Joe R. Lansdale's "On the Far Side of the Cadillac Desert with Dead Folks," which focuses on how a zombie apocalypse brings out the worst in both the dead and the living, an issue films avoid embracing with Lansdale's graphic detail until the twenty-first century.

In 1986, three years before penning "On the Far Side of the Cadillac Desert with Dead Folks," Lansdale published *Dead in the West* (1986), a more lighthearted version of a zombie outbreak, and the first zombie Western, which illustrates how quickly innovation was changing zombie fiction during this golden age. While zombie films were adding brain-eating (*The Return of the Living Dead,* 1985, directed by Dan O'Bannon), experimenting with zombie hordes, and creating fast zombies (*Nightmare City*, 1980, directed by Umberto Lenzi), some zombie fiction was venturing into darker areas, such as zombie prostitution and pedophilia, adding often unsettling but unquestionably innovative twists to the mythology. Richard Laymon, for example, introduces the notion that zombification can be undone in *One Rainy Night* (1991). In the novel, a mysterious black rain transforms people into violent, crazed (and overtly sexual) psychopaths. The main characters do what so many have done before and after them—they shoot, stab, and crush their altered friends and neighbors. Then they discover that if they had simply washed off the black rain, the affected would have returned to normal. This raises complicated moral questions not found in your typical fend-off-the-zombie-horde, Romeroesque survival tale. One of the key tropes of zombie film at the time is that it is morally okay to shoot infected family members in the head because they aren't themselves anymore, but in the world of *One Rainy Night*, we discover—after the fact—that they actually *were* still themselves.

By the 1990s, zombies could be found in print everywhere. A series of seven novel adaptations of the *Resident Evil* video games was penned by S.D. Perry from 1998 to 2004. Laurel K. Hamilton's popular Anita Blake series includes zombies even though the series is primarily about vampires. Zombies can be found even in the work of authors with significant critical stature. Joyce Carol Oates, for example, writes about a serial killer (fashioned after Jeffrey Dahmer) who is attempting to create a zombie in her 1995 novel *Zombie*. Zombies were so popular that publishers even dug into the past and resurrected previous works, such as Theodore Roscoe's *A Grave Must Be Deep* and *Z Is for Zombie* (originally serialized in *Argosy* in 1937), both of which were reprinted in 1989.

Despite this surge in popularity, zombie literature, which had originally inspired zombie film, for the most part still lagged film. Many of the literary works being written continued to take their lead from film. In the twenty-first century, this relationship flipped, and zombie fiction became the ground for innovation in the zombie genre. Plenty of works were being written in the same vein as works from the 1980s and 90s, such as Tim Lebbon's *Fears Unnamed* (2004), David Wellington's *Monster Nation* (2004), Simon Clark's *Stranger* (2002), Scott Nicholson's *The Harvest* (2003), Walter Greatshell's *Xombies* (2004), J. Knight's *Risen* (2004), and Bentley Little's *The Walking* (2000). In 2006, zombie novels crept into the literary mainstream with works such as Max Brooks' immensely successful *World War Z* and Stephen King's *Cell*. However, beneath the gloss of mainstream publishing, new ideas were taking shape, ideas that moved the genre beyond the zombie ghoul in their exploration of fresh narrative territories. Carlton Mellick III explores such territory in *The Steel Breakfast Era* (2003), which hyperbolizes battles with zombie hordes to the point that mountains of "corpse parts"[23] threaten to block the heroes' escape route. Brad Gooch cleverly applies zombie mythology in his story of a young, gay man who self-identifies as a zombie and goes in search of a master, a trip that ultimately leads him to Haiti.[24] James Lowder's three-volume edited collection of zombie stories (2001–03) for Eden Studios (a gaming company) offers numerous innovations on the zombie myth. Short story collections and novels offered by boutique publishing houses became the proving ground for fresh approaches to the zombie, approaches that would only later appear in film.

One example from Lowder's trilogy worth noting is Daniel Ksenych's "The Other Side of Theory," which appears in *The Book of All Flesh* (2001). The story is the earliest example I have found of what I call the "zombie channel"—a corpse deprived of his/her essential self that has had that vacated space filled by some other consciousness. Albert Parsons in "The Other Side of Theory" is a test subject who travels to another dimension. He returns dead, but still able to move and talk. He appears to be the same man who left. But Parsons is changed. Something else now occupies his mind, something for which he is a channel, something that he passes to others by biting their flesh. Outside of print, we do not see a zombie channel until 2005 when Sam Hamm adapts Dale Bailey's short story "Death & Suffrage" for an episode of the *Masters of Horror* television show called "Homecoming."[25] Ksenych's clever innovation was to fill the space left by the loss of self with something (or someone) else. Hamm's teleplay does the same, as does King's *Cell* (2006), in which the zombies eventually develop hive consciousness, in a manner similar to the zombies in Brian Keene's innovative Rising series (2003–15). King touches on the idea, but Keene fully embraces it. Keene's zombies are like Romero's zombie ghouls; they are the resurrected dead, and they nibble on the living, but each is occupied by a conscious entity attempting to escape "the void."[26] The souls of the living depart at death, and that space is filled with intelligent, highly organized entities that kill to make new flesh vessels for their friends. The human soul is gone, as Martin in *The Rising* (2004) explains to a zombie priest: "You may have taken the body of a man of God, but you couldn't touch his soul!"[27] Keene further advances the zombie narrative by having all living things on the planet subject to transformation, thereby illustrating the existential principle informing much of the zombie's twenty-first-century appeal—that the struggle for survival is always, in the end, an exercise in futility.

Zombie literature has come a long way from the Haitian zombie drones of the 1930s to the flesh-starved creatures we find in Keene's Rising series, or in Len Barnhart's Reign of the Dead trilogy (2004–13), or in Wellington's novels, or in Robert Kirkman and Jay Bonansinga's ever-growing series of novels based on *The Walking Dead* series of graphic novels and teleplays (2012–), or in hundreds of other zombie works that have been published in the past thirty years. Admittedly, many works are derivative and repetitious, but a surprising number of short stories and novels are daring and innovative and help lead the enduring myth into more and more interesting territories.

Understanding zombie mythos requires the acknowledgment of zombie literature as an ongoing source of creative innovation and its history as part and parcel of the zombie landscape. When scholars and aficionados exclude written representations of zombies in favor of visual representations of zombies, they overlook the ineluctable fact that most visual representations begin as screenplays and therefore, like novels and short fiction, originate with writing. Consider the opening of Romero and Russo's script for *Night of the Living Dead*:

EXT. CEMETERY—DUSK
It is an ordinary dusk of normal quiet and shadow. The gray sky contains a soft glow from the recent sun, so that trees and long blades of grass seem to shimmer in

the gathering night. There is a rasp of crickets, and the rustle of leaves in an occasional whispering breeze.[28]

Compare this to the following passage from Hearn's "The Country of Comers-Back" (1889):

It is a breezeless and cloudless noon. Under the dazzling downpour of light the hills seem to smoke blue: something like a thin yellow fog haloes the leagues of ripening cane,—a vast reflection. There is no stir in all the green mysterious front of the vine-veiled woods. The palms of the roads keep their heads quite still, as if listening.[29]

While one might dispute the literary merit of these two examples, it would be difficult to argue that they do not share the same genus. They are both literature, and their similarities reflect the fact that virtually all representations of zombies outside of oral tradition begin with the written word, making examinations of the written word critical to our understanding of the living and the dead.

NOTES

1. Cf. Kyle William Bishop's *American Zombie Gothic*, 217.
2. Weeks, *Among Congo*, 248.
3. We might characterize this movement as a shift from Lacan's *objet petit a* to Kristeva's abject.
4. St. John, *Hayti or the Black Republic*, 160.
5. Hearn, *Two Years*, 369–70.
6. *Ibid.*, 369.
7. *Ibid.*, 186.
8. *Ibid.*, 174.
9. I outline nine classifications of zombies in "The Zombie as Other: Mortality and the Monstrous in the Post-Nuclear Age." Two of these, the zombie ruse and the zombie ghost, are not actually zombies by any definition. The other seven are the zombie drone, zombie ghoul, tech zombie, chemical zombie, psychological zombie, bio zombie, and cultural zombie.
10. Seabrook, *Magic Island*, 93.
11. In dramatic works of the period, the influence of Seabrook is undeniable, but many of the authors of these works claim that other works influenced theirs. An argument can be made that some of those works were less influential than the authors' claims might indicate, and that they were mentioned largely to justify the use of the word "zombie" without fear of legal ramifications from Amusement Securities Corporation, which owned the rights to the film *White Zombie* and fought early on to maintain control over the term "zombie." (Cf. *Amusement Securities Corporation v. Academy Pictures Distributing Corporation*)
12. Hurston, Interview.
13. Lovecraft, "Reanimator," 230–31.
14. Hurston, Interview.
15. "Dreary Black."
16. Tremayne plays loose and free with geography in the novel, taking the name of his island from St. Maquelon off the coast of Newfoundland and claiming it is "north of Carriacou" (10), an island that actually lies in the Caribbean between Grenada and Saint Vincent and the Grenadines.
17. Dendle, *Zombie Movie Encyclopedia*, 4.
18. *Ibid.*, 13.
19. Works such as R. Chetwynd-Hayes' "The Ghouls" and Ramsey Campbell's "Rising

Generation," both published in 1975, retain the idea of zombies as beings that are raised from the dead through mysterious means and then exploited as a workforce.

20. Dendle, *Zombie Movie Encyclopedia*, 7–8.

21. Curt Selby was the pen name of Doris Piserchia, whose writing career spanned 1966–83.

22. I argue that to qualify as a zombie, a person (or entity) must exhibit some loss of essential self; merely being a reanimated corpse is insufficient. This important distinction allows us to dismiss people brought back through CPR, defibrillation, or, like Lazarus and Jesus, through mystical means. Furthermore, it creates a uniform definition that applies to the earliest manifestations of the term as well as the most recent.

23. Mellick, *Steel Breakfast Era*.

24. Gooch's protagonist is the type of zombie that I refer to as a "cultural zombie"—a character that displays the basic characteristics of a zombie (particularly the loss of some essential, defining self), but whose zombification does not involve supernatural elements. Trevor Reznik (Christian Bale) in *The Machinist* (2004, directed by Brad Anderson) is an excellent example.

25. Bailey's original story was first published in 2001, around the same time as Ksenych's "The Other Side of Theory," but Bailey's reanimated dead still maintain their original identities. They are zombie ghosts who maintain their essential selves and thus do not qualify as actual zombies. If they did, zombies would have to include Lazarus, Jesus, and a lot of emergency room patients among their number. Zombie ghosts sometimes fallaciously appear in zombie anthologies—works such as Clive Barker's "Sex, Death and Starshine" (1984), which was included in *The Mammoth Book of Zombies*, despite the fact that the resurrected Shakespearean actors in the story have intact identities and do not properly belong to the canon. In Hamm's adaptation of Bailey's story, however, the zombies are reimagined as vessels for something else, and their essential selves are absent.

26. Keene, *The Rising*, 297.

27. *Ibid.*

28. Romero and Russo, *Night of the Living Dead*, 1.

29. Hearn, "The Country of Comers-Back," 61.

The Attributes and Qualifiers of Literary Zombies

BERNARD PERRON

Mapping the transmedial world of the living dead and paraphrasing the famous lines of SWAT team officer Peter Washington in *Dawn of the Dead* (1978, directed by George A. Romero), I have written elsewhere: "When there's no more room in a medium the dead will walk another one."[1] As Max Brooks has noted in *The Zombie Survival Guide*, "[z]ombies are migratory organisms, with no regard for territory or concept of *home*."[2] This tendency of the zombie *as monster* provides a metaphor for its performance as a transmedial phenomenon whose migratory activities can be mapped and analyzed. At the same time, we must also acknowledge that "[a] zombie is always a mass event; a chance encounter with a zombie multiplies with the regularity of massproduction [sic]. One becomes the many."[3] Following this logic, there were few undead-themed literary works in the 1980s and 1990s, including *Zombies! Stories of the Walking Dead* edited by Peter Haining (1985), *The Mammoth Book of Zombies* edited by Stephen Jones (1993), *Book of the Dead 1* and *2* edited by John Skipp and Craig Spector (1989 and 1992), *Zombie!* by Peter Tremayne (1981), *I, Zombie* by Curt Selby (1982), *The Breeze Horror* by Candace Caponegro (1988), and *Wet Work* by Philip Nutman (1993). However, the turn of the 2000s marked the advent of a real gathering of living-dead literary works. To refer back to Jennifer Rutherford's observation: one did become the many.

To chart the rising in literature around what is commonly identified as the zombie renaissance in popular culture, my essay focuses on novels. Since it is the portrayal of "*homo mortis*"[4] that has led me to consider what is distinctive in each of its media representations, I study from a formal perspective the links between films and novels, the mediation introduced by the use of words, and the importance of descriptions of zombie attributes in literary fiction.

Just Like in the Movies (or Not)

In an assertion often quoted, Peter Dendle has highlighted that "[z]ombies are ... the only creature to pass directly from folklore to the screen, without first having an established literary tradition."[5] Doubtless, after the voodoo zombies and following *Night of the Living Dead* (1968, directed by George A. Romero), the most important and constant reanimated corpse invasions have been sighted in films. The first thing we witness when we lose ourselves in contemporary zombie novels is the weight of the modern cinematic tradition.

This weight is so heavy that it produces in these novels a sense of hyperreality: zombie novels are fictions that are not only modeled on other fiction, but also self-consciously deploy their models to build their diegetic sensibility. Jean Baudrillard has famously argued that "[s]imulation is no longer that of a territory, a referential being, or a substance. It is the generation by models of a real without origin or reality: a hyperreal. The territory no longer precedes the map, nor does it survive it."[6] As the map precedes and engenders the territory, so novelists are captivated by the "map" of zombie cinema and take it as a basic point of reference. Hence, in order to make sense of the postapocalyptic world into which they are overwhelmingly falling, many characters don't refer to their (fictive) reality or to other novels, but to the movies. In S.D. Perry's *Resident Evil: Umbrella Conspiracy* (1998), the first novelization of the video game *Resident Evil* (1996, developed by Capcom), after special agent Chris Redfield has come across and shot a man with a "deathly pale" face whose "eye sockets glittered with hunger," he weighs in on what is happening, thinking he has watched "enough late-night movies" to know that even if he can't believe it, these are "*Zombies*."[7] A soldier is bitten and turned into a monster "like something out of a zombie movie" in Craig DiLouie's *Tooth and Nail* (2010), and this correlation "explained everything."[8] In Jonathan Maberry's *Patient Zero* (2009), a doctor illustrates the nature of the threat that the counterterrorism taskforce is facing with an explicit analogy: "You know that movie, *Night of the Living Dead*? Well, I think 'living dead' is a pretty good name for what we got here."[9] Soon after, he explains the infection with yet another film: "Ever see the movie *28 Days Later*? No? You should."[10] As for Jack Barnes, the main character of Robin Becker's *Brains: A Zombie Memoir* (2010), he discovers very promptly at the beginning of his story that a virus has "hit the world like a terrorist attack" and explains, "That's the genius of George Romero. His initial trilogy ... was prescient in the grand tradition of science fiction becoming fact.... Imagine a virus that turns corpses into the walking dead, and someone, somewhere, will develop that virus."[11] The zombie mythology introduced by Romero forms the basis of the understanding of the undead invasion, imbuing the novels with a pronounced metafictional dimension.

The relationship between contemporary zombie novels and the cinematic zombie tradition is described well by Patricia Waugh's definition of metalanguage and metafiction as "writing which consistently displays its conventionality, which explicitly and overtly lays bare its condition of artifice, and which thereby explores the problematic relationship between life and fiction."[12] Indeed, many authors place the fictional world imagined by the director of *Night of the Living Dead* at the center of their own creations and play with the essence of the fictional characters' "real life." Romero himself is not just a filmmaker within the near-future world of Mira Grant's *Feed* (2010); he is "considered one of the accidental saviors of the human race."[13] This salvage is the result of his Dead Cycle: "Fans of Romero's films applied the lessons of a thousand zombie movies to the reality of what had happened. They traded details of the attacks and their results over a thousand blogs from a thousand places, and humanity survived."[14] Those survivor tips are applied by others as well. *Resident Evil*'s Chris Redfield is happy to see that "[a]pparently head shots *were* the best way to kill a zombie, just like in the movies."[15] Because zombies shouldn't exist in the rational world of Rhiannon Frater's *The First Days: As the World Dies* (2008), and since they feel they are suddenly "living in a horror movie,"[16] Jenni, the housewife, advises Katie, the prosecutor, when a zombie is coming toward them: "Just shoot him in the head. That's how it works in the movies."[17] A living dead creature in Daryl Gregory's *Raising Stony Mayhall* (2011) states that, to improve on the procedure shown in "every movie about the undead ever made—including the documentaries," it is better that "you knock him [another living dead creature] the fuck down. Then you walk up close, about two feet away. *Then* you shoot him in the head."[18] For characters in zombie novels, then, zombie cinema has provided instruction in not only the basic principles of zombie disposal, but also some of the finer points of technique.

In some cases, the metafictional interplay between print works and their cinematic predecessors takes another turn as characters express uncertainty about the applicability of fiction to their "real-life" experience. For example, even though police officer Eddie Hudson in Joe McKinney's *Dead City* (2010) says that, like one of those zombies in the movies, there was nothing behind the face of a man who has just bitten his partner,[19] he still doesn't realize what monsters the human community is encountering and how people should defend themselves. In another instance, at the school where the action of Darren Shan's *Zom-B* (2012) is mainly taking place, after a knife is driven into the head of a zombie, the teenagers initially wonder if this method works in real life as it does in movies.[20] Later, the protagonist B Smith says, "I've seen enough horror films to know a fully paid-up member of the living dead when I see one. They don't move as stiffly as most movie zombies, but they have the vacant expression."[21] Romero's rules might be put forward and turned to in order to survive, but they're also questioned in relation to the nature of the walking dead, and sometimes the Romero canon is explicitly treated as a resource of dubious reliability. With the aim of finding a way to grasp what is happening, Viktor, the young brother of the adolescent Flora, whose grandfather has suddenly risen from the dead in John Ajvide Lindqvist's *Handling the Undead* (2005), has been watching Romero's *Day of the Dead* (1985). Shaken by what he has seen, he asks his sister if she thinks the dead are dangerous as they are in the movie. Flora answers, "The movie … it's all made up." She wonders in return if Viktor believed in elves and hobbits like in *Lord of the Rings* and closes the conversation by staring at the black monitor and asserting, "In real life they're nice. At least, they don't want to hurt anyone."[22] "What real life?" we, the readers, are wondering.

Nonetheless, the characters in these and certainly others novels don't seem to have watched the filmic evolution of the zombie from the Romerian living dead to the infected. Consequently, they remain puzzled by the new breeds they encounter. This confusion plagues the housewife of *The First Days,* who thinks she knows what kind of horror movie her world has fallen into because of her "steady diet of zombie flicks": "'A Romero movie,' Jenni agreed, then frowned. 'They aren't supposed to be so fast. They're supposed to be slow. Very slow.'"[23] These monsters come to break "all the fucking zombie rules!"[24] Yet it's not so much the speed as the mindfulness that is problematic. One character running a website on zombies before the plague of *Dead City* gives a police officer a quick lecture in "zombie studies."[25] He distinguishes three kinds of zombies: the Hollywood zombies seen in movies, the Haitian voodoo zombies, and the philosophical kind. He concludes that the people walking around don't really fit into any of the categories.[26] Because they are still alive, therefore more likely infected, they raise moral questions revolving around the issue of consciousness. The creatures met in Brian Keene's *The Rising* are well and truly dead. However, Jim, the dad, on his way to save his son, remarks to the Reverend traveling with him that although they eat humans, they don't eat the whole body as in the movies, "where they rip a victim apart, gnawing every last scrap of meat off the bone."[27] He had observed earlier that the risen dead were also smarter than those on the silver screen.[28] In point of fact, the human walking dead of *The Rising*—because here other animals (such as rats, squirrels, birds, or deer) can be infected, too—talk, use tools, drive, ambush survivors, etc. The zombies in S.G. Browne's *Breathers: A Zombie's Lament* (2009) don't fit the traditional mold, either. They are third-class citizens trying to fit back into society, and for them, the screening of *Night of the Living Dead* becomes "a moment of clarity."[29] In *Raising Stony Mayhall*, the zombies instead watch *White Zombie*

(1932, directed by Victor Halperin) when they get together[30]; the screening is a nice reflexive gesture about their enslavement. In all these narratives, zombie cinema is invoked with the aim of creating intertextual play with its conventions.

Although the depiction offered by Romero in his movies constitutes an unavoidable foundation for comprehending modern literary zombies, novelists also are telling their own original stories and, above all, working with the mediality of the words. This media specificity is an important source of meaning and thus another core focus of this essay.

The Name(s) of the Living Dead

Studying the connection between horror and image, Éric Dufour has rightly aimed at the differentness of images and words. For him, the image "is the sensitive, and the sensitive, it is what is given, what I passively receive and that I still have to decipher, to understand, that is to identify and to determine." What is given is "the pure existence, the fact that this thing or event is given to me in a naked way. It is precisely this immediate donation, that is to say, the pure *to exist*, that writing cannot preserve."[31] The sensitivity of the image is what explains, according to Dufour, why we have, for instance, no difficulty in talking about a piece of erotic literature but can't speak of a pornographic one. It is the same thing with horror, which is more the domain of the image. For Dufour,

> Writing and speaking mark the advent of the analysis, and thus of the discursive mediation.... While speaking and writing dissolve and decompose a whole into its elements (the analysis), the image, on the contrary, restores its ontic charge, its inertia and its gravity, in a word, its presence. Or the speaking understands and explains; it rationalizes and supposes an innate donation on which it establishes a foothold and from which it occurs, while the image gives and shows without explaining anything: to show is certainly to direct at, to indicate, but it is not yet to identify and to determine.[32]

The cardinal notion of the discursive mediation underlined by Dufour can be addressed from two main angles: the decomposition of the whole and the act of identification. As I'll deal with the former in the next section, I'll concentrate now on the latter.

Clearly, novelists approach their writing with the knowledge that the world, events, and characters they'll present are not given "in a naked way." This awareness actually leads to a great concern for the labels applied to the living dead. This is not to say that attention is not given to names in a visual medium (the reanimated corpses have, for example, many nicknames in Robert Kirkman's comic book series *The Walking Dead* [2003–]) or that the way things are identified and dubbed isn't invariably referring to both their denotation and their connotation. Nevertheless, in literature, the term brought to play in order to designate the monsters is the "foothold" from which the understanding arises. We can identify three ways of using names: the hyperreal approach, the descriptive opposition, and the qualifying terminology.

The first way is the most interesting. In line with the notion of a simulacrum, novelists recall with the sole usage of "zombie" the whole modern hyperreal meaning of the monster. Brooks has put the emphasis on this right at the start of his celebrated *World War Z: An Oral History of the Zombie War*:

> For me, it will always be "The Zombie War," and while many may protest the scientific accuracy of the word *zombie*, they will be hard-pressed to discover a more globally accepted term for the creatures that almost caused our extinction. *Zombie* remains a devastating word, unrivaled in its power to conjure up so many memories or emotions, and it is these memories, and emotions, that are the subject of this book.[33]

The weight of the word is so heavy that the Centers for Disease Control and Prevention are avoiding it in *The First Days*: officials are "calling [them] reanimated corpses [or "reanimates" and "reanimated dead"]…. Nobody wants to say *zombie*."[34] It is just the opposite in *Feed* for one significant reason: "Calling zombies 'the infected' creates an artificial feeling of security, like we can somehow avoid joining them. Well, guess what? We can't."[35] Existing in the shadow of humans, the ghouls in *Raising Stony Mayhall* don't "use the Z-word."[36] They don't like that term—or "living dead," "walking dead," and "undead"—insofar as it's "not only inaccurate but offensive to our people and prejudicial to the attitudes of noninfected humans"; they prefer the term "Differently Living."[37] In Daniel Waters' *Generation Dead* (2008), the dead teenagers need to be identified as "living impaired" or "differently biotic persons."[38] Similarly, in Joan Frances Turner's *Dust* (2010), the fifteen-year-old Jessie never calls herself "zombie" because she finds it "racist," yet the zombie community nicknames humans "hoos."[39] The diegetic scrutiny of the term "zombie" thus becomes a tool for interrogating both the power of language and the language of power—from the ability of a single word to elicit fear or hate to the political uses of words to marginalize groups that are deemed dangerous or undesirable.

In the second category, alternative names are used in opposition to introduce new types. For instance, Mark Spitz, the member of a civilian sweeper unit, meets two types of victims of the pandemic that has devastated the planet in Colson Whitehead's *Zone One* (2006): the "standard-issue skels," who crave human flesh, and "the stragglers," who are frozen in place, stuck in one living moment.[40] The world of Shan's *Zom-B* is also inhabited by two kinds of zombies: the *reviveds*, who are the "ordinary, mindless" ones, and the *revitaliseds*, "who can think and act the way they did before they died."[41] Since they are in an underground lab, we learn in more detail than in any other novel the new bodily (non)functions of these *revitaliseds*: they can't blink, don't breathe, can live with no heart, have no digestion, and can't taste anything, but they have improved senses of hearing and smelling. Inasmuch as the citizens rising from their graves in *Handling the Undead* don't seem to behave like Romero's monsters and the authorities do not really know what they are confronting, the awakened dead are straightforwardly referred to as "reliving."[42] Such coinages of new terms and taxonomies suggest the possibilities for innovation that zombie writers are exploring.

In the third category, the bynames underline a particular quality of the undead. The "slugs" and "meatskins"[43] of Alden Bell's *The Reapers Are the Angels* (2010) highlight their unwieldiness. The "(non-)breather" foregrounds the absence of a vital sign (in fact, "non-breather" is used only once at the beginning of chapter seven of *Breathers*; "breather" is employed in *Raising Stony Mayhall*, too). The label "Mad Dogs"[44] (or "Maddies," as the civilians go by the "Hajjis"[45]) of DiLouie's *Tooth and Nail* stresses the animality of the creatures. The drive of eating flesh is as well salient in the "hungries"[46] met in M.R. Carey's *The Girl with All the Gifts* (2014); however, Carey is careful to note their mental condition as the hungries toggle between two states: frozen in place most of the time, but very sensitive when they smell prey, hear it, or catch sight of it.[47] It is also quite interesting to remark that the zombies are, in the first page of *Pride and Prejudice and Zombies* (2009), the contaminated classic of Jane Austen, christened "the unmentionables"[48]; this designation somewhat suggests that they have been at all times present but were not acknowledged before the mutations created by Seth Grahame-Smith. In the village guided by a Sisterhood at the center of Carrie Ryan's *The Forest of Hands and Teeth* (2009), the loved ones brought back to life are designated as "the Unconsecrated"[49] to underline the blasphemous nature of the fiend. In all of these instances, the qualities highlighted by the various labels are central to the novel's vision.

The names given to the living dead are, in the end, the expression of two main degrees of being distinguished by the capacity to understand things, to gain knowledge, and to use skills in an efficient way. On one hand, the zombies remain unstoppable thoughtless monsters, the spreading virus infecting and destroying humankind. On the other hand, and above all, they have evolved.

The States of Decay

The mutation of the living dead addresses an important critical issue raised by, among others, June Pulliam: "[the] lack of free will generally makes zombies flat characters, unable to fully appreciate the wretchedness of their condition, unlike vampires, who frequently wax philosophical about being doomed to hunger for living blood. Thus, zombies are generally not the protagonists of stories about them."[50] Her assertion was formulated differently later in her encyclopedia entry: "Literary zombies are generally flat characters, which is to be expected, since they are typified by the mindlessness of their drives. Notable exception can be seen in Tim Waggoner's hard-boiled dark fantasy *Necropolis* (2004) and Brian Keene's *The Rising* (2003) and *City of the Dead* (2005), novels that feature intelligent zombies."[51] Insofar as Gary the med student has succeeded in keeping his faculties while becoming a walking corpse in David Wellington's *Monster Island: A Zombie Novel* (2006), or as Stony the zombie messiah has kept his human abilities in *Raising Stony Mayhall*, they are certainly more exceptions to add to the list. That being said, literature offers yet a new opportunity. Since the ghouls lose the ability to speak when they come back to life, their mental existence is more difficult to communicate in an audiovisual medium like movies—at least without the use of a voiceover. However, to invoke the notion introduced by May Sinclair, writers can render the "stream of consciousness" of any character.[52] They can achieve this effect, as Dorrit Cohn foregrounds in *Transparent Minds: Narrative Modes for Presenting Consciousness in Fiction*, "because fictional consciousness is the special preserve of narrative fiction."[53] Thus, it does matter if zombies factually speak or not at one point in the story. They are telling from a first-person perspective all their thoughts about the new (un)life and its conditions as well as reflecting on their past human existence. This is what Andy Warner in *Breathers*, Jessie in *Dust* (the zombies communicate amongst themselves through waves of sound), R in Isaac Marion's *Warm Bodies* (2011), and B Smith in *Zom-B: Underground* do. For instance, in an incident that links first-person zombie narration to the zombie novel's intertextual dialogue with cinema, Andy Warner declines to have another portion of his mother's ribs because "I know that in the movies, zombies devour limbs and buckets of internal organs and can't seem to get enough. But that's just more Hollywood propaganda. Breathers are as rich and filling as a double chocolate soufflé."[54] As for Jessie, she horribly misses being human and talks about "stupid things like missing what human food tasted like: strawberries, potato chips, ice cream."[55] Novels such as *Brains: A Zombie Memoir* and McKinney's *Memoirs of the Walking Dead: A Story from the Zombie's Point of View* (2010) take the idea of recounting someone's undead personal experiences a step further.

Whether zombies are mindless or still intelligent, they have to be seen for what they are: creatures transgressing the categorical distinction of living and dead. With this perspective, it is hard not to challenge the comment made by John Clute and David Langford in their short entry in *The*

Encyclopedia of Fantasy: "Zombies are difficult to make interesting in prose—*Walking Dead* (1977) by Peter DICKINSON being a notable exception—but are vividly present in countless ZOMBIE MOVIES."[56] Now present in a myriad of print works, the living dead are no less "interesting" in writing than in movies although they are not revived with the same mediality. Following the dual model of fantasy literature developed by Denis Mellier, zombie novels exemplify the "fantastic of the presence" (as opposed to the "fantastic of the uncertainty"). This mode "accentuates the expressive values of the fantastic by offering strong visual forms using descriptive and hyperbolic processes. Its narrative structures play in suspense pending the spectacular unveiling."[57] The "fantastic of the presence" elaborates a "poetics of the explicit" and of excess. It gives precedence to showing and grants the most expressive force to explicit and visual descriptions. It is worth recalling here Dufour's distinction between images and words. Because it doesn't have the "immediate donation" or the "pure *to exist*" of the image, writing needs to decompose "a whole into its elements (analysis)."[58] For example, in a scene where a groaning zombie totters toward Daryl Dixon in the forest during "Always Accountable," the sixth episode of season six of AMC's *The Walking Dead* (15 November 2015), I can only capture a certain amount of detail from my "sensitive point of view" in the course of the sixteen seconds and five shots during which I watch the ghoul approaching until he gets an arrow in the skull. I can see that it's a man; his face is skeletal with teeth well in view; he wears pants; he has no skin on his upper body; his rib cage is emptied of any wet organ; and he is starting to be covered by moss and leaves, which makes him look like a walking tree. But I don't pay attention to his hair, his ears, his eyes, his hands, his feet, etc. While I'm writing this, I'm performing exactly what the description does: translating in a succession what the senses mostly register in simultaneity and stopping the course of action in order to create an image or a perception in the reader's mind.

Obviously, contemporary undead novels include their share of blood and gore, of greedy mouths, of teeth, hands, and nails ripping and biting human flesh, of intestines falling out of open bellies, etc. The living dead display the incompleteness of horror monsters, showing missing limbs and sometimes half a face. Along with the depiction of these gruesome or macabre scenes, and even more interestingly, the novelists strive to enlighten, to give an "expressive force" to the images and sounds of zombies; this is their greatest contribution to zombie culture. For instance, the eyes of the undead are "like shriveled grapes,"[59] "vacant and milky white, like candle wax,"[60] "have all the red-rimmed sunkenness of an ancient animal,"[61] and "remain fixed with an alien stare."[62] The eyes of one of the reliving "were watery brown; it was like staring into a muddy pool where nothing was stirring. No response."[63] Like college-professor-cum-zombie Jack phrases it, "If eyes are windows to the soul, then Marie's soul had left the building."[64] It is what the detective in *Patient Zero* feels: "This wasn't the deadeye stare of a shark, nothing like that. This was freak-show stuff because there was nothing there; it was like looking into an empty room.... I saw terror and hopelessness there. I saw death."[65] The creatures growl and groan. They also "issue a hiss of animal hatred," "scream like jungle animals," moan "like lost souls," and "set up a dreadful howl of unnatural need."[66] If the Mad Dogs are obviously "howling in the dark," they might not be "growling when they make that noise, they are actually talking, but their throats have become partially paralyzed so it comes out as a creepy gurgle."[67]

The advent of zombies is consequently the advent of the determination of their undead attributes. In *Dust*, and in continuity with the previous section about names, the living dead are distinguished according to their stages of decay. To a young girl having just joined her gang, Jessie explains that if she's already a rotter who will stay this way for a certain period of time since she was embalmed, she'll go through phases: (1) a bloater when the bacteria really start breaking the insides down; (2) a feeder when the bugs start hatching; (3) a dusty when the body is in dry decay; and (4) a skeleton.[68] The non-breathers like Andy must regularly consume enough formaldehyde to keep at bay the decomposition of their bodies and internal organs.[69] The precaution, moreover, focuses on the largest organ of the body, which is taken more into account in the novels than the films: the skin. Bell is all too aware of its importance in *The Reapers Are the Angels*: "Death is all about skin.... It dries to paper thinness, it shrivels and tautens around the knuckles and the other bones to create shrink-wrapped skeletons. It changes color—gray then brown then black, but it frequently holds its hair follicles in place."[70] The color transformation is what hits the reporter Mahler the most when he digs out his grandson in *Handling the Undead* and sees a thin "dark green, olive-coloured" layer.[71] While "Stony's skin was a brownish gray—the color of last night's pork chop, his sister Alice said—and dry as paper,"[72] the skin of the first boy that the agent of the United Nations Postwar Commission meets in *World War Z* "was cold and gray as the cement on which he lay."[73] Marked with sores, it's the same skin color that Elizabeth's friend Charlotte has in *Pride and Prejudice and Zombies*.[74] It's also what happens to Carey's hungries when they can't feed: "Grey threads have broken the leathery surface of their skin in a network of fine lines, crossing and re-crossing like veins."[75]

The dryness of the skin doesn't, however, elude the varying degrees of putrefaction of the flesh. This in fact underscores an aspect that novels exploit much more than films, video games, and comic books. Because they are not working in a(n) (audio)visual medium, the writers depict and rely a great deal on the smell of the zombies who "can be considered walking noses, very stinky walking noses."[76] So, before they see or hear the reanimated corpse coming to attack them, the characters building barricades in Robert Kirkman and Jay Bonansinga's *The Walking Dead: Rise of the Governor* (2011) can smell "that black, oily, mildewy combination of rotting protein and decay—like human waste cooking in bacon grease."[77] The putrid scent of decay assaults the senses of the humans and calls to mind many things. "The stink is incredible, the dense sour-milk stench of the infected."[78] Its foul smell is like (1) "that *of* carrion,"[79] (2) a "muddy mixture of must and putrefaction, oil and rancid shit,"[80] (3) "a sickly, butcher shop odor. The reek of roadkill and offal and rotten meat,"[81] or (4) "a strong smell of—*what is it called*—Havarti. Aged cheese."[82] Of all, only the United Nations representative lowers the impact of the fumes in *World War Z*; he realizes that the living dead are surprisingly bereft of odor and possessed a "scentless stink."[83] Such an observation inverts the perspective on this sense. Following Brooks' observations in *The Zombie Survival Guide*, the undead have a more acute sense of smell insofar as they rely on it more.[84] The threat of the hungries in *The Girl with All the Gifts* is, for example, derived from this primitive sensorium. If they get the scent of the humans, they'll follow them for a hundred miles.[85] This is why the latter need to be "sprayed from head to foot with e-blocker"[86] in order to avoid being nose-catching and spotted. It is also through a "strange chemical smell" that Jessie will discover in *Dust* that the life of one and all is about to change.[87]

*   *   *

Writing about *Night of the Living Dead*, Jamie Russell has accentuated a key theme of zombie fiction: "Romero never lets us forget that this is a film about the body. Or, to be more accurate, the horror of the body."[88] If the nature of the living dead remains a showcase for film and TV make-up departments, it is as well one for the novelists. They can display all their skills in making this horror into words, that ability to name, to define, or to describe the undead. This is as inescapable as the invasion, and this is also where one of the great pleasures of the written dead lies. As a matter of fact, like an aficionado of undead fiction, I must say that I react most of the time as the Doctor of *Patient Zero* in front of rotting zombies: "It's beautiful, man, absolutely freaking beautiful."[89]

NOTES

1. Perron, "Zombie Escape and Survival Plans."
2. Brooks, *Zombie Survival Guide*, 17.
3. Rutherford, *Zombies*, 65.
4. Wellington, *Monster Island*, 22.
5. Dendle, *Zombie Movie Encyclopedia*, 2–3.
6. Baudrillard, *Simulacra and Simulations*, 1.
7. Perry, *Resident Evil*, 74.
8. DiLouie, *Tooth and Nail*, 125.
9. Maberry, *Patient Zero*, 163.

10. *Ibid.*, 166.
11. Becker, *Brains*, 4.
12. Waugh, *Metafiction*, 4.
13. Grant, *Feed*, 23.
14. *Ibid.*, 99.
15. Perry, *Resident Evil*, 105.
16. Frater, *First Days*, 27.
17. *Ibid.*, 29.
18. Gregory, *Raising Stony Mayhall*, 193.
19. McKinney, *Dead City*, 19.
20. Shan, *Zom-B*, 153.
21. *Ibid.*, 8.
22. Lindqvist, *Handling the Undead*, 216.
23. Frater, *First Days*, 27.
24. *Ibid.*, 229.
25. McKinney, *Dead City*, 192.
26. *Ibid.*, 101.
27. Keene, *Rising*, 106.
28. *Ibid.*, 43.
29. Browne, *Breathers*, 238.
30. Gregory, *Raising Stony Mayhall*, 164.
31. Dufour, *Cinéma d'horreur et ses figures*, 49–50 (translated freely).
32. *Ibid.*, 50 (translated freely).
33. Brooks, *World War Z*, 1.
34. Frater, *First Days*, 63.
35. Grant, *Feed*, 40.
36. Gregory, *Raising Stony Mayhall*, 111.
37. *Ibid.*, 151.
38. Waters, *Generation Dead*, 3 & 101.
39. Turner, *Dust*, 17 & 8.
40. Whitehead, *Zone One*, 48.
41. Shan, *Zom-B: Underground*, 27–28.
42. Lindqvist, *Handling the Undead*, 106.
43. Bell, *Reapers Are the Angels*, 12 & 6.
44. DiLouie, *Tooth and Nail*, 6.
45. *Ibid.*, 170 & 14.
46. Carey, *Girl with All the Gifts*, 3.
47. *Ibid.*, 71.
48. Austen and Grahame-Smith, *Pride and Prejudice*, 7.
49. Ryan, *Forest of Hands and Teeth*, 2.
50. Pulliam, "Zombie," 724.
51. *Ibid.*, 741.
52. Sinclair, "Novels of Dorothy Richardson," 57.
53. Cohn, *Transparent Minds*, vi.
54. Browne, *Breathers*, 209.
55. Turner, *Dust*, 140.
56. Clute and Langford, "Zombies," 1048.
57. Mellier, *Littérature fantastique*, 32 (translated freely).
58. Dufour, *Cinéma d'horreur et ses figures*, 50 (translated freely).
59. Perry, *Resident Evil*, 236.
60. McKinney, *Memoirs of the Walking Dead*, 123.
61. Bell, *Reapers Are the Angels*, 106.
62. DiLouie, *Tooth and Nail*, 151.
63. Lindqvist, *Handling the Undead*, 54–55.
64. Becker, *Brains*, 16.
65. Maberry, *Patient Zero*, 19.

66. *Ibid.*, 19, 237, 249, 258.
67. DiLouie, *Tooth and Nail*, 151.
68. Turner, *Dust*, 73–74.
69. Browne, *Breathers*, 10–11.
70. Bell, *Reapers Are the Angels*, 205.
71. Linquist, *Handling the Undead*, 130.
72. Gregory, *Raising Stony Mayhall*, 18.
73. Brooks, *World War Z*, 7.
74. Austen and Grahame-Smith, *Pride and Prejudice*, 120.
75. Carey, *Girl with All the Gifts*, 178.
76. Niedenthal, "Doux parfum de dégoût," 203–04 (original English version).
77. Kirkman and Bonansinga, *Rise of the Governor*, 35.
78. DiLouie, *Tooth and Nail*, 70.
79. Maberry, *Patient Zero*, 20.
80. Bell, *Reapers Are the Angels*, 17.
81. Keene, *Rising*, 36.
82. Lindqvist, *Handling the Undead*, 130.
83. Brooks, *World War Z*, 226.
84. Brooks, *Zombie Survival Guide*, 7–8.
85. Carey, *Girl with All the Gifts*, 3.
86. *Ibid.*, 68.
87. Turner, *Dust*, 61.
88. Russell, *Book of the Dead*, 67.
89. Maberry, *Patient Zero*, 168.

Love, Connection and Intimacy in Zombie Short Fiction

Laura Hubner

This essay looks at how integral human values of love, connection, and intimacy are reexamined and given new meaning in contemporary zombie stories. To some extent, zombie apocalyptic landscapes seem to obliterate these values as survival unleashes the death of identity and the gradual collapse of social boundaries and significances. However, zombie texts also provide insight into what the prospect of survival means, raising fundamental questions about existence and the motivation for living—as a human being. Underlying these questions are larger political concerns with the boundaries of war and peace and the broader philosophical concerns about what is intrinsic to a "human" with respect to consciousness, self, and being—concerns that have long been important to zombie fiction.[1] While some stories ask us to appreciate the lost values of the pre-zombie world, many use the "new" world as a springboard to explore different ways of looking at love, connection, and intimacy or to provide insight into problems within current society. Many zombie narratives de-romanticize love, liberating it from its ceremonial qualities, but a popular contemporary twist on the traditional survival story is the suggestion that connection and intimacy are in fact necessary motivators for survival. Looking at short stories by a range of authors (including Adam-Troy Castro, Nancy Kilpatrick, Robert Kirkman, David Moody, Susan Palwick, and Michael Swanwick), I suggest that the short fiction format, through its use of epiphanies and an impulse to economize, is able to amplify these concerns to the point where they frame the narrative.

Increasingly, zombie stories function as a means to explore the debilitating effects on health of contemporary afflictions such as loneliness, isolation, and disconnection. This idea that connection is essential for humans to thrive is not new. In 1871, Charles Darwin proposed in *The Descent of Man, and Selection in Relation to Sex* that there is a notable cycle of compassion leading to increased fitness, mass, and strength:

> In however complex a manner this feeling may have originated, as it is one of high importance to all those animals which aid and defend one another, it will have been increased through Natural Selection; for those communities, which included the greatest number of the most sympathetic members, would flourish best, and rear the greatest number of offspring.[2]

Since the new millennium, increased instances of mental isolation and related health issues in the USA have led to prioritized research into links among well-being, happiness, and health. For example, the work of Joseph Raz within the philosophical field has taken a renewed interest in human connection to consider contemporary understandings of well-being, arguing that "instinct for survival, or desire for ever greater longevity, has nothing to do with well-being. It is not the desire, which many of us also have, to have a good life. In general, the quality of people's life is independent of its duration."[3] In other words, instinctual drives to eat, to keep alive, and to have a long life are not the same as drives for happiness and well-being, which involve perceiving value in the life we are leading. While the motivational drivers of survival and well-being may be independent in the sense that being motivated to survive may not be connected to the impulse for happiness, contemporary research has continued to drill down into the broader social significance of well-being and its link to health. Recent social researchers have added support to the work of contemporary psychological theorists[4] who have emphasized that human connection is important not only for well-being and health, but also for survival itself.

These kinds of studies are a result of what has been seen as a waning sense of social connection in contemporary America: "Household sizes are decreasing and biological family and friends are more geographically and emotionally disconnected from one another than ever before."[5] This disconnection has led to the rise in feelings of loneliness and a sense of seclusion from others, with twenty-five percent of Americans reporting in 2004 that they had no single close confidant at all.[6] Studies by developmental psychologists have argued that intimacy and close tenderness in the form of a loving, compassionate relationship are essential components of a human life, particularly emotional support, such as empathy and affectionate concern for and by another, and specifically the *perception* of support from others.[7] Social connection amounts to "closeness, intimacy, and affection," which have enormous health benefits such as an inverse correlation with dementia, and, as Emma Seppala, Timothy Rossomando, and James R. Doty argue, "social connection needs to be positive and affectionate and perceived as such."[8] It is the *perception* of social connection that really determines health rather than an actual quantity of social connection.[9]

Contemporary zombie stories provide a fantastical space to consider the fundamental question of what motivates humans to live at all, especially at a time when the basic fabric of social interaction seems to be breaking down, even when time is ostensibly freed up and communications increased by the advancement of new technologies since the 1990s. Swanwick's "The Dead" (first published in 1996) projects a generally dystopian vision of America's future, but it is also a plea to contemporary society, which is seen as bereft of intimate connection, for a revival of solidarity and compassion between people. Based in Manhattan and featuring zombies that are not ravenous monsters driven to eat and infect humans but commodities that are produced, bought, and sold, "The Dead" is clearly a reflection on the increasingly global corporate landscape of the 1990s. It provides a cautionary view of life with no emotional intimacy or human connection but also critiques individualist passions, or negative human drives triggered by personal ambition. The zombies present no direct physical danger to humans; the threat lies rather in what the use of the zombie means for the future of humanity. The story is narrated by Donald, who describes being waited on by zombies during a business dinner with ex-colleague and casual sex partner, Courtney. She proposes that he switch from his current position to join Koestler Biological, a company that uses reanimated dead bodies to perform various tasks and services, arguing that the product has become viable as an economical alternative to real ("blue collar") labor.

"The Dead" warns of the potential unethical and amoral practices that might be opened up by rapidly developing technologies, driven by human greed for profit and power. It is in keeping with science fiction stories, Swanwick's usual field of writing, which foretell the demise of human connection in the service industry when nonhuman alternatives, such as machines or robots, take over.[10] Here, though, the new superefficient product is a zombie rather than a robot, thus adding a sense of repulsion and the macabre to this vision of the future. The narrative clearly draws inspiration from the soulless drone or slave associated with the folkloric voodoo zombie recounted by American writers who had travelled to Haiti during the early part of the twentieth century (as outlined in the introduction and first essays of this volume). The story is also a commentary on the problems already manifest in contemporaneous Western society, most overtly evident in the strategies of emotionless and cold-blooded businesspeople in hot pursuit of finding innovative ways of reducing labor costs. While slavery is ostensibly consigned to the history books of a colonial era, trading with humans remains ever present in various forms of human exploitation, such as sex trafficking, domestic slavery, and illegal adoption. Nevertheless, handling *dead* human bodies as goods is clearly something of a taboo, providing an element of fantasy that unsettles what it means to be human. The subversive elements of Swanwick's story resonate with Rosemary Jackson's assertion that fantastic literature "opens up, for a brief moment, on to disorder, on to illegality, on to that which lies outside the law, that which is outside dominant value systems."[11] However, Jackson's overall argument is that most forms of the fantastic tend to restore a sense of order by the close of the narrative, or—as with the Gothic—a restored sense of order challenged only by a lingering ambiguity (that disorder *might* return). What makes many apocalyptic zombie fictions distinct is their tendency to stretch this subversive potential further, beyond "a brief moment," so that a gaping rupture remains. There is an abiding sense that the previous life will not return, even in a destabilized form. In "The Dead," this finality is alleviated only by the cautionary message aimed at the silent, disempowered masses to wake up from our current zombified slumber.

The vocabulary and style employed in "The Dead" emphasize parallels with the evolving society, seen as passionlessly driven by profit at the cost of human connection. The dead human products are given the sanitized name "postanthropic biological resources," alluding to the human body as a material source that has economic value. At the time this story was published, the term "human resources" was beginning to replace "personnel" across a range of workplaces, including those less corporately inclined, and it has since become commonplace for human bodies to be counted in relation to units of currency.[12] As Toby Venables notes, zombie films and literature do not always simply convey a dread of the future, but can also shine a light on the contemporary city as it stands: "Ultimately, perhaps, the greatest fear evoked by the modern zombie mythology is not that we will become the undead, but that, somehow, we already are, rendered so by the city, and by modern life; anonymous, directionless, disconnected from the land, from history and from traditional notions of community—without soul, without meaning."[13] The fear thus embedded in zombie narratives is that the contemporary city breeds anonymity and disconnection, eroding any sense of community spirit or meaningful being. In a number of zombie films, parallels have been made metaphorically between zombies and consumers, an image iconized explicitly in George A. Romero's *Dawn of the Dead* (1978), when hordes return aimlessly to roam the shopping malls. Swanwick draws similar parallels, depicting city-dwellers as already dead, made collectively powerless and apathetic by inequality, but beyond this, he creates a blurring in "The Dead" so that it is unclear at key points whether the narrator is commenting on the present or an imagined future, on humans or zombies. This blurring is particularly prominent about two thirds of the way into the story when, in a significantly isolated paragraph (configured with an additional line space before and after it), Donald recounts a hallucinatory vision of Manhattan at night—a city of corpses "all waiting for the years to pass and the flesh to fall from their bones."[14] The condensation opened up by the short story form provides license for this one insulated paragraph (couched as a dream) to gain emphasis that it would be difficult to achieve in a novel, thus providing a powerful interlude to assert its message. We might see it as a crucial pause, or reflection. It allows insight into the story's central "point," a freeing from "reiterations" and "repetitions" that Austin Wright suggests are key features of a longer novel: "And the cessation of reiteration may be what produces that impact, epiphany, or revelation."[15] This snapshot of citizens as corpses offers a profound image of contemporary life. The catastrophe of waiting to die, rather than connecting compassionately, is something that is prominent in the stories examined later in this essay, where the active benefits of love, of connecting intimately, and of loving being alive become a central focus.

"The Dead" is narrated in first person, from Donald's perspective, to some extent making him a figure to identify with as a symbol of postcolonial conscience, but as the story progresses, this identification begins to fracture. Donald's presence and marked disapproval of Courtney's profession, "peddling corpses" as he terms it, help steer the reader's responses, providing a moral barometer, as does his uncomfortable note of the sanitized term for human bodies used in the contract: "A certain product."[16] He is also actively repulsed by the idea that they will be trading bodies from Africa,[17] contextually at a time when "fair trade" as a concept, and later as a brand, was starting to take force on a global scale. However, Donald's ongoing objectification of Courtney makes him a shakier figure, and as the narrative progresses, it also becomes apparent that he will have to comply with the order. Towards the end of the story, when Courtney refuses to have sex with Donald but instead leaves him a "present" in his hotel bedroom—in the form of an "ethereal," beautiful dead woman—he rushes to Courtney's room and accuses her of "necrophilia." He holds onto an old world, one in which human connection is intricately linked with (natural) sex: "That thing's just an obedient body. There's nothing there—no passion, no connection, just … physical presence."[18] But the fact that he is a problematic figure presents deeper layers, and Courtney's statement that they have "equity" now has a feminist edge. Courtney's devaluing of human life seems to have some degree of gravitas, honesty, and sense to it, compared with the inadequacies of the "old world" with its fabricated passions and the false fantasies of desire set up by systems of prostitution, and (sexual) human relationships more generally.

The story closes with Donald looking out over Manhattan at a "vast necropolis"—at the disproportionate numbers of the poorer population who will soon be out of work. Their only source of income will be selling themselves as future dead bodies, thus taking the concept of insurance to a new level, based around a reverse system of payment. The prospect suggests a criticism of a wider culture of insurance, propelled and paralyzed by fear, safeguarding for a less oppressed future, as if already dead, or waiting to die. The ending presents the quandary of whether these living dead citizens have enough vigor to fight the "corpses" for their lost jobs. The first condensed paragraph of the final passage expresses the narrator's fear of the masses rising up. The next (penultimate) brief paragraph, consisting of three short sentences, offers the alternate option that nothing would happen. The final sentence, significantly isolated as a final paragraph, declares: "God help me, but I didn't know which one scared me more."[19] As Scott D. Emmert argues, the "formal compression" enabled by the short story often means that there is "greater importance on the ending, which arguably functions differently in short stories than in novels."[20] The concluding proclamation in "The Dead" is testament to Emmert's claim that short fiction endings are often "the most violent force in the story."[21] Despite its ostensive ambivalence, the final statement delivers a clear message; the thought that citizens would not come together compassionately and unite is an extremely worrying prospect on a global level. The story presents the inherent problems of a world with no intimacy and no human connection, at the same time offering a critique of both the individual and collective passions and prejudices that motivate the human race, together with the unequal distribution of wealth and power, resulting in apathy. Such a nihilist vision is also a call to act, to wake up and to resist the drives of unthinking scientific and technological advancement, specifically. Philosophically, the story advocates acting on the vital energy that connects us as people, living and working together to achieve significant change.

A number of stories since the millennium have focused on what the living dead might be able to tell us about the intrinsic joys of living (that we might have lost). Palwick's "Beautiful Stuff" (first published in 2004), also featuring an undead population very different from the ravenous human-killing zombies that have become the norm, is a response to politicians' exploitation of 9/11 as a reason for war and in turn a reflection on how victims of the attack might respond, if they were able to speak, to the war campaigns that have been raging in their name. The story suggests that, given the chance of a moment of life, a day to live again, the dead would perceive the chance for life radically differently from how the living perceive it.

"Beautiful Stuff" values the immediate connection to be felt by appreciating tangible beauty in the present moment, a love that can be sensed at the fingertips by simply being alive. The revived corpses are childlike and find it virtually impossible to lie. They are drawn to living creatures and flowers, to playing with food and making mud pies, ignoring their relations' "impassioned statement of devotion,"[22] which is depicted as programmatic and artificial. When Rusty, a revived victim, is brought to the bandstand podium to speak to audiences, families, reporters, and cameras, primed to stress the need to retaliate, for troops to redress the evil, he instead finds it hard not to chase a butterfly and speaks of the pain caused by dying, urging the audience to put an end to any further killing. His message, to "[e]njoy the beautiful stuff while you have it," is initially misinterpreted as a statement of greed and possession until he corrects the emphasis—"No. Just enjoy. Look at it. Don't fight."[23] As the last words that Rusty says before the story's finale, they have an added emphasis and a prevailing wisdom that might be lost in the multiple reiterations of a novel. The purity of the revived dead predominates over societal artifices, shallow declarations of devotion, and wars fought in the name of love.

Like "The Dead," "Beautiful Stuff" spells out its meaning in the closing paragraph, in which all of the living dead are described as being "in love," but the associations of this love, though intense for the moment, are different from those associated with clinging or claiming ownership. Rather, the alert beings are alive to the sounds and sights of the sunny park—a bird, a scarf, and an empty milk carton. Thus "Beautiful Stuff" speaks politically against taking revenge for the sake of harmed loved ones. It advocates realizing a love divorced from possessive passion, a joy in the object or living being near at hand, in and for all its temporariness. In short, the zombies are represented as superior in many ways to the living humans surrounding them. While "The Dead" and "Beautiful Stuff" are unusual because they do not take place in quite the conventional zombie apocalypse setting, there has been a movement toward depicting humans as worse than zombies, and many narratives have begun to focus on the extremes that humans can go to, under stress, in order to survive. For example, in Kim Paffenroth's novel *Dying to Love* (2006), the survivors are former inmates who beat the new prisoners and rape a child. As Margo Collins and Elson Bond argue, "because they can think, humans are potentially more horrific than their undead counterparts."[24] While the loss of human will has traditionally been a subject of fear in zombie narratives, "Beautiful Stuff" celebrates this loss. The human compulsion for power, revenge, passion, and ownership comes under severe scrutiny. The moral of this antiwar story is that society should form immediate connections in the present moment, rather than waste time fighting for an illusion forged in the name of a past alliance or in defense of the future.

However, the staple of contemporary zombie novels and films has been the theme of survival, empathizing with the human survivors against the mass horde, and this has been one of the main focal points of contemporary short stories as well. Key to these narratives is considering how well an individual will fare using primal survival skills in an apocalyptic landscape, especially when the main signifiers of contemporary civilization—such as technology, capitalism, and education—no longer have value. While this focus on survival has clear individualist elements, drawing on the fear of being taken over by the faceless masses, there is also the growing sense of a collective heroism underlying contemporary representations of survival. As Shawn McIntosh has observed, "protagonists must also work together to try to overcome the zombie masses and survive."[25] With respect to survival, many stories, like their cinematic counterparts, have typically dwelt on the essence of love and being, and whether an individual should (or is able to) kill a previous loved one once that person has turned into a ravenous zombie. This tradition can be seen in earlier stories such as Stephen King's "Home Delivery" (1989), which depicts a woman killing her returned zombie husband in order to save the child within her, and more recent stories, such as David Wellington's "Good People" (2010), which similarly centers on sacrificing a three-year-old child.

While it is thus commonplace for zombie fictions to explore a de-romanticized vision of love in the face of survival, and often the final chances of survival are very bleak, romanticism has sometimes remained in the guise of the individualist hero.[26] The stories explored for the remainder of this essay mark a departure from some of the traditional narratives where survival is the key driver for existence. These stories of survival form part of a recent tendency within short fiction to focus on the notion that life is not worth living if there is no human contact, or even that human contact is vital to survival.

Kilpatrick's "The Age of Sorrow" (2007) suggests that the touch, smell, and sounds of another material being are necessary not only to curb loneliness but also as a crucial part of survival. The female protagonist is the sole survivor in a world of zombies. In this altered state, as is often the case in zombie narratives, she has started to be honest with herself all the time, realizing that in her previous life she detested her job and made ill-considered choices in the name of love (for Gary, who ended up having an affair). After her parents' divorce, she became disconnected from her father, feeling no familiarity with "his voice, his scent, his touch."[27] She realizes that humanity as a whole has made bad choices. Now, in this new life, choices are simpler—to live or to die. Despite being extremely adept at survival, having mastered the use of solar panels and the cultivation of vegetables, she wonders if the zombies, her only companions, seek her out for connection, as lonely as she is: "If I cease to survive, will they?"[28] Following a dream of sunny fields covered with wildflowers, the scent of lilac and the feel of Gary's electric touch, she realizes she needs contact with another—and goes out to meet her death just so that flesh can meet flesh; the zombie's fingers and foul odor are sensed as flowers. The story's central message is articulated at the start and end, thus framing the narrative structurally. The first sentence of the story, "Grief had taken hold of her long ago,"[29] is resolved by the closing solace: "for the first time in a long time her sorrow evaporated into the wind."[30] This framing, enforced by the condensation of the short story format, permits a philosophical prominence that is able to eclipse the narrative ending (the protagonist's death). As Emmert suggests, "the endings of short stories often enforce an interpretive re-orientation by requiring readers to 'sweep back through the story' and judge its details in relation to the finale."[31] Consistent with this observation on the short story format, the closing of "The Age of Sorrow" presents a reevaluation of the story's emphasis. Similar to "Beautiful Stuff," "The Age of Sorrow" highlights the unnecessary artifices and protocols of civilization. Ultimately, it values intimate flesh contact above survival; death is preferable to a life with no contact.

The introduction to Kirkman's "Alone, Together" (2010) in *Living Dead 2* states the importance of human psychology in survival.[32] The story relates Timothy's past life with his perfect, intelligent, and funny girlfriend until his world falls apart, and he constructs a new life in the zombie apocalyptic world with Alicia. Even though he has had no real choice and misses his previous relationship, he realizes nevertheless that he has never known anyone as intimately as he does Alicia. The high ideals he once had are abandoned. His world revolves around wanting to find her things she might value. However, it transpires through the course of the story that the death of her ex was not accidental, and that Timothy had chosen not to step in and help, thus aiding the cause of his death. The use of the present tense and first person emphasizes the urgency: "I tell her because I love her. I tell her because I respect her. I tell her because I hope she'll forgive me."[33] While he believes they will be stronger for having no secrets, the revelation of his lie makes her desperate, and she leaves the next morning, taking everything—food, supplies, weapons:

> Whether she's meant it or not, she has killed me.
> I won't last more than five days alone.
> Truth be told—without her, I don't want to.[34]

These final three sentences of the story, each presented on the page as a new line, move towards the final revelatory declaration. It is precisely the "concision" of the short story that, as Valerie Shaw argues, is able to "dramatize a moment of revelation which brings a character to full consciousness for the first time in his life."[35] The ending cements the story's central philosophy, as is the case in the other short stories explored in this essay. Love itself is here a survival source; Timothy does not see the point in continuing without Alicia. Love in the sense of human intimacy and connection is necessary not just to enhance life, but as a crucial element of survival. The story's point that Timothy thrives when believing that he has a special connection with Alicia relates to the studies by developmental psychologists Seppala,

Rossomando, and Doty, who argue that social connection needs to be *perceived* for it be effective in stimulating health and well-being.[36]

Castro's "The Anteroom" (2010) contemplates a living limbo in which zombies have awakened to the atrocities they have carried out and have nothing to do but wander in a barren landscape, surrounded by those haunted by the people they have killed. We are placed in the position of a conscience-ridden zombie as the story addresses the reader as subject, using second-person narration. One of the "fellow prisoners" compares these shattered souls with the dementia patients she used to nurse, and the "dangerous stage most people don't know about."[37] The point she makes is that while this state is in no way as terrible as Hell, there is no room in Heaven: "You scream until you run out of breath and stand there panting as you wait for an answer. But nobody answers. No body answers.... You are alone."[38] The story thus makes conscious parallels between zombie violence and dementia, and the sense of a unified self is shaken up, fracturing the concept of a "them" and an "us" and the conventional "othering" of the zombie. As Collins and Bond argue, the new social anxiety, distinct from the consumerist concerns of earlier zombie texts, is the interstitial place between zombie-humans and human zombies: "Ultimately, modern zombie stories reflect our fear of loss of identity."[39] This fear can be linked back to the intricacies of Cartesian dualism: "But what then am I? A thing which thinks. What is a thing which thinks? It is a thing which doubts, understands, [conceives], affirms, denies, wills, refuses, which also imagines and feels."[40] The importance here is about *perception* (not so different from more recent philosophical findings), since René Descartes continues through the course of his essay to argue that even if what surrounds us is false, a dream, then at least it seems that I see these things, hear these things, and feel these things. If we relate this in turn to more recent studies of well-being and human connection, human identity is crucially entwined with not simply consciousness or conscious thought, but imagination and feeling—perceiving that something is there, some sense of connection.

The final story to be examined in this essay, "Who We Used to Be" (2010), by British writer Moody, communicates the need to live and love in the present moment, even at the risk of danger. It illuminates the problems of attempting to hold on to the past, wasting time on unimportant rituals, surviving rather than thriving. It contemplates the close details of a family's remaining days after all human life is over—"when more than six billion lives were abruptly ended."[41] The family members are thus positioned—suddenly—in limbo, where it is clear that their lives are over, already never the same again; we witness the gradual draining of the remnants of their life. This immediate switch means the end of the world, or human life, so that the story constructs no "them" and "us" division between zombies and humans—but rather all humans have died suddenly: and as if it were no more than a "blip," minutes later "every last one of the dead got back up again and tried to carry on."[42]

Clearly, as in the pre-zombie world of "The Age of Sorrow," no real intimacy exists in their everyday lives, and the stresses of contemporary British life are given full rein in Moody's descriptions of the domestic setting. The moment happens for Simon when he is working as usual in his home office on a Saturday morning, looking at business projections; it is taking up much more time than he had anticipated, but the work is deemed necessary to support the obligatory house, car, and holidays. The process means missing valuable time with his son, Nathan, and his wife Janice is only superficially satisfied, sustaining consumerist urges, having just returned from shopping with bags of unnecessary clothes. Therefore, both Simon and Janice already waste too much time on ritualistic, repetitive, and vacuously commercial pursuits when the sudden paralysis hits.

"Who We Used to Be" urges that humans be driven by love and inspiration rather than fear and prejudice, arguing that they should not exist only to prolong something long past, as Janice and Simon do, shutting out the outside world and the dead surrounding them, by closing blinds and blocking the living room door. Stylistically, their goal is singled out, with the two short sentences, given a separate paragraph, emphasizing the irony of the words: "They were safe. The house was secure."[43] Although they are reanimated as suddenly as they died, it transpires that they have been revived only in an increasingly debilitated state. To survive even for a limited time, they must become virtually dormant, avoiding the hazards of outside life, which causes bodies to ooze with lumpy brown liquids and fracture, as flesh falls away from tattered insides. Simon and Janice scarcely endure throughout the story, preoccupied with maintaining their survival (or rather the continuance of their newly undead state), for as long as possible; inevitably their speech is impeded, their energy is drained, and their bodies decay, until it is, finally, over. The notion of keeping alive, dragging out the inevitable, clearly relates to contemporary (Western) ways of handling terminal illness and the imminence of death, using medication and technology to keep death at bay for as long as possible when, as Moody argues, the "kindest and most sensible" option might be to let go.[44]

"Who We Used to Be" echoes "The Anteroom" in that it portrays people clinging on, like dying patients unable to take control of their final hour. This critique of thoughtlessly continuing along the same track is stressed from the opening sentence of Moody's story, which notes the greatest "irony" of all—that people disregarded their own eradication and simply carried on.[45] The story raises ultimate questions concerning the purpose of living—not only the human motivation for extending one's life, but also the way to pursue a meaningful (or even happy) life. By exploring a changed situation or a limited lifespan, the story prompts us to think about what should motivate us to live, or how to be alive, suggesting that contemporary life is for many a slow living death when we become "for too long increasingly focused on the irrelevant."[46] As well as opening up many of the familiar quandaries about how humans might cope in an apocalyptic setting, or on being or becoming one of the living dead, the focus on such a survival here also poses questions about contemporary life as it already is, revealing the lost joys of living, forgotten amidst contemporary responsibilities and (increasing) dependence on the securities of new technologies allegedly based on aiding comfort and communication. The story comments on the intricate and diverse ways that can prompt people to cling to the familiar, even if the original goal or impetus for that form of life is long dead.

While the final episode of "Who We Used to Be" opens with the summary that Simon and Janice lasted another eighteen days, long after their brain activity ceased, lying at extreme ends of the living room, the concluding paragraph concentrates on their son Nathan who lasted only a single day. In contrast to his parents, he had opted to act, similar to the undead in "Beautiful Stuff." He attempts to play football, climb a tree, play with animals, and explore a forbidden part of the garden. While Simon and Janice fail to do anything but keep the house secure, thinking about who they were in the past and everything that they have lost, their son is driven by a love of (and connection to) the moment. The story presents a guide to adopting a more fulfilling way of being, to be alive to change, and to accept death. The message is that safety can be a living death, that in carrying on, life becomes stale, a mere reflection of what once was. The child embodies the philosophy of engaging with the environment and living things, venturing into unknown and potentially dangerous territories, facing rather than securing (or insuring) for the future.

"Who We Used to Be" might be seen as an acting out of the prophetic vision in "The Dead," when Donald sees the city of corpses waiting for the years to pass and the flesh to fall from their bones. The difficulty in contemporary society, many of the stories explored in this essay remind us, is recognizing what the spark of "now" really is. This impulse, emphasized stylistically by the candid use of language and framing of the short story format, has become cannily prophetic. Since these stories were published, "wellbeing," "value," and "mindfulness" have grown into corporate buzzwords, endorsed by government initiatives and policies, as part of an allegedly transparent way of dealing with mental health issues and feelings of disconnection. It might be said that these buzzwords have become a way to maintain the status quo and in some instances to increase the efficiency of the human resource. To leave this nominally supportive environment can be a fearful prospect. The stories bring us back to a straightforward contention: that contemporary society needs to be driven by love and inspiration rather than fear, and that being alive should not consist of living in a number of successive pasts, or of safeguarding the future, but should be more focused on the moment and the values of human connection.

NOTES

1. See, for example, Mason's philosophical inquiry: Mason, "Galvanic 'Unhuman,'" 193–207.

2. Darwin, *Descent of Man,* 111.

3. Raz, "Role of Well-Being," 283.

4. See, for example, Cacioppo et al., "Loneliness and Health," 416, and Pressman et al., "Loneliness, Social Network Size, and Immune Response," 297.

5. Seppala, Rossomando, and Doty, "Social Connection and Compassion," 412. Seppala, Rossomando, and Doty also cite the work of Hobbs and Stoops, "Demographic Trends in the 20th Century," 33, to support the claim.

6. Seppala, Rossomando, and Doty, "Social Connection and Compassion," 412.

7. *Ibid.,* 414.

8. *Ibid.* Summarizing the work of Fratiglioni, Wag, and Ericsson, "Influence of Social Network on Occurrence of Dementia," 1315–19.

9. See, for example, Seppala, Rossomando, Doty, "Social Connection and Compassion," 419.

10. There are striking parallels in general with the recent British-American television series *Humans*, which debuted 14 June 2015 on Channel 4 and AMC, and the film *Ex Machina* (2015, directed by Alex Garland), but significantly Swanwick's story is not about the question of whether there is consciousness beneath the surface of the seemingly lifeless, artificial being, or indeed what consciousness is, but more about the impact on humanity, and thus the boundaries between the living and the dead remain less blurred than in many later representations.

11. Jackson, *Fantasy,* 4.

12. It is worth noting that some of the technologies mentioned in the story are prophetic. For example, the ability to access information on an optic chip by a simple eye movement is becoming increasingly more likely with developing technologies, such as the Google Glass.

13. Venables, "Zombies, a Lost Literary Heritage," 216.

14. Swanwick, "The Dead," 104.

15. Wright, "Writer Meets the Critic," 18.

16. Swanwick, "The Dead," 104. There are haunting parallels with the rhetoric of Nazi authorities, as evidenced in a memo, written in an early stage of the Final Solution, that euphemistically refers to the people being exterminated as the "load," "pieces," and "merchandise" (see Katz, "Ethic of Expediency," 255–56). Swanwick's caution against the extremes of capitalism in contemporary life matches Steven B. Katz's argument that the "ethos of expediency" that frames the discourse of the Nazi memo also drives technological capitalism, often taking "precedence over human convenience, and sometimes even human life" (*Ibid.,* 271).

17. The story can also be seen to provide a self-conscious nod to the problematic representations of race historically embedded in the "Cinematic Voodoo Zombie," as articulated in Kyle William Bishop's investigation of *White Zombie* (1932, directed by Victor Halperin) as a "perpetuation of the imperialist model of cultural and racial hegemony." Bishop, "Sub-Subaltern Monster," 141.

18. Swanwick, "The Dead," 106.

19. *Ibid.,* 107.

20. Emmert, "Naturalism and the Short Story Form," 81.

21. *Ibid.,* 81.

22. Palwick, "Beautiful Stuff," 139.

23. *Ibid.*, 147.

24. Collins and Bond, "Off the Page and into Your Brains!" 202.

25. McIntosh, "Evolution of the Zombie," 10.

26. This is evident to some extent in Max Brooks' *World War Z: An Oral History of the Zombie War* (2006), a novel that has been seen as distinctly American in its violence and a "testimony to the rise of heroism in a world that was forced to overcome its differences in order to fight a common enemy" (Baldwin, "*World War Z* and the End of Religion," 414). Brooks revisits ideas of heroism in his short story "Steve and Fred" (2010) in which Steve, initially depicted saving the day on his motorbike with a girl on the back, is finally revealed to be actually holed up in a toilet, parodying the traditional individualist hero, along with masculine valor.

27. Kilpatrick, "Age of Sorrow," 334.

28. *Ibid.*, 342.

29. *Ibid.*, 332.

30. *Ibid.*, 344.

31. Emmert, "Naturalism and the Short Story Form," 81.

32. Kirkman, "Alone, Together," 3.

33. *Ibid.*, 16.

34. *Ibid.*

35. Shaw, *Short Story*, 8.

36. Seppala, Rossomando, Doty, "Social Connection and Compassion," 414. Summarizing the work of Fratiglioni, Wag, and Ericsson, "Influence of Social Network on Occurrence of Dementia," 1315–19.

37. Castro, "Anteroom," 53.

38. *Ibid.*, 55.

39. Collins and Bond, "Off the Page and into Your Brains!" 204.

40. Descartes, "Meditations on First Philosophy," 10.

41. Moody, "Who We Used to Be," 315–16.

42. *Ibid.*, 316.

43. *Ibid.*, 324.

44. Moody, "Introduction," 315.

45. Moody, "Who We Used to Be," 315.

46. *Ibid.*

Analyzing Late Modernity with a Corpse

Max Brooks' Zombie Understanding of Modernity

MARCUS LEANING

Max Brooks' 2003 *The Zombie Survival Guide: Complete Protection from the Living Dead* (hereafter *ZSG*) and 2006 *World War Z: An Oral History of the Zombie War* (hereafter *WWZ*) present us with two thoughtful and surprisingly complex zombie texts. Zombies are polysemic and have been considered to serve a number of purposes; they function as texts to which we can attribute different meanings, including the death of civilization,[1] a mirror that reflects our own weakness in the face of global consumer capitalism,[2] and a "modern monstrous"—an "other" against which we define our humanity.[3] In this essay, I contend that when considered through a theoretical framework drawn from the work of a number of European sociologists, Brooks' work and the "story-world" therein can be used to understand social life and experience in contemporary times. This approach characterizes the current period of time as late modernity—a period in which risk and high levels of individualization are recognized as centralized narratives. Though Brooks' work has been subject to critical engagement from various perspectives, such as the far right[4] or broadly socialist,[5] the interrogation offered here from a European sociological perspective affords a fresh critical lens through which to consider both texts by Brooks and perhaps the wider presence of zombies in popular culture. It also affords an opportunity to consider how the issues of risk and individualization can be articulated through zombie literature.

This essay commences with an overview of two of Brooks' main contributions to zombie literature, then moves on to identifying a number of themes in his work and his story-world or zombie universe. These themes are then considered in the light of the work of a number of European sociologists, and through Brooks we are able to envisage and even interrogate particular aspects of late modernity, such as the manufacture of risk and the drive to individualization.

Max Brooks' Zombie Books and His Zombie Universe

Brooks' texts have served to define and increase the popularity of longform zombie literature. The addition of a zombie motif to a pre-existing literary or cultural convention is an effective method by which the zombie meme has spread, leveraging new market sectors for zombie-infected texts. However, while the body of zombie literature is growing fast, it proves increasingly difficult to define its edges. In addition to their home in horror, zombies find themselves deployed in pseudohistorical fiction such as Seth Grahame-Smith's 2009 *Pride and Prejudice and Zombies* (Jane Austen is graciously accorded a byline); choose-your-own-adventure-style texts, such as Max Brailer's 2011 *Can You Survive the Zombie Apocalypse?*; mock children's books, for example, Michael Teitelbaum and Jon Apple's 2012 *The Very Hungry Zombie: A Parody*; and even a political treatise—Daniel Drezner's 2014 *Theories of International Politics and Zombies*. In these examples, the texts parasitically draw upon prior existing genres and literary traditions, creating hybrid texts that stretch the boundaries of both the zombie and the host genre. Jonathan P. Eburne contends that such zombie texts pose a self-awareness of the conventions of zombie fiction,[6] though they also draw equally heavily on the conventions and rules of the host genre. Brooks' two texts continue this approach and skillfully utilize prior existing literary genres to extend the reach of the zombie further.

The *ZSG* is a comedic instructional text that offers methods, techniques, and general information that could be used to survive a zombie apocalypse. In style, it references a tradition of instructional texts that describe the means and methods of survival in different settings. Guidelines for dealing with dangerous situations and surviving in extreme conditions have long been available as training resources for military and survival-oriented individuals. Such texts offer guidance on surviving in the wild,[7] surviving everyday disasters,[8] or surviving times when the ordinary mechanics of law, order, and civilization have broken down.[9] These texts have also found a ready market beyond those who may directly need such information. Numerous guides that detail techniques used by military personnel, survival "experts," and "preppers"—people who seek to prepare for the collapse of civilization—have been published for popular audiences. The rhetoric of survival has also found its way into the titling of various guides for what are clearly not extraordinary situations, such as parenting teenagers,[10] teaching,[11] and being a fashion designer.[12] A further derivation of this is the production of texts for surviving disasters whose occurrence is uncertain—from the possible (terrorist attacks and nuclear war[13]), the generally pessimistic (the collapse of society and slipping into a new "Dark Age"[14]), and the unlikely (robot uprisings[15]), and moving into the parodic (alien invasions or being a vampire[16]). While texts in the last category are written with the authorial tongue firmly in cheek, in some instances, the authors may be seeking to educate about particular aspects as well (Daniel Wilson, the author of the book on robot uprisings, has a Ph.D. in robotics, and the text includes significant details of much current robotics research). In this category are also a number of texts about surviving the zombie apocalypse. Survival guides and manuals for how to thrive in the zombie apocalypse have proven popular, with a number of alternate texts being published—for example, Michael Thomas and Nick Thomas' 2009 *Zompoc: How to Survive a Zombie Apocalypse*, Gerald Kielpinski and Brian Gleisberg's 2011 *Surviving the Zombie Outbreak: The Official Zombie Survival Field Manual*, and Sean Page's 2013 *Zombie Survival Manual: From the Dawn of Time Onwards*.

Brooks' *ZSG* is possibly the best known in its textual class. The *ZSG* comprises an introduction, six chapters, and a list of historical recorded attacks. The six chapters cover a range of theoretical and practical topics, such as the cause and nature of zombies, guidance on fighting them, survival in various spaces, escape and attack strategies, and long-term survival in a zombie-infested world. Each chapter is divided into sections; this structure mirrors that of instructional guides that divide information into discrete parcels or steps to follow. The book includes numerous simple illustrations that closely resemble those found in packaged instructions and guides (the illustrations were created by Max Werner, a freelance artist and book cover illustrator; Werner has also produced illustrations for Rick Curtis' *The Backpacker's Field Manual*). Similarly, in tone the text draws abundantly upon the instructional text genre; it postulates potential problems that could occur in a zombie apocalypse and then offers solutions and strategies for dealing with such problems. Furthermore, the advice is delivered in a simple and straightforward manner, and it defies possible conflation or ambiguity of meaning, a tenet central to good instructional writing.[17] While the initial premise may be fantastical, the responses and advice Brooks offers are thoughtful and in many ways no different from advice given in the survival guides for nonfantastical situations. With respect to the value of staying in a basement during a disaster, for example, the advice that Brooks offers is similar to that given by Cody Lundin and Kylene Jones.[18] Brooks notes that he conducted numerous interviews with specialists in order to gain insight into how to survive particular situations.[19] However, while Brooks concurs on the specifics of such advice, he offers a more positive, longer-term prognosis for the future of humanity, and across both texts is an underlying possibility of salvaging Western, late-modern civilization—a theme to which I will return later.

Like the *ZSG*, *WWZ* also emerges from a particular literary tradition. Its title and style draw explicitly from Studs Terkel's *The Good War: An Oral History of World War II* (1984)—a link Brooks himself notes.[20] Terkel's work itself is situated in a long history of using the recollections of participants in events—Ritchie argues the first oral histories were compiled by scribes and historians in Zhou dynasty China (1046–256 BCE), with Herodotus engaging in a similar practice in Greece several hundred years later.[21] Brooks adopts this approach, and the story of the zombie war is told through the recollections of numerous war participants. This oral history approach affords the novel a new perspective on the zombie apocalypse, one not told from the angle of a single person or group of individuals encountering zombies, but from a bird's-eye-view of the total global war. Because of this approach, the only consistent character is the narrator, though a number of characters get a final additional entry at the end of the book as well as their main stories. The book is divided into nine sections plus acknowledgments, with each section consisting of a number of interviews with participants. Through these interviews, Brooks reports on the course of the war.

The story commences in China with the initial outbreak, which is spread through organ trading, human trafficking, an incompetent state (which stages a conflict with Taiwan to cover up the outbreak), and then fleeing refugees. This occurrence leads to outbreaks in the rest of the world, the largest of which occurs in South Africa. In Israel, the early warnings are taken more seriously: the Warbrunn-Knight Report is produced, and an isolationist plan is put into place, which helps to save the country (though does itself result in a civil war). The USA does not instigate any systematic plan, and this failure to act is attributed to the weakness of the CIA and other government agencies, which have been financially unsupported for years, and the unscrupulous marketing of an ineffective inoculation, *Phalanx*. As the contagion spreads, "The Great Panic" commences with millions fleeing. After Iran closes its borders to refugees fleeing from Pakistan, the two countries engage in a nuclear war and effectively destroy each other. Following the overrun of New York, the U.S. military forces a plan for a defense of Yonkers, though this is a disaster due to the inappropriateness of modern weapons on zombies and poor planning that results in a lack of effective ammunition. Millions of Americans flee north to Canada; however, due to insufficient equipment, housing, and food, over five million die in the first winter. In South Africa, a retired Afrikaner apartheid strategist produces what becomes known as the *Redeker Plan*, a strategy based on a plan for white survival during a black insurgency. The *Redeker Plan* involves sacrificing large areas and many lives to guarantee the survival of particular areas. In the USA, it involves the government's retreat behind the Rocky Mountains to a safe zone that can be defended. The plan is adopted in many countries to great success, and the course of the war with zombies gradually begins to turn. At a meeting aboard a U.S. battleship seven years after the initial outbreak, the U.S. president announces a plan to attack the zombies and recapture the USA. This plan, known as the "Road to New York," involves the use of new tactics supported by a restructured U.S. economy. This plan works and is then used in other countries until, twelve years after the war began, the zombies are defeated when China is deemed cleared. Despite victory's being declared, though, many zombies survive in the wild, and they still pose a threat.

The postwar world is dramatically different from the prewar one. Many countries have changed: China becomes a democracy known as the "Chinese Federation"; Russia has transformed into the "Holy Russian Empire," governed by a priestly class that is responsible for killing the infected; Tibet becomes a free country, and Lhasa the world's most populous city; Mexico adopts the Aztec name *Aztlán*; Israel and Palestine become "Unified Palestine"; Cuba retains its sovereignty by developing a vibrant economy; and the USA remains intact and democratic, though its economy is radically different—now based on Keynesian economic principles and universal health care rather than classical or neoclassical economic models. Such dramatic changes to the political systems across the world are imbued with a distinct political vision. Right-wing reviews of the book have contended that such a vision is an articulation of Brooks' liberal values—that the USA remains a democracy but adopts Keynesian/Rooseveltian New Deal-esque principles reveals much of Brooks' underlying leftist stance. However, the transition to the postzombie world and the solving of the problems encountered in reaching it owe much to an assertion of the drive to individualization away from collective and state action.

The book contains numerous instances of commentary, or even in-jokes, on the politics at the time of writing—indeed, Brooks notes that he was conscious of this and was happy for his work to be fixed in the politics of the time.[22] However, the political commentary in the text attracted considerable criticism from various reviewers: right-wing reviewers critiqued the text, accusing it of an affirmation of a liberal agenda,[23] while left-wing reviewers critiqued its support of various racial agendas and its representation of countries other than the U.S.[24] The diversity in reception of Brooks' work indicates that the ideas raised in the books trigger debate and have resonance in a contemporary, non-zombie-infected world.

Across both texts, Brooks maintains what Christy Dena refers to as a stable "fictional world."[25] This approach integrates real-world characters (Nelson Rolihlaha Mandela[26]), characters arguably based on real-world people ("The Whacko" Vice-President,[27] who is based on Howard Dean after Dean's electoral collapse in the New Hampshire Democratic primary following the "Dean Scream,"[28] and the "Big Guy," the president of the USA, based on Colin Powell[29]), politics, and physical phenomena with fictional devices, the chief of which is the existence of zombies. However, while the zombies appear the most fantastical aspects in Brooks' zombie universe, all components—even those that are manifest in the real world—are constructions or at best interpretations. That is, though we may be able to discern aspects of Brooks' world that also seem to appear in our own and identify aspects that are obviously not present, such as zombies, we must be cautious of affording any aspect a greater degree of significance in the text. Thus if we engage critically with the texts, we may find ourselves focusing on the more fantastical elements, such as the zombies. However, it is those aspects that have a greater degree of verisimilitude that may afford richer insight.

Brooks' Zombie Creation Myth and Risk in Late Modernity

Central to any zombie story is the "zombie creation myth," or explanation of how people become zombies. Kim Paffenroth describes the origin used in a number of films:

> For some reason, recently dead human beings suddenly start getting up and walking around again. They no longer have human minds, however.... They are zombies....
> The exact cause for this outbreak is usually left unstated, but is sometimes briefly and cryptically described as "mysterious radiation" from a space probe returning from Venus (*Night of the Living Dead* [1968, directed by George A. Romero]), or divine judgement (*Dawn of the Dead* [both 1978, directed by Romero, and 2004, directed by Zack Snyder]), or, more scientifically, some kind of disease or virus (*Dawn of the Dead*), or most likely a biological weapon got out of hand (made explicit in *Resident Evil* [2002, directed by Paul W.S. Anderson] and *28 Days Later* [2002, directed by Danny Boyle]).[30]

A selection of other zombie creation myths used in films, books, and other media include a chemical spill (the film *Hell of the Living Dead*, 1980, directed by Bruno Mattei), an opened plague pit (the book *Zombie Apocalypse!*, 2010, by Stephen Jones), the bite of a Sumatran Rat-Monkey (the film *Braindead*, 1992, directed by Peter Jackson), an airborne virus (the book *The Zombie Autopsies*, 2011, written by Steven Schlozman), or a universal, viral-induced propensity to become a zombie after death as long as the brain is intact, though neither the origin of the virus nor how it is spread is revealed (*The*

Walking Dead comic [2003–, written by Robert Kirkman] and TV series [2010–, created by Frank Darabont]). Most zombie creation myths involve the basic premises that once the initial event has occurred, the creation of new zombies occurs easily and that the contagion spreads more quickly than it can be prevented, cured, or stopped. Moreover, the cause, spread, and failure to check the outbreak of zombies are often linked to a failure (or complicity) on the part of the state or big business.[31]

In Brooks' story-world, zombies are caused by the Solanum virus, a highly communicable virus that is spread by fluid exchange, typically occurring during an attack by a zombie. Any victim who is not killed by the initial attack will sicken and die within twenty hours before reanimating as a zombie, which is then intent on attacking others. In naming the virus "Solanum," Brooks uses a name that in nonzombie literature refers to a genus of flora that includes tomatoes, potatoes, various nightshades, and (entertainingly) Solanum nigrum L, colloquially known as Branched Calalue, which is identified as a constituent part of Haitian voodoo zombie poison.[32] Brooks thus draws upon a range of different zombie creation myths to present a new one. The use of the term "Solanum" adds a degree of depth to the myth; by incorporating a term from an extant zombie myth, Brooks utilizes a wider set of signs, which adds verisimilitude if not credibility to the myth.

For Brooks, the rapid spread of the virus and the high numbers of zombies present a seemingly insurmountable problem for humanity. The zombies seem unstoppable; even the immense and incredibly sophisticated armory of the U.S. military forces using modern weapons and tactics is unable to defeat the zombies in open battle (the Battle of Yonkers[33]). Moreover, the very nature of modern warfare, relying as it does on "shock and awe," does not work on zombies as they feel no fear.[34] Modern science is similarly unable to offer a solution; there is no cure, nor can the virus be immunized against.[35] Indeed, rather than defeating the Solanum virus, the complicity of the Federal Drug Administration, the UN, and other state and governmental agencies with pharmaceutical corporations in the release of the false vaccine, Phalanx, exacerbates the problem.[36]

Zombies thus present a natural phenomenon or hazard that modern science is unable to defeat, mitigate, or adapt to. The ability of the apparatus and expert systems of the modern state to deal with global problems and hazards, along with the fear of such a phenomenon, is understood to be characteristic of late modernity. Anthony Giddens defines many contemporary societies as "risk societies": they are "increasingly preoccupied with the future (and also with safety), which generates the notion of risk."[37] It is important to note that Giddens does not assert that we live in an age of greater hazard (he rightly notes that life in the Middle Ages was far more dangerous than life in contemporary society); instead, a risk society is a society characterized

by *manufactured* risk—the widespread assumption that there are new phenomena or "risk environments for which history provides us with very little
previous experience."[38] In earlier eras, we could defer to tradition (in pre-
modern societies) or to corporate and governmental systems (in modern
societies) to mitigate risk—we could turn to private insurance or to the wel-
fare state. But in a late-modern risk society, the threat comes not from outside
nature or external human action but from *manufactured* risk, the direct consequence of our very response to external threats—what we do to ameliorate
external risks becomes itself a new level of threat to us. Moreover, we become
increasingly aware that we are at risk both from external risk and from the
very actions that we take to mitigate that risk. This manufactured risk has
occurred as the disembedding processes of modernity have lifted us out of
a close relationship with both tradition and the systems and practices that
insulated us from direct understanding of issues of local and global risk.[39]
The shift in how we understand the world from the power of religion and
(uncritically engaged) tradition to one of the scientific and bureaucratic
rationality of modernity results in our becoming aware of greater risks from
both our environment and humanity's own development, especially science
and technology. Thus, risk in late modernity not only is caused by *external*
threats but also occurs as a side effect of human attempts to deal with external
risks; because of the supercomplexity of modern life and science and technology, our very efforts to mitigate external risk result in new, widely understood risks. Ulrich Beck determines risk to be and to result from modern
society's "systematic way of dealing with the hazards and insecurities"[40]—
this "manufactured risk" is the consequence of human action, the unintended
consequences (and failures) of science and technology and of bureaucratic
systems implemented to deal with external risks. For example, to alleviate
the problem of food shortages, which are in part caused by insects, insecticides were developed and used to increase crop yields. Yet we now make conscious decisions to consume organic fruit and vegetables specifically to avoid
crops that have been treated with insecticides, as there is a belief that the
insecticides can harm humans. A *manufactured* risk (the problem of ill health
caused by insecticides) now exists alongside an extant natural one (hunger
caused by insects' feeding on crops).

In Brooks' story-world, the attempted cover-up of the initial zombie
infections, the systemic failure of the U.S. state to deal with outbreaks, the
entrepreneurial actions of pharmacological companies, and the complicity
of national and international agencies in the production of a false immu-
nization result in the Great Panic. For Brooks, manufactured risk accelerates
and facilitates the zombie threat; millions flee to Canada where they die due
to ill preparedness and a lack of knowledge of how to survive—it is not the
zombies who kill them, but their own attempts to escape the threat.[41] Zombies

on their own would be bad, but in a late-modern world, they find allies in how risk society engages and experiences threats.

Self-Sufficiency and the Individualized Self

Present in both of Brooks' books is a strong commitment to the potency of individual action to alter immediate and longer-term circumstances. The *ZSG* offers an alternate form of action to that of a centralized state's engaging and solving problems. Irony aside, the aim of the *ZSG* is to empower the individual for the zombie apocalypse, to equip an individual with resources to survive and thrive in a zombie-infected world. The guide thus supports an approach to living in which individuals are more responsible for their own self-interest (not to mention survival) than in the prezombie world, where the state and other systems could (in theory) be relied on to protect individuals by holding a monopoly on the legitimate use of force. Following the emergence of the zombie, however, individuals must now take on this responsibility to a degree. Individuals can be advised on how to protect themselves and survive, but the state can no longer guarantee their protection. This shift in determining responsibility in terms of basic conditions of survival between the pre- and postzombie worlds accentuates a process defined by Zygmunt Bauman,[42] Beck and Elisabeth Beck-Gernsheim,[43] and Giddens[44] as that of individualization—the restructuring of class and other forms of macro identity, forming categories whose result is that individuals are required to make decisions about issues that they previously could have left to social systems, state agencies, and others. In this situation, Giddens argues, the self becomes a project, a task towards which we devote increasing amounts of time and energy.[45] Bauman describes individualization as "the emancipation of the individual from the ascribed, inherited and inborn determination of his or her social character.... '[I]ndividualization' consists in transforming human 'identity' from a 'given' to a 'task'—and charging the actors with the responsibility for performing that task."[46] Similarly, the all-encompassing requirements and continuously conscious action of focusing upon individual and familial survival advocated in the *ZSG* refocus attention onto self-action and away from reliance upon wider social systems, which Bauman would term "obligatory *self*-determination."[47] It is important to note that for Bauman, Beck and Beck-Gernsheim, and Giddens, individuals do not choose individualization; they have it forced upon them by the trajectory of change occurring in societies as they progress through modernity.

In *WWZ*, these issues are further developed. There are multiple instances in which the formalized and heavily bureaucratic institutions of the state prove ineffective against the zombie threat—for example, the CIA's failure to detect the outbreaks in China.[48] Indeed, on a number of occasions, the mechanisms of the modern democratic state—such as the requirement of public consent for large-scale actions[49]—actually impede the fight against the zombies. Similarly, the characters in *WWZ*, and indeed assumed readers of the *ZSG*, have been thrust into the zombie world and have to make new choices and decisions. The possibility of the characters' survival now resides with themselves and their actions rather than with state agencies, as it did previously. While Bauman, Beck and Beck-Gernsheim, and Giddens consider the process of individualization to be a very gradual one that emerges in middle modernity but slowly intensifies in late modernity, the zombie apocalypse radically alters this time scale, and individualization occurs not across generations but in years, months, weeks, and even days. Characters in *WWZ* are violently thrown into the zombie apocalypse with little or no time to adjust to the new world in which they must live.[50]

The degree of verisimilitude of Brooks' story-world and books is enhanced by the degree to which it is consonant with the themes noted here of risk and individualization. This is not to argue that Brooks explicitly wrote his texts in this manner; rather, the story-world acquires its validity and truthful appearance through Brooks' skilled use of social norms, preoccupations, and values. Indeed, it may be that the unusual genre styles of the texts—the use of the survival guide and oral history—afford opportunities to engage with sociological structures and interpretations that other, more traditional approaches to zombie storytelling are not able to do—that the unconventional styles Brooks uses may indeed facilitate a greater degree of resonance with contemporary life than other texts that relate the direct experience of characters in seeming real time.

Furthermore, the positive conclusion to *WWZ* (humans survive and the zombies are almost completely beaten) and the self-empowering nature of the *ZSG* both indicate that for Brooks, zombies pose a challenging but surmountable threat; humanity will triumph, though in a very different world. Humanity, and in particular Western civilization and its inherently progressive intent, can be salvaged from the threat of zombies, but only through the recognition of new forms of risk and a greater degree of engagement with individual action. Salvation for humanity and individuals comes through conscious, reflexive engagement with the new reality. Similarly, a theme common to the work of Bauman, Beck and Beck-Gernsheim, Beck and Edgar Grande, and Giddens is the assertion that core aspects of modernity and particularly its progressive and cosmopolitan intents can be salvaged from the critique of postmodernity and other philosophical and ideological challenges.[51] It is not argued that Brooks is in some way constructing zombies as a form of existential threat, but rather that his reader can seek to understand zombies though the literature of late modernity and in particular the sociology of

Bauman, Beck and Grande, Beck and Beck-Gernsheim, and Giddens, which afford us a fresh critical lens on zombie texts. Simultaneously, Brooks' zombie texts and story-world afford us a fairly original method of approaching the work of Bauman, Beck, Beck and Beck-Gernsheim, Beck and Grande, and Giddens and indeed some of the internal forces of late modernity. Perhaps, then, zombies constitute a new method of sociological inquiry.

NOTES

1. Alderman, "Meaning of Zombies."
2. McNally, *Monsters of the Market*, 210.
3. Conrich, "Infectious Population," 15.
4. Hood, "World War Z."
5. Schaefer, "World War Z."
6. Eburne, "Zombie Arts and Letters."
7. See Wiseman, *SAS Survival Handbook.*
8. See Wiseman, *SAS Urban Survival Handbook.*
9. See Jones, *Provident Prepper*, and Lundin, *When All Hell Breaks Loose.*
10. See Geltman, *Survival Guide to Parenting Teens.*
11. See Thompson, *First Year Teacher's Survival Guide.*
12. See Gehlhar, *Fashion Designer Survival Guide.*
13. See Lane, *Concerned Citizen's Guide to Surviving*, and Kearny, *Nuclear War Survival Skills.*
14. See Ballou, *Long-Term Survival.*
15. See Wilson, *How to Survive a Robot Uprising.*
16. See Mumfrey, *Alien Invasion Survival Handbook* (W.H. Mumfrey is a pen name for Grant Murray), and Dicce, *You're a Vampire—That Sucks!*
17. As advanced in Gerson and Gerson, *Technical Writing.*
18. Authors of *When All Hell Breaks Loose* and *Provident Prepper*, respectively.
19. Pierce, "Interview: Max Brooks."
20. *Ibid.*
21. Ritchie, *Doing Oral History*, 1–2.
22. Pierce, "Interview."
23. See Hood, "World War Z."
24. See Schaefer, "World War Z."
25. Dena, *Theorising the Practice*, 328.
26. Brooks, *World War Z*, 110.
27. *Ibid.*, 146–51.
28. Walsh, "Battle Cry That Backfired."
29. Brooks, *World War Z*, 147–51.
30. Paffenroth, *Gospel of the Living Dead*, 2–3.
31. See McIntosh, "Evolution of the Zombie," 14.
32. Davis, *Passage of Darkness*, 97.
33. Brooks, *World War Z*, 92–104.
34. *Ibid.*, 104.
35. *Ibid.*, 4–5.
36. *Ibid.*, 54–59.
37. Giddens and Pierson, *Conversations with Anthony Giddens*, 209.
38. *Ibid.*, 210.
39. Giddens, *Consequences of Modernity*, 35–36.
40. Beck, *Risk Society*, 21.
41. Brooks, *World War Z*, 121–30.
42. See Bauman, *Liquid Life*; Bauman, *Individualized Society*; and Bauman, *Liquid Modernity.*

43. See Beck and Beck-Gernsheim, *Individualization*.
44. See Giddens, *Modernity and Self-Identity*.
45. Giddens, *Modernity and Self-Identity*, 75.
46. Bauman, *Individualized Society*, 144.
47. *Ibid.*, 145.
48. Brooks, *World War Z*, 121–30.
49. *Ibid.*, 52–53.
50. *Ibid.*, 63 & 73.
51. See Beck, *Reinvention of Politics*; Beck, *Power in the Global Age*; Beck, *Cosmopolitan Vision*; and Beck and Grande, *Cosmopolitan Europe*.

Dispatches of the Dead
World War Z *and the*
Post-Vietnam Combat Memoir

W. Scott Poole

> This is my rifle. There are many like it, but this one is mine.
>   My rifle is my best friend. It is my life. I must master it as
> I must master my life.
>   My rifle, without me, is useless. Without my rifle, I am use-
> less. I must fire my rifle true. I must shoot straighter than
> my enemy who is trying to kill me. I must shoot him before
> he shoots me. I will.
> > —Rifleman's Creed, USMC

> "One guy with a rifle, that's all you need, right?"
> > —Todd Wainio, veteran of World War Z

In Max Brooks' *World War Z*, the catastrophic "Battle of Yonkers" ends all hope that the U.S. military can put a quick end to "the Great Panic," the dead rising.

The most embittered moments in the novel are found in Brooks' fictional oral history with Todd Wainio, a young veteran made "old before his time" by what he experienced in the northern suburbs of New York. On that fateful day, the U.S. Army attempted to stop the streaming millions of infected coming out of Manhattan with the same kind of high-tech weaponry that warfighting doctrine in the American military has leaned on since the First Gulf War in 1990. Wainio grasps for American historical experiences with which to describe the struggle, thinking first of Pearl Harbor. But no, he says, "This was more like Little Bighorn … [a] panic train." Wainio wonders aloud in his interview about why his commanders failed to deploy troops on top of buildings and shopping centers: "They could have put a whole company right above the A&P," he angrily recalls.[1]

Myopic military leaders marshaled the full array of their technological prowess rather than, in Wainio's telling, depending on the individual soldier. "Dude, we had everything," Wainio remembers, "Bradleys, Humvees.... Stinger surface-to-air missile sets." He concludes this description of the armament deployed against the millions of zombies by bitterly describing these plans as utter failures dreamt up by "Fucktards.... Tight-assed, narrow-minded" generals who were "probably pissed off from so many years of brush-fire war." The panoply of tactical weaponry, even as it shredded zombies to bits, failed to take out their brains or prevent the panic of troops not trained to make the necessary headshots. The military and civilian leadership in Washington failed to wage the right kind of zombie war, an American kind of war. The results proved disastrous. The horrific Battle of Yonkers became a rout of American forces and initiated a despairing phase of World War Z that seemed likely to end in the complete destruction of humanity.[2]

The American soldier did not fail, Wainio insists. Political leaders and the Pentagon failed. Wainio cynically describes how the military attempted to redeploy the "shock and awe" tactics of the Second Gulf War, but that the very nature of an enemy with limited brain activity and a necrotic nervous system prevented them from being either shocked or awed. Instead of following the obtuse schemes of "fucktard" generals, Wainio insists that the American army could have prevented the disaster through the archetypal mythic act of American manhood, one the stretches back beyond the genocidal dreams of Manifest Destiny on the western frontier to the Minutemen of Concord and Lexington. "[O]ne guy with a rifle," Wainio assures the oral historian, "That's all you need, right?" This war needed "professional soldiers" and "trained marksmen" instead of generals and politicians with their slogans, assurances to the media, and expensive toys.[3]

Brooks' imaginary zombie war, a fiction from which readers can draw a variety of contradictory political conclusions, employs the myth of "one guy with a rifle" that has become integral to a segment of American culture over the last four decades. Since the Vietnam era, many white, middle-class Americans struggle with the politics of remembering lost wars, rejuvenating American manhood, and holding desperately to notions of American exceptionalism.

Brooks' ability to distill competing imagery into a set of easily recognizable cultural tropes made his novel successful among readers from a wide range of political persuasions. Despite the obvious desire to entertain, certain ideological assumptions in *World War Z*—and his earlier 2003 *The Zombie Survival Guide*—have become part of a peculiarly American apocalyptic fantasy that depends on the idea of "one guy with a rifle." It's a fantasy that assumes frontier myths and applies them to contemporary debates about issues as diverse as gun rights and the appropriate response to the Islamic State. Along the way, these assumptions picked up significant cultural baggage from the Vietnam era, especially the complicated texts produced by veterans of America's most costly Cold War defeat.

Brook's fiction of a zombie war employs an image of the American warrior cultivated in a number of influential, and bestselling, memoirs of Vietnam. All of these texts, written from differing ideological perspectives, have in common a distrust of the institutional state combined with an elegiac defense of the veteran. Many of these texts, especially after the 1980s, also claim that if the American warrior could only be unleashed on the enemy, he'd win all our wars and guarantee our safety.

This fantasy has wider implications for American life beyond the kinds of entertainment we enjoy. The continuing construction of a contemporary paramilitary zombie fantasy represents one product of Brooks' effort. This fantasy fuels elements of American gun culture, the adulation accorded to morally problematic figures such as "American Sniper" Chris Kyle, and the transformation of the inherently flexible metaphor of the zombie into a survivalist dream of what Richard Slotkin famously called "regeneration through violence." The post–Vietnam combat narrative has played a central role in questioning, revising, and, eventually, celebrating this core American myth. A slow trickle of such memoirs in the 1970s, some of them significant literary achievements, became a deluge of narratives in the 1980s. Many of the latter, churned out by ghost writers, represent mass-market paperback revisions of the Vietnam War. Increasingly, the weary veteran reflecting on combat became the story of "the real American hero," the warrior who fought an inhuman, faceless enemy with immense skill, courage, and an indefatigable belief in the nobility of the cause.[4]

The importance of such works has generally been ignored in discussions of Brooks' novel. The author himself has acknowledged Studs Terkel's *The Good War* (1984) as his own literary model. Both books are structured by memories of individuals whose personal lives are pulled into the whirlwind of a larger history, a struggle that engulfed civilians as well as soldiers.[5]

World War Z owes something more to *The Good War* than its style and structure. Much like Terkel's nonfiction classic, Brooks' imaginary oral history was written in the shadow of national catastrophe. At the time of *World War Z*'s publication, many Americans had spent three decades attempting to overcome the cultural crisis created by the country's defeat in Vietnam. By 2006, 9/11, the "war on terror," and the Iraq War further angered these unquiet spirits, some of which politicians assured us had been laid to rest by the apparent dominance of American military power after 1991 and the end of the Red Army as a countervailing balance to U.S. adventurism. The sudden dominance of American military power made a seemingly unstoppable zombie apocalypse, rooted in new fears, a powerful narrative strategy. The new realities of the twenty-first century created the context for Brooks' work, as well as its popularity, in much the same way that the 1980s shaped *The Good War*. Terkel's assumptions behind his oral history of World War II intertwined with the cultural currents of the 1980s, a complex historical moment in which the American reading public needed "a good war" to remember, just as it required a "greatest generation" to have won that war.

The title of Terkel's book, published during a presidential administration that urged Americans to leapfrog the experience of Vietnam, reveals the ideological needs it served. Terkel, of course, created his oral history from the perspective of the populist left and had no use for Reaganism. He, in fact, is famous for one of the great oral histories of American labor, simply entitled *Working* (1973), and maintained a lifelong commitment to the labor movement. Yet his oral history of "the workingman's war" could also appeal to the populist right's interest in mass crusades that ignore the concerns, and rational arguments, of cultural elites.

World War Z inherited this ideological complexity along with a new set of uncertainties about America's role in the world. In the months following 9/11, most of President Bush's circle of advisors demanded a series of military interventions that went far beyond neutralizing Al Qaeda. Indeed, Secretary of Defense Donald Rumsfeld, we now know, initiated plans for an invasion of Iraq within hours of the collapse of the Twin Towers.[6] These advisors offered an idea as expansive as George F. Kennan's view of "containment," the guiding principle of American foreign policy in the Cold War era. However, the circle that advised George W. Bush insisted on more grandiose plans than Kennan's. They proposed a global mission to destroy America's enemies in Asia, the Mideast, and the horn of Africa.[7]

Bush's 2002 State of the Union address famously made what, in an era of more careful political rhetoric, would have amounted to a declaration of war. He asserted that America faced an "Axis of Evil" that included Al Qaeda, Iran, Iraq, North Korea, and the Afghani Taliban, as well as a smattering of anti–American terrorist organizations. The United States would consolidate hegemonic claims across the globe, secure access to oil in the Middle East, and wreak vengeance for September 11 in a war with no visible end. The Department of Defense bundled these hydra-like efforts to secure American supremacy under the designation "Operation Enduring Freedom." In the days after 9/11, this amorphous war effort received a moniker that suggested its original, far-reaching ambitions: "Operation Infinite Justice."[8]

Brooks published *World War Z* as the Iraq War bogged down these elaborate schemes. When the novel appeared in 2006, sectarian violence had torn apart the allegedly liberated country, and by the end of the year, the U.S.

Army admitted its failure to quell the outbreak of factionalism. The Republican Party faced an utter debacle in the midterm elections, losing both the House and the Senate, while the Democrats, in a victory without historical precedent, did not lose a single incumbent, open seat, or governorship. The failure of the Iraq War represented the leading issue.[9]

Zombie hordes, unthinking and uncaring, seem to move against America and its interests in this construction of geopolitics. The specter of American military defeat by waves of half-crazed, fanatical insurgents reproduced the cultural and political nightmare of the early seventies for many Americans. Tight government control kept the reportage of military causalities to a minimum, and the Bush administration forbade film and photographs of the dead being returned home, hoping to prevent the phenomenon of the Vietnam-era "body bag" returning home. Charities for "wounded warriors" sprang up, though often wrapped in the sentimental language of patriotic sacrifice and carefully avoiding the possibility that American foreign policy could be held responsible for the maiming of young, mostly working-class Americans. Only in more recent years have stories surfaced of what an IED does to the human body or what combatting insurgents defending themselves against an invading army does to the psyche of the soldiers of that army.[10]

Brooks' novel manages to conflate various American anxieties about its warrior fantasies in the age of an amorphous "War on Terror" while reaching back to a significant amount of confusion, and moral reflection, from the Vietnam era. The "oral history" of the zombie war puts into the mouths of veterans sentiments that reflect what cultural historian Tom Engelhardt has called "the end of victory culture" in the aftermath of defeat in Vietnam. Engelhardt claims, in a 2007 updated edition of his work, that American exceptionalism in war and historical experience had a kind of "sequel ... that crashed and burned within a scant few years, leaving the Bush administration standing in the rubble of its own imperial project."[11]

Zombies rose out of that rubble. *World War Z* unfolds on an international stage, and American voices are not the only fictional commentary we hear speak convincingly of "the Great Panic" and the global conflict that followed. A builder of zombie fortresses in "The Province of Bohemia, the European Union" explains how he put into practice his idea of building strongholds for the living in some of the more isolated regions of Eastern Europe. A resident of Kyoto describes turning himself into a warrior monk in the midst of a plan for a complete evacuation of the Japanese home islands' 128 million people.[12]

However, references to the global war are still structured by America's experience in *World War Z*. Our oral historian touches down in Finland primarily to hear about the work of American special forces units doing mop-up work against "Zack," or "Gs," nicknames given to the zombie menace reminiscent of Vietnam era shorthand for the enemy as "Charlie," "VC," or the highly racialized term "gook." The politics of America's relationship with China forms the basis for a Chinese sailor's memory of his life aboard a renegade nuclear sub. Even when describing the horrors borne by a Russian veteran, Brooks structures the passage with material from the American experience of Vietnam and the Iraqi insurgency in which civilians are perceived as the enemy in disguise.[13]

The novel, presented as a global experience of the zombie apocalypse, can be read as a story of America's successful effort to rediscover its own myths so that it can win the war. Wainio's description of a war that could be fought only by "one guy with a rifle" becomes prophetic. Time and again, we are told of various government failures to respond adequately to the threat. Officers and military planners "interviewed" for the novel complain that the public wanted "a blitzkrieg smackdown" impossible under the conditions that the president and the joint chiefs faced.[14] Some of these very same planners are forced to admit that the individual American infantryman and specially trained commando snipers of the so-called "Alpha Teams" are largely responsible for America's successful campaign against the zombie menace. In fact, Travis D'Ambrosio, an American general who commanded "Allied" forces in World War Z, explains that these elite units, "though their battle record is sealed for the next 140 years," represent "one of the most outstanding moments in the history of America's elite warriors." Not without irony, however, this same general describes how "after Vietnam," he found a generation uninterested in military service, a laxness that, when the zombie war began, meant that "we were almost too weak and vulnerable to stop them."[15]

This evocation of Vietnam and an alleged present state of military unreadiness jostles uncomfortably with D'Ambrosio's claim that only with the help of indefatigable American infantry and elite sniper units could the war have been won. In such contradictory claims, we see the cultural conflicts inherent in the post–Vietnam combat narrative and the cultural discussion that made them possible, inexplicable paradoxes that appear again in post–Iraq, and post–World War Z, reconstructions of the meaning of American manhood and of America's role in the world.

World War Z maintains a profound cynicism about various American institutions ranging from the Pentagon to the media to the state itself. Meanwhile, the veterans of the zombie war tend to valorize the experience of the lone wolf soldier or, occasionally, soldierly camaraderie. Similar ideas are absolutely central to the post–Vietnam combat memoir. The collapse of the American war effort in Vietnam precipitated a crisis of myth in American culture. The genre of the combat memoir emerged very quickly in the war's wake as individual soldiers sought to explain their own trauma and, in some cases, explain away the first real defeat of the American nation-state. Collectively, they created new cultural myths to shore up, or to critique, deeply held ideas about American exceptionalism, American innocence, and American manhood.

The atmosphere of these works, a cloudy mixture of stirring heroism and cynicism, found its way into *World War Z. Dispatches* (1968), by war correspondent Michael Herr, stands *sui generis* in the earliest efforts, offering memoir, oral history, and direct reportage with the closest the printed word can come to featuring a rock-and-roll soundtrack. Herr's direct, acerbic style made it an iconic literary account of Vietnam compared by critics to the works of Orwell and Hemingway. Herr's work employs many of the same themes as later combat narratives. His grunts are young men grown old in war, eyes hollow from what they've had to see and had to do. His soldiers are, like Todd Wainio in *World War Z,* men who have "one of those faces ... all the youth sucked out of the eyes.... Life had made him old, he'd live it out old."[16] Like Wainio in the fictional zombie war, these young men, old before their time, did not lose the war. At worst, they have been fooled by the "overripe bullshit" employed by politicians, and a few of them employ the phrases their commanders and politicians have told them to use: "Hearts and Minds, Peoples of the Republic, tumbling dominoes, maintaining the equilibrium of the Dingdong by containing the ever encroaching Doodah." Herr gives his readers the sense that Cold War rhetoric represented a declension of language, policy points becoming slogans that degenerate into meaningless phrases repeated by rote. Like Brooks' soldiers in the front line of the zombie war, cliché and propaganda have become part of the fog of war.[17]

Much of *Dispatches* offers a running critique of what Herr simply calls "the Mission," an omnibus term for how the men fighting the Vietnam War understood the protean aims of the United States in Southeast Asia. "The Mission" becomes an idea void of content by the time it's explained by political leaders, the State Department, and even Nixon. When General William Westmoreland claimed he needed another quarter of a million men because he could see "the light at the end of the tunnel," Herr describes Washington elites "leaning so far out to hear some good news that a lot of them slipped off the ledge and said they could see it too."[18]

Herr uses both the hellish experiences of the men on the ground and the nature of the enemy they fought to make his case against "the Mission." When one soldier who spends his time tossing grenades into the vast tunnel system used by the National Liberation Front (NLF) in Tay Ninh City heard about Westmoreland's claim, Herr writes that he responded, "What does that asshole know about tunnels?" Meanwhile, enemies that can pop in and out of hiding take on the characteristics of an undead army, undefeatable because they are unkillable. NLF units "are engaged and wiped out" only to reappear "at full strength." In the aftermath of the Tet Offensive, "pop grunt mythology" speaks darkly of an enemy that won't stay dead. As one general describes the zombie army of *World War Z*, they are the only force ever massed that can truly wage a total war.[19]

Brooks makes a point of having his veterans deny any particular political views in *World War Z*, a rhetorical tool found in most Vietnam memoirs. Philip Caputo's *A Rumor of War*, an account of his time in Vietnam as a Marine lieutenant, joined *Dispatches* in becoming one of the earliest and most highly regarded post–Vietnam memoirs. Appearing in 1977, it describes Caputo's two years in Danang with the first regular American unit to serve on the ground. He insists that his memoir "does not pretend to be history. It has nothing to do with politics."[20] In spite of these assertions, Caputo does have a very clear message about what he came to see as the futility of the conflict, lives wasted by incompetence and anticommunist fanaticism.

A Rumor of War shares the tendency of the genre to mock military leadership while giving compelling accounts of the individual soldier and even romanticizing the camaraderie between warriors. Caputo parodies the leadership in Danang in the summer of 1966 when, despite clear signs of an impending attack from the NLF, the officer corps frittered away time reading, practicing square dance calls, and issuing pointless orders that Marines with "non-regulation cloth name tags sewn above the left pockets of their shirts" should remove them. While growing numbers of NLF troops massed for an attack on an American-held airfield, the general staff sent orders complaining that circulation of the *Marine Corps Gazette* had dropped and requesting that officers renew their subscriptions.[21]

The complex layers of Caputo's narrative do not allow for the one-dimensional celebration of the American rifleman found in most Vietnam combat memoirs. The grunts in Vietnam can be terrified by the possibility of NLF snipers to the point that they shoot wildly into the darkness at "a chimera" and risk giving their positions away to actual snipers. A private named Morrison has delusions of grandeur and tells Caputo that he has an idea to win the war all on his own "in the boonies creeping and crawling and ambushing Cong along the way.... We'd waste the shit out of them."[22]

Here we have returned to the American frontier myth and to *World War Z*'s "one guy with a rifle." Morrison, an absurd figure in Caputo's account, ironically represents the kind of American warrior readers wanted in later accounts of Vietnam. His idea of fighting "in the boonies creeping and crawling and ambushing" became exactly the kind of hero celebrated in the 1980s and 1990s in the combat memoir, as well as in other kinds of American fictions about re-fighting the war. By the time of the publication of *World War Z* and the growth of paramilitary zombie culture, playing this new version of what Herr had called "cowboys and Indians" became the epitome of American warrior manhood.

After Caputo's and Herr's work, Frederick Downs' 1978 memoir *The Killing Zone* became a bridge to a new kind of Vietnam combat narrative. Described unfairly in 1986 by historian George C. Herring as a "gung-ho" account of the conflict, *The Killing Zone* does not strike the contemporary reader as engaging in much flag waving, particularly after the enormous number of "real American hero" tales that have appeared since the Reagan years.[23] Downs claims in a short preface that hostility from the American public, hostility he allegedly experienced firsthand in one strange incident, led him to try and tell the story of "the day-to-day life of an infantryman on the ground." An infantry lieutenant like Caputo, Downs provides a narrative that centers on the experience of the platoon he commanded. Also like Caputo, he claims he will avoid airing his political views and simply explain "what it was like to fight in Vietnam."[24]

Downs manages a tone that appears balanced and objective. The popularity of the book among veterans in the 1970s and 1980s largely grew out of his ability to summon the sights, sounds, smells, and horrors of his, and their, personal trauma. He does not flinch in his description of burning down villages made up mostly of women, children, and old men on his early "search and destroy missions." His only comment on this practice is that he accepted it as a way to win the war.[25]

Sinewy prose and reflective honesty cannot hide a politics of nostalgia for the veteran trying to do the right thing under impossible circumstances in Downs' account. A tank sergeant tries to kill a group of alleged "Viet Cong" prisoners, and Downs refuses. The anecdote suggests the moral clarity of "one guy with a rifle." He understands this war better than someone who lives the less stringent life of a tank sergeant.[26] Much like Downs' account, the lone infantryman in *World War Z* becomes both hero and victim of a leadership that fails to grasp the situation on the ground. Again and again, Downs describes the individual rifleman as key to the entire American mission and yet also left to himself in an impossible situation in which "the night belonged to the enemy" and the only occupied territory became what a rifleman was "standing on at the time." The "sweep and clear" missions of *World War Z* are fought by the same kind of individual warriors.[27]

Downs does nothing to defend American policy in Vietnam, and his shrug-of-the-shoulders attitude toward the kind of war his superiors asked him to wage suggests a deep cynicism about America's war aims. Most telling of all, he pays tribute to the bravery of his enemy, both as he's engaged in killing and when he returns to Vietnam on a goodwill visit following the war. This has a peculiar resonance with Brooks' Wainio, who, while seemingly understanding that "Zack" has no brain capacity for courage, fear, or camaraderie, tells the oral historian that he wouldn't mind seeing one of the zombies mutilated (but still walking) from the high-tech explosives used at Yonkers because he's "always up for meeting a fellow veteran."[28]

The Reagan years transformed the Vietnam combat narrative in substantial ways. The focus on the individual soldier and a deep distrust of American institutions remained. In contrast to earlier Vietnam memoirs, however, the writing became unrepentantly political and went beyond focusing on the individual soldier's experience to initiate a full-throated glorification of the warrior untrammelled by home-front liberalism, the world of diplomacy, or even a chain of command. The idea that forces that did not understand the zombie war led to the early disasters of World War Z comes directly from this new sort of combat memoir. David Donovan's *Once a Warrior King* (1985) became one of the first in a long line of memoirs (and men's adventure tales) to celebrate the "Spec Ops" soldier and launch jeremiads about how the war effort had been stabbed in the back at home by the press, liberal politicians, and antiwar protestors. Al Santoli's *To Bear Any Burden* (1985) suggests, with a sentiment echoed by Brooks' General D'Ambrosio, that the post–Vietnam generation of Americans lost their will to fight.

This new kind of memoir had its genesis in Reaganism's cultural project of forgetting in order to remember properly. Reagan, in 1980, urged Americans to get over "the Vietnam syndrome" in a speech to the Veterans of Foreign Wars in which he complained about the alleged "shabby treatment" of veterans of the war and the refusal of many Americans to see it as a "noble cause." As with other "lost cause" movements that aim at cultural revitalization, Reagan sought to reorient the meaning of history itself and urged Americans to renounce any sense of "guilt" in order to prepare for an ongoing struggle.[29]

Reagan's landslide election victory less than three months later suggested that Americans desired this story. They wanted faceless, nameless, brutal enemies who, zombie-like, moved in hordes against American interests. They also wanted to hear a story of the singular American warrior taking out this amorphous menace, preferably with a headshot that secured "the kill." In this mythology, the problem of Vietnam, the challenge of situating defeat in the myth of American exceptionalism, found resolution.

The lunatic logic required for this historical revision claimed that America had not lost the Vietnam War because the real America had not fought it. The idea of "self-imposed restraint" became, according to cultural historian James William Gibson, one of the war's enduring myths. Gibson writes that "defeat … could only be explained by arguing that the full powers of the heroic American warriors of legend had not been unleashed."[30] Gibson assembles an enormous body of evidence to show that "warrior dreams"-obsessed American film and fiction led to the proliferation of military-grade firearms among private citizens and even influenced American foreign policy. Every veteran of World War Z, American or otherwise, echoes these sentiments. In Brooks' novel, the politicians don't understand, the generals want to fight a kind of war that differs from the one that they've inherited, and no one has properly steeled himself/herself. America must rediscover itself to save the world.[31]

In the two decades before the publication of *World War Z*, substantial portions of American culture and politics marinated in a romanticized notion of the singular American warrior, the kinds of weaponry he brought to bear, and the idea that Americans confronted a world of enemies whose motivations remained opaque but represented a threat to American freedom nonetheless. *Soldier of Fortune* magazine, with its combination of right-wing politics and detailed articles on field-stripping military-grade weapons, had a circulation of over 200,000 by the mid–1980s. The enormously popular film *Red Dawn* (1984, directed by John Milius) imagined a paramilitary response to a Soviet occupation of America. A paperback series called *The Executioner* told the fictional story of Vietnam vet Mack Bolan, who slaughters piles of Mafia dons, communist revolutionaries, and various "Third World" terrorists in hundreds of virtually identical books.[32]

Why would *World War Z* engage in such ideological work after the Red Army no longer stood in the way of America's geopolitical goals? At the end of the Cold War, even with the United States an unchallenged superpower, such fantasies remained essential to the project of American rejuvenation. Could we declare victory? The Vietnam combat narrative lurched far to the right, feeding revenge fantasies and making a fetish of men with guns at war. Richard Marcinko's *Rogue Warrior* became a publishing phenomenon in the early 1990s. It functioned as a sort of novelization of *Rambo: First Blood Part II* (1985, directed by George P. Cosmatos) in that it allowed the American public the satisfaction of seeing the lone warrior at last unleashed on Southeast Asia, seemingly winning the war that had been lost.

Rogue Warrior quickly became a number one *New York Times* bestseller with its story of a Navy SEAL—"one guy with a rifle"—who, as the title suggests, seemed well on his way to winning the war in Vietnam all by himself despite the interference and bumbling of his military and civilian commanders. In fact, even the lower rungs of the command structure are incompetent. Marcinko, or rather his ghost writer John Weisman, describes characters like "Colonel Shit and Polish," who becomes so disoriented by Viet Cong successes that he locks himself in his "radio room … listening to chatter" while Marcinko has to salvage a victory from a "VC" attack. Meanwhile, his lieutenant commander lacks "those ineffable, deadly hunter's qualities that make great warriors great warriors." While warriors are being great warriors, the top levels of American military strategy are simply "pencil-pushing Pentagon assholes."[33]

World War Z's embattled warriors, such as Wainio, show a similar disdain for state institutions and bureaucratic systems, but in Marcinko's world, it's not only the command structure that deserves contempt. In the foreword to *Rogue Warrior*, contributed by the same person who ghosted much of the rest of the text, we find Marcinko described as "a gung-ho young SEAL officer ... [who] operated behind enemy lines." Others may have "hid behind barbed wire and sandbags," but Marcinko and his unit "hunted the Viet Cong on their own turf."[34] This profound lack of respect for the American grunt appears in other examples of what Nick Turse has called "the best-selling paeans to snipers, commandos and Navy SEALS" that constitute the real American hero narrative. It's almost as if the grunts "humping" through the jungle have become a disgraceful image, out of line with the archetypal American hero, existing now as traumatized ghosts at the feast in the party to rejuvenate America.[35]

Brooks departs most radically from the "real American hero" mythos when he recreates a much more democratic, if no less violent, American myth. In an important departure from the spec-op/cowboys-and-Indians narratives of the 1980s and 1990s, anyone can become "one guy with a rifle" in *World War Z* (including women). In the aftermath of the Battle of Yonkers, a new American army with a new war-fighting doctrine emerges. The "grunts" that had fought and won the zombie war had basic physical stamina and skills, but mostly they simply had been people who could learn to make headshots and psychologically endure the endless routine horror of watching piles of undead form walls of rotting flesh in front of them.[36]

This departure from the flood of commando narratives does not deter Brooks from ultimately reaffirming the mythos of American exceptionalism. Toward the end of *World War Z*, our intrepid oral historian returns to talk to Wainio, who lived to fight in the counterpart of the disaster at Yonkers, the Battle of Hope, New Mexico. The new American army has rediscovered itself and disposed of all the high-tech military hardware. Now hardened soldiers sit for hours in tight two-line formation, the front lines firing expertly and taking out Zack with headshot after headshot while the second line waits to step up. A constant supply of food, water, and, most importantly, ammo makes its way to the front. "One shot one kill at one shot per second" becomes standard operating procedure. It works. The American marksman—one could say simply the American sniper—wins this war.[37]

Early in the novel, Wainio sounds like Herr, Caputo, or Downs in his cynicism and utter bitterness toward the military establishment. In the new dawn of Hope, New Mexico, he's become the rejuvenated American warrior. Notably, Wainio's description of this new kind of war begins with a loving appreciation of the kind of gun the grunts are now carrying, the SIR (Standard Infantry Rifle) that "looks like a World War II gun."[38] The American warrior has reclaimed the weapon of his fathers. Wainio explains the weapon, in some detail, as a modification of the Soviet AK-47, also made in an equally deadly Czech model, used in numerous Cold War conflicts in which it proved superior again and again to the M-16. Such extended descriptions of the weapons available to the individual soldier became a staple of the "real American hero" genre from Marcinko to, in recent years, Kyle's *American Sniper* (2012). The latter spends entire chapters detailing the specification of the kinds of weapons SEALS employed in combat. At the time of Kyle's death, a new book (also ghostwritten) appeared, simply called *American Gun*, which claimed to explain all American history through the weapons carried by individual soldiers in varied historical eras.[39]

The fetishistic appreciation of firearms has become a staple of the zombie paramilitary fantasy, connecting it with the far right position on gun ownership and use in American politics and culture. Kelly Baker's *The Zombies Are Coming!* explores this connection between stockpiling weapons, racism, and the zombie fantasy. Baker writes of "the intimate relationship of zombies to American gun culture." She cites evidence of the zombie apocalypse's use to sell "Zombie Max" ammunition for high-powered rifles, as well as "zombie targets" that include one member of the undead with an uncomfortable resemblance to Barack Obama.[40]

Baker also connects *World War Z* with the apocalyptic fantasies abroad in American culture—and perhaps within the military itself. Brooks has become a frequent speaker at a variety of the American military's disaster preparedness training events. Baker quotes journalist Spencer Ackerman as saying that the author of *World War Z* has become "a cult hero inside the army. I've found his books on practically every forward operating base I've been on in Iraq and Afghanistan."[41]

Americans with dreams of fighting off hordes of enemies at the end of time are surely impressed by how seriously the military takes the zombie fantasy. Brooks' *The Zombie Survival Guide* reads like a deadpan stylization of the warrior fantasy of Americans who collect weapons and plan for the coming of some kind of apocalypse while expecting no aid, and perhaps some interference, from state and federal authorities. Brooks' manual offers an obvious parody, though it's not clear from our current culture of doomsday prepping that everyone is in on the joke.[42]

Notably, when *The Zombie Survival Guide* provides a history of "Recorded Attacks," relatively minor outbreaks of the zombie epidemic before *World War Z*, Brooks creates a character that easily could have come from the pen of Marcinko's ghostwriter when an undead rising occurs in Southeast Asia. A "special forces sniper" operating on the Laotian border, and thus part of the very real secret war waged by the CIA in both Laos and Cambodia, moves with his unit against a village that's allegedly become a center of communist guerrilla activity. Instead, it's a village under siege by hordes of another kind of enemy. The unit calls in air support, and "napalm plastered the area." The village had been destroyed in order to save it.[43]

World War Z appeared at an ideal moment in the zeitgeist, the atmosphere heavy with another failed American war. Brooks' novel produces a pastiche of several eras of American war memory. Brooks, obviously with plenty of help from his readers, created an ideologically confused text that changed the direction of zombie fictions in America.

Kyle William Bishop's prediction that the "zombie invasion subgenre" would grow in popularity has proven true. Many of these narratives register what Bishop calls "post–9/11 anxieties about potential terrorist attacks."[44] But, perhaps more than registering anxiety, they also serve ideological uses. A fantasy of fighting off the zombie invader buoys up a view held by many Americans, particularly white males, that their investment in American power, and the privileges that accrue to them because of it, are threatened by dangerous, faceless, ever-changing hordes of enemies that must be dispatched. The fantasy of killing the invader of one's country or one's house has become deeply fetishized by this portion of the American public. The "one guy with a rifle" mythos helped to make Kyle's *American Sniper* a best-selling war memoir and a successful feature film in 2015 (directed by Clint Eastwood). Kyle's account of his activities as a SEAL in Iraq, ghostwritten by a team that included one of Marcinko's collaborators, refights the Iraq War. In this alternate history presented as a firsthand account, Kyle actually finds those fictional weapons of mass destruction used by the Bush administration to justify the invasion. "Operation Iraqi Freedom" becomes, rather than a destabilization of the entire region with consequences that continue to unfold with the emergence of the Islamic State, a simple war against "savages" in which "the bad guys" are defeated. Notably, these "savages" are faceless zombie-like hordes that because of "drugs" and "religion and adrenaline" can "take several bullets without seeming to feel it." The horde presses forward unless a warrior who knows how to stop it emerges.[45]

Kyle died in 2013, not in the ruins of Ramadi, but from a shot fired by a fellow Iraq War veteran whom he believed he could help through a kind of shooting range therapy. An equally bizarre incident in Kyle's tragic story represents another haunting version of how the "real American hero" becomes a vessel for paramilitary fantasies of slaughtering the inhuman Other. Kyle claimed, falsely, to have turned the top of the New Orleans Superdome into a sniper's nest, taking out thirty looters in the aftermath of Hurricane Katrina. In this fiction, "one guy with a rifle" defends property against the horde. The fetish of the gun and the killer and the wild frontier reached its apogee.[46]

World War Z succeeds brilliantly in its ability to tell a monster tale as oral history, turning zombies into an enemy that overwhelmed the world, utterly transforming human history. Readers can find in the book a number of political alternatives, some of them shaped by a conception of American exceptionalism and manhood held in tension with history since at least 1968.

Brooks' use of themes from the combat narratives from Vietnam, whether he consciously imitated them or simply absorbed them from forty years of warrior fantasies, deserves our attention when considering the novel's larger cultural significance. Many Americans still chase the ghosts of Vietnam, Iraq, and Afghanistan. The popularity of farragoes such as Kyle's *American Sniper* suggests that many Americans long for the sublimity of violence inflicted on a faceless enemy horde. In this desire for regeneration through violence, we, to paraphrase Žižek, see how fantasy scenarios can hide from us the true horror of our situation.[47]

NOTES

1. Brooks, *World War Z*, 93.
2. *Ibid.*, 94.
3. *Ibid.*, 100.
4. Slotkin argues that a mythic notion of the American frontier as a place for the American spirit to find renewal though separation from ease and civilization and engaging in "savage war" appears again and again in both the experience of and the narrative myths created around the Vietnam-era warrior and even recent combat narratives (see his *Regeneration Through Violence*). Most pertinent to this essay is his further elaboration of this idea in *Gunfighter Nation*; on zombies and the gun culture, see Herman, "Gun Owners Are Obsessed with Zombies." A number of events, such as the "Outbreak Omega" weekends, allow shooters to live out zombie fantasies dressed in full tactical gear ... while skirting American gun laws by having the chance to fire full-auto weapons "for a small fee" (see Polk, "Outbreak Omega Shows Zombie Shooting").
5. In a September 10, 2012, interview with NPR, Brooks describes himself as a "history nerd," but when asked about the influences on *World War Z*, only the Second World War receives mention (see "What College Kids Can Learn"). The acknowledgments of *World War Z* mention Terkel, filmmaker George Romero, and a somewhat obscure author, General Sir John Hackett, who wrote a 1982 novel entitled *The Third World War*.
6. Engelhardt, *End of Victory Culture*, 309. Engelhardt's claim comes from notes transcribed by an aide to Rumsfeld and later reported by CBS News.
7. See the NSA online archive of declassified documents, especially the September 30, 2001, memo from Rumsfeld to Bush that asserted that if the war didn't bring about a "significant change to the political map of the world," then U.S. efforts would have failed ("Secret U.S. Message to Mullah Omar").
8. Ignatieff, "America's Empire Is an Empire Lite."
9. Jones, "Why the Democrats Won."
10. Bumiller, "U.S. Lifts Photo Ban on Military Coffins." The ban had essentially been in place for eighteen years although the second Bush administration renewed it in 2003 and 2008.
11. Engelhardt, *End of Victory Culture*, xii.
12. Brooks, *World War Z*, 187 & 224; Terkel's oral history of World War II had similar nods to the global experience. He talked with a Russian veteran, a Londoner who experienced the blitz, and a survivor of the dropping of the A-Bomb on Hiroshima.
13. *Ibid.*, 50, 78–79, 238; on the use of the term "gook" and how it became a racialized omnibus term used by American soldiers confronting foreign populations across the world, see Turse, *Kill Anything That Moves*, 49.
14. Brooks, *World War Z*, 53.

15. *Ibid.*, 52–3.
16. Herr, *Dispatches*, 16.
17. *Ibid.*, 20.
18. *Ibid.*, 47.
19. *Ibid.*, 3, 71, and Brooks, *World War Z*, 274. The NLF was founded in Vietnam in 1960 to achieve the unification of both segments of the country. By 1962, a grassroots communist organization formed the core of the NLF. The military arm of the NLF became known as the "Viet Cong" in military slang, apparently a corruption of the term "Victor Charlie" that served as a NATO designation of Vietnamese communists.
20. Caputo, *Rumor of War*, xiii.
21. *Ibid.*, 184–85.
22. *Ibid.*, 99–100, 141
23. Herring, "Vietnam Remembered," 152.
24. Downs, *Killing Zone*, "Preface."
25. *Ibid.*, 31–32.
26. *Ibid.*, 64–66.
27. *Ibid.*, 111, and Brooks, *World War Z*, 285.
28. Brooks, *World War Z*, 104.
29. Reagan, "Peace."
30. Gibson, *Warrior Dreams*, 9.
31. Gibson also exposes the myth of "self imposed restraint" with statistics that show the enormous commitment of personnel and firepower unleashed on North Vietnam and the "Viet Cong" that essentially held the loyalty of vast parts of South Vietnam. The USA dropped at least eight million tons of bombs in Vietnam, four times the tonnage used in all of World War II. Meanwhile, close to half of all military personnel from the army, marines, and air force served in Vietnam with somewhere between 200,000 and 300,000 personnel serving in the Navy's Seventh Fleet off the Vietnamese coast at any one time. The United States threw the full weight of a superpower's military might against the North Vietnamese Army and the People's Liberation Army of South Vietnam.
32. Gibson, *Warrior Dreams*, 43–47, 34–35. The best introduction to the Mack Bolan phenomenon can be found in Pendleton, *Executioner's War Book*; by 2015, this series and numerous spinoffs had sold 200 million copies.
33. Marcinko and Weisman, *Rogue Warrior*, 160, 220, 266.
34. *Ibid.*, xiii.
35. Turse, *Kill Anything that Moves*, 267. More examples appear in Kyle, McEwen, and DeFelice, *American Sniper*, 93, 223. This attitude about Vietnam and Iraq war veterans needs further exploration. I would connect it to the strange phenomenon in American politics in which saber-rattling rhetoric and a desire to expand American military power often conjoin with votes to slash veteran benefits and attempts to shame veterans whose political worldviews diverge from the far right.
36. Brooks, *World War Z*, 275.
37. *Ibid.*, 278.
38. *Ibid.*, 274.
39. See Kyle, McEwen, and DeFelice, *American Sniper*, 77, 112–20, 143–46, and Marcinko and Weisman, *Rogue Warrior*, 51, 97, 284–85. Gibson calls this fetish "the hero's magic weapons" and believes it's tied to the desire, on the part of the NRA and American gun culture, both to own illegal weaponry and to fight even the most rational of proposals for gun control (*Warrior Dreams*, 93–95).
40. Baker, *Zombies Are Coming!*, LOC 330, 464, 511; *Guns and Ammo* has actually published a "Zombie Nation" guide to the apocalypse.
41. Baker, *Zombies Are Coming!*, LOC 511; cf. Ackerman, "Army's Disaster Prep."
42. Brooks, *Zombie Survival Guide*, especially the Introduction, 29, 41–51. The ideological conflicts in Brooks' work can be seen in his urging zombie preppers to obey gun laws, since, after all, "simpler weapons" rather than "paramilitary death machines" are most effective in dispatching the undead. However, later in the text, we learn that "nothing is more important than your primary firearm" and receive the kind of detailed, affectionate, technical

discussions about military-grade weapons that American culture has been having with itself since the 1970s.

43. Brooks, *Zombie Survival Guide*, 228. This famous quote, which has come to symbolize American failure—and brutality—in Vietnam, came out of the mouth of an army major describing the destruction of Ben Tre, a village considered an NLF base of operations ("Major Describes Moves," 14). See also Kyle, McEwen, and DeFelice, *American Sniper*, 168, 280, 361.

44. Bishop, *American Zombie Gothic*, 206.

45. Kyle, McEwen, and DeFelice, *American Sniper*, 280, 361, 168.

46. DeBerry, "'American Sniper's' Preposterous Post-Katrina New Orleans Story." References to the American frontier conflated with legends of "The Old West" and Kyle's constructed persona appear throughout *American Sniper* (see especially 12–15, 17–20, 222).

47. Žižek, "Fantasy as a Political Category," 89–91.

Carrie Ryan's
Romance of the Forest
Mudos, Young Adult
Novels and the Gothic

CORY JAMES RUSHTON

Carrie Ryan's zombie books, collectively called The Forest of Hands and Teeth after the first novel in the trilogy, borrow from the traditional Gothic, a genre ancestral to contemporary horror narratives. Set at least several decades after a zombie apocalypse, the trilogy follows three female narrators across two generations as they alternately flee zombies (called the "Unconsecrated" or "Mudos") and search for love. Read against a text such as Ann Radcliffe's seminal 1791 *Romance of the Forest*, Ryan's books echo several features of the Gothic, even as they participate in the expected tropes of the zombie genre. This essay argues that Ryan's use of the Gothic extends beyond interest in the traditional setting of Gothic story, the ruins of an older, rejected world (usually some vestige of the Catholic Church or the *ancien régime*). Ryan's heroines can appear passive, requiring their male love interests to save them, a Gothic trait also inherited by Stephenie Meyer's Twilight series (itself an apparent influence on Ryan's trilogy). Ryan's female heroines, like Radcliffe's, struggle against oppression by religious or aristocratic authority and operate in a world where parents are either absent or inadequate. The core tension in the series is the relationship between the sharp individuality of the three teenaged narrators' voices and the pull of the social endemic to the zombie genre, in which survival depends on groups working together in the common cause (a generic trope demonstrated, more often than not, by failure to cooperate). The protagonist of the first book, Mary, is orphaned when her mother chooses existence as a zombie in order to follow her dead husband into the forest; Mary, in the next book, abandons her own adopted daughter to seek out her former home in the forest.

I make no claim that *The Forest of Hands and Teeth*, or its sequels, meets all the requirements for a proper Gothic novel, only that it borrows Gothic traits just as the Gothic itself borrowed from earlier literature to make claims for itself (and it does so more explicitly than other horror texts, despite the DNA that they share with the Gothic). Neither do I claim that Radcliffe's *Romance of the Forest* is a source for Ryan's novels, although it is clearly not coincidental that of all possible Gothic novels, I have chosen that book, with that title, to act as Ryan's interlocutor. In many ways, the trilogy's true generic home is not the zombie or horror, but romance.

The Gothic genre is famously difficult to define, but it does have certain universally acknowledged key features: settings which often include abandoned medieval ("Gothic") structures, often religious ones; innocent heroines under duress, usually at the hands of evil aristocrats or religious authorities; a pronounced lack of sexual restraint on the part of these menacing figures. These are all found in the genre's original text, Horace Walpole's 1764 novel *The Castle of Otranto*. In *Otranto*, an aristocrat named Manfred (Lord of Otranto, although not the rightful one) attempts to marry an innocent heiress named Isabella to his own sickly son Conrad. When Conrad is killed by a giant helmet that mysteriously falls from the sky, Manfred conspires to divorce his wife and marry Isabella himself. Isabella flees to the protection of a friar, whose son Theodore becomes her protector. Theodore is later given Otranto when the ghost of Alfonso, the former lord betrayed by Manfred, reveals that Theodore is Alfonso's grandson. A further prophecy, that only Manfred's blood can erase his crimes, is fulfilled when he kills his daughter Matilda, thinking her to be Isabella. This is a family saga, with the committing and subsequent expiation of sins stretching out over three generations of children, lost and found. Walpole himself, when he claimed the initially anonymous novel for himself at its second printing in 1765, laid out what he called "rules" for the new genre, which was "an attempt to blend the two kinds of romance, the ancient and the modern" (by which he meant medieval and contemporary, respectively). The Gothic's characters should "think, speak, and act, as it might be supposed mere men and women would do in extraordinary positions."[1] In practical terms, this meant (as in *The Castle of Otranto*) old ruins, family secrets, bad behavior amongst the ruling classes, realistic responses to baffling supernatural events, and a focus on the fears of heroines.

But as with all genres, the Gothic is more than the sum of its trappings. The Gothic explores contemporary anxieties through the exploration of an abandoned past. At its origin, the Gothic—so called as a result of Walpole's subtitle to *The Castle of Otranto*, "A Gothic Story"—was deeply concerned with history and with historical rupture. Manfred's usurpation is obviously a matter of political rupture, set in a medieval and aristocratic past. As Jerrold

E. Hogle remarks, the Gothic is "founded on a quasi-antiquarian use of symbols that are quite obviously signs only of older signs," all distanced from whatever meaning they once had; Walpole, in particular, "made his references to the distant past distinctly *hollowed-out* ones, allusions to what was largely empty as well as distant for him."[2] For Walpole, one aspect of England's past that required hollowing out was its previous Catholicism, lingering within Protestant English society and physically present within the landscape as cathedrals, monasteries, and churches. The form of the Gothic building stood in for ancient, half-spoken, partially suppressed prejudices and beliefs. Subsequent social unrest, resulting in revolutions and attempted revolutions, heightened anxieties around the loss of traditional modes of social life. The French Revolution had a particularly strong impact on the genre, especially in the hands of perhaps its greatest early practitioner, the English author Ann Radcliffe.

Radcliffe was so much an early influence on subsequent Gothic that one alternate name for the genre was "the Radcliffe romance." Robert Miles, noting that Keats called her "Mother Radcliff," argues that "to a very real extent 1790s Gothic writing happened within her shadow."[3] Radcliffe was very much a second founder of the genre. Her two best-known innovations to the Gothic are an expansion of the trope of the heroine's flight from masculine threat, and a relentless debunking of the supernatural elements that she herself evokes and describes.[4] *The Romance of the Forest* exemplifies these two features. Radcliffe tells the story of Adeline, a young woman who turns out to be the heir to an estate currently held by a usurping false Marquis; this Marquis wishes to marry Adeline but is also the murderer of her father. Two young men fall in love with Adeline, one the son of her first protectors (Pierre de la Motte and his wife) and one the son of her second protector (the benevolent Arnaud la Luc). Adeline and the de la Mottes spend time in a ruined abbey owned by the Marquis, and, after fleeing that situation due to the Marquis' advances, with la Luc's family in Savoy. The novel ends when the king restores justice, in a move that speaks to Radcliffe's essentially paternalistic worldview, while the false Marquis kills himself, and Adeline marries la Luc's son, called Theodore. Radcliffe's father-worship is found throughout the novel, as Adeline encounters and moves past several inadequate father figures before finding la Luc (who will become her father-in-law) and the king (who will use his patriarchal authority to force a happy resolution of the novel's convoluted problems).

Radcliffe's novel establishes a language of architecture that Ryan's books borrow. The very word "Gothic" is used five times in the long description of the ruined abbey in which the main characters take refuge (twice on 15, thrice on 20). The ruined nature of the building, key to the genre, is made clear: "The greater part of the pile appeared to be sinking into ruins, and that, which had withstood the ravages of time, shewed [sic] the remaining features of the fabric more awful in decay. The lofty battlements, thickly enwreathed with ivy, were half demolished, and become the residence of birds of prey."[5] Ryan echoes the way that predatory, creeping nature can take over a place of former spirituality, in the form of the "Cathedral" that sits at the metaphorical heart of Mary's village.

> To my left is the village itself. From up here the houses are even smaller, the Cathedral a hulking shape that dominates the sunset boundary, its graveyard all that stands between the large stone building and the fences lining the Forest. From here I can see the way the Cathedral has grown awkwardly, wings sprouting off the central sanctuary at strange angles.[6]

This building is the home of the Sisterhood, the real political power in the village and, unlike Radcliffe's abbey, is a living place. But we soon learn that the Cathedral's spiritual presence is partially an illusion, even faintly parodic, as Sister Tabitha explains, "Did you know that long, long ago, centuries before the Return, this building used to belong to a plantation? Used to house a winery?" Tabitha states that the wine was "made elsewhere" and that the winery was abandoned when the "soil failed."[7] There are real questions about when Ryan's zombie apocalypse begins: Gabry suggests in *The Dark and Hollow Places* that it is "[o]ver a century and then some," while Annah thinks the Dark City has survived "hundreds of years" after the Return,[8] but it is clearly in America, where there have not been many century-old wineries. Ryan's early recourse to the religiosity of "Cathedral" indicates how steeped her vision is in the trappings of the Gothic, even to the point of further hollowing out the already hollowed Catholic tropes.

Like *The Castle of Otranto* and *Romance of the Forest*, Ryan's The Forest of Hands and Teeth trilogy is a family saga, but one set against a series of postapocalyptic events and organized around three communities: Mary's village in *The Forest of Hands and Teeth* (and to a lesser extent, the first Gabrielle's separate village); the seaside town of Vista in *The Dead-Tossed Waves*; and the Dark City in *The Dark and Hollow Places*, confirmed to be New York City.[9] The broad outline of that postapocalyptic history emerges, through mostly oblique references, across the trilogy. In the immediate aftermath of the first zombies, coastal communities retrench enough to survive while the communities of the Forest are fenced off, with marked paths in between them, as part of a concerted effort to halt the epidemic at the place where it was apparently strongest. In *The Dead-Tossed Waves*, readers (including Gabry) are given confirmation that the fence system was put in place as a refuge for "dignitaries, scientists, women and children," a "series of interconnected nodes" in touch with each other but also partially self-contained; nonetheless, the system serves to eventually and ironically channel the zombified inhabitants of one village down to the others.[10] Vista operates as a port for traders who find the ocean safer than the roads, until the rise of a pirate culture. The Dark City is the heart of a loose Protectorate with its armed Recruiters, who rebel and impose a brutal military regime between the second and third books, prompting a mass exodus from the City.[11] The Protectorate was liberal enough to allow the rise of a troubling zombie-worshipping cult, the Soulers, and illiberal enough to insist on Recruiter service both as the only path to citizenship and as a method of punishment for youthful transgressions.

The events of the trilogy are set in motion when a girl, Gabrielle, arrives in Mary's village from one of the others, whose existence is known only to the Sisterhood. Mary encounters this strange and unexpected person as a shadow in the window or a voice in the dark, one that she feels closely resembles herself—a classic doubling trope.[12] Gabrielle's subsequent death as a captive of the Sisterhood results in a rare kind of zombie, a Fast One or Breaker, which continues to follow Mary and her friends as they escape their overrun village. The Fast Ones develop when a zombie is created in isolation, away from others, in a nod to the social anxieties of both the Gothic and the zombie genres. Loneliness is not only a source of perverse strength but also a guarantee that the new zombie will burn out faster than others of its kind. Simultaneously, it is impossible not to see Ryan's creation of the Fast Ones as an acknowledgment of one of the zombie genre's great debates: fast versus slow zombies, a question popularized in the current generation by director Danny Boyle's highly successful *28 Days Later* (2002). Gabrielle's red coat, which Mary finds unnaturally bright compared to the somber colors of her village, marks her as she stalks the group through the forest. This flash of bright red on a doomed girl seems uncomfortably close to the red coat worn by a young Jewish girl in Steven Spielberg's *Schindler's List* (1993), a girl who is equally doomed albeit in a very different way. Gabrielle functions as Mary's double, promising the possibility of travel outside the village while also suggesting Mary's metaphorical imprisonment through her literal captivity. Her death sets Mary free but also haunts her, driving her to the ocean.

The trilogy takes place over two time periods, making it a generational novel: Mary's escape from the village and arrival at the ocean in the first book, which leads to the stories of the twins Abigail/Gabry and Annah in the second and third books, respectively. Mary appears in the second book as caretaker of Vista's lighthouse, before she departs for the Forest hoping to find her village again; Gabry also appears in the third book. Gabry's adventure begins when she accompanies some other teens outside the walls of Vista in order to be with her friend Cira and Cira's brother, Catcher, who is Gabry's initial love interest. Attacked by zombies, several die and Catcher is bitten; he turns out to be immune, both zombie and not zombie, and basically invisible to them. Attempting to visit Catcher outside the walls, Gabry meets Elias, a Recruiter who has infiltrated the Souler cult (who worship the undead). Eventually, Gabry accompanies Elias, Catcher, and Cira into the Forest in search of Mary. Finding Mary and her village, they all flee a Recruiter party that is hunting them, and Gabry reads the Sisterhood's record of the village's history. Elias and Gabry are separated from the others and flee to the Dark City, accidentally awakening a zombie horde on their way. Gabry falls in love with Elias. The third book begins with the scarred Annah trying to leave the Dark City, and seeing her identical but unscarred sister going into the City (one of the trilogy's moments of explicit doubling). Gabry is arrested, and Annah, Catcher, and Elias try to save her from the Recruiter fortress, an island. The Recruiters discover Catcher's ability to pass the undead safely and blackmail him by threatening his friends if he does not work for them. The zombie horde awakened at the end of the second book reaches the Dark City, and Annah improvises a hot-air balloon out of old blankets, allowing the protagonists to flee the Recruiter island. Catcher and Annah fall in love, resolving Annah's jealousy towards her sister.

As with most texts, Ryan's The Forest of Hands and Teeth trilogy's sources are not limited to the obvious (zombie apocalypse texts descended from George A. Romero's films) or the classically "literary" (the Gothic), although most students of popular culture have felt the temptation of the latter. To link a piece of modern pop culture to an earlier, often canonical, text or series of texts is to make a claim for the later text's worthiness. In fact, the Gothic itself was defended by precisely this rhetorical, literary-historical move: Radcliffe fills Romance of the Forest with poetry, particularly with allusions to Shakespeare, in an explicit attempt to valorize her work as part of the English tradition and not a light deviation from it. Ryan does the same thing when Mary finds a collection of Shakespearian sonnets, and she uses their traditional numbering as a way of leaving messages for her adopted daughter: the number of the sonnet linked to the safest path through the numbered villages of the Forest. Yet Ryan has sources nearer to hand, as well. Her Sisterhood, which controls Mary's village until its destruction, is most easily compared to two antecedents: the Bene Gesserit Sisterhood from Frank Herbert's classic Dune series (1965–85) and the religious dictatorship of Margaret Atwood's The Handmaid's Tale (1985).

The Bene Gesserit are probably the closer model, with their long-term genetic planning for a messiah, although Atwood's dystopian religious state is probably better known now. Both occur in diegetic worlds in which the normal birth cycle has been complicated by issues of politics and health. Gabry learns, from the records of Mary's village (Village 18), that the villages of the Forest were highly variable, some filled with scientists and leaders, others serving as refugee camps. Village 18 "was the latter, an abandoned field station left staffed by a handful of monastic nurses" whose religious doctrine became the village's organizing principle, while Sister Tabitha explicitly suggests to Mary that the Sisterhood's purpose is the preservation of "strong bloodlines" to ensure humanity's survival as a species.[13] Mary's nascent rebellion, interrupted but abetted by a zombie invasion led by her dead double Gabrielle, is all about love as opposed to prearranged marriages as social duty. While that rebellion eventually succeeds both for Mary and for the next generation of heroines, it does so against the grain of the narrative to some extent, for these heroines are still more passive than not, obsessed with whether the boys love them back, and finally achieve happiness largely through those boys.

A key feature of the Gothic is the threatened heroine, the damsel who is not only in distress but is more beautiful for it. Radcliffe's Adeline is introduced in precisely this way: "a beautiful girl, who appeared to be about eighteen" and whose "features were bathed in tears," a figure who sinks at La Motte's feet; La Motte "found it impossible to contemplate the beauty and distress of the object before him with indifference,"[14] the two elements of her disheveled appearance being of equal and linked importance. Although Adeline will resist evil and seek out answers about her past, she remains entirely dependent on the kindness of male strangers (including father figures both inadequate, as La Motte, and benevolent, as La Luc, who also happens to be the father of her future husband—this family connection, providing a new father through marriage, is not a coincidence). The Gothic heroine is largely incapable of helping herself, and modern horror inherits this generic trait. The oddity of Ryan's trilogy is that it is produced after *Buffy the Vampire Slayer* (1997–2003, created by Joss Whedon), an explicit attempt to build a heroic narrative around the traditional cheerleader victim (an inversion of that Gothic trope), and contemporaneously with Katniss Everdeen from The Hunger Games trilogy (2008–10, written by Suzanne Collins). Ryan's heroines sometimes act as though they are in the same mold as Katniss or Buffy, but they are very much like *Twilight's* Bella Swan: a passive heroine waiting for the men to finish fighting over her. Mary is torn between love interests in the first book, but her relationship with her mother and her longing for the ocean keep her from being too simple a figure. Gabry and Annah are almost entirely concerned with their romantic longing, with Gabry's affections moving to Elias while Annah's move, in a more complex way, to Catcher, the boy whom Gabry rejects.

Gabry is so distracted by her early love for Catcher that she nearly dies at the teeth of a recently turned friend; only Catcher saves her, and he is bitten as a result. When her new love interest, Elias, is caught on something while crossing a bridge, Gabry saves him by calling on Catcher to save him; she spends the rescue scene thinking about their first kiss with her eyes closed.[15] Travis, Mary's love interest in *The Forest of Hands and Teeth*, dies saving her.[16] The trilogy's passive heroines are not the only Gothic holdover that now looks problematic: the crippled Daniel, one of the villains introduced in the second book, is a figure to be pitied and feared partly because of his limp, but also because his limp both reveals and causes the deformation of his personality. This classic disability trope is everywhere in the Gothic, most explicitly in texts such as Mary Shelley's *Frankenstein* (1818) and Robert Louis Stevenson's *The Strange Case of Dr Jekyll and Mr Hyde* (1886), in which monstrous physical qualities act as a proxy for disabled bodies. Tellingly, when a female protagonist (Gabry) finally tries (rarely) and actually succeeds (more rarely) in an act of self-defense, it is against a disabled character. Rather than attempting to trouble traditional gender and ableist norms, here Ryan merely plays them against each other.

Annah, the protagonist of the third book, encapsulates this tension, attached as it is to the series' persistent gender norms and teen-romance generic expectations. While exploring the old subway system, Annah is scarred in a childhood encounter with "a tangle of razor-sharp wire" meant to trap Unconsecrated—another ruin of the past, now disfiguring the future— and is obsessed with her own perceived ugliness.[17] This perception is a major strand in the final novel's eventual resolution, but it sits oddly in a postapocalyptic world. Does the scar stigma make sense in a world suffering through centuries of a zombie apocalypse? One explanation might be the lingering influence of Walpole, as Annah does act as a real person might act or feel regardless of her exceptional circumstances. The problem is that Walpole's modern, reasonable person is not contemporary here, but trapped in a vicious future. Whether the scar stigma does or does not make sense, Annah's stigma matters for the novel in problematic ways: her belief that her body-length scars have kept her safe from rape does not reflect society's current understanding of what rape is, for example.[18] When Annah sees Abigail/Gabry on the bridge into the city at the start of *The Dark and Hollow Places*, we've been given literalized doubles in place of Mary/Gabrielle.[19] The scars become the difference between the twins, as when Annah sees "herself" (the clean, unscarred Abigail version of herself) flirting with her initial love interest, Elias.[20] Teenage angst replaces the diegetic cohesion of the trilogy: in a world of zombies, fascist military dictatorships, and a desperate hand-to-mouth existence, Ryan's novels suggest that people might still be obsessed with physical perfection.

Despite this emphasis on teenage sexual and romantic desires, the trilogy is more violent than it is sensual, unwilling to show sex, even in a world where life is short and parents mostly absent. The moment when Gabry and Catcher almost begin a relationship describes the act of falling in love in a manner that the trilogy also uses to describe the transition to zombiehood, as Catcher remembers suddenly seeing her as something other than his little sister's friend: "I realize how right he is. How we still see people as who they were before and maybe not as they are now."[21] As the trilogy begins, Mary's mother is unable to accept that her husband is gone, that his wandering body no longer contains what made him her husband. Her love for her husband blinds her to the realities of life, and unlife, in a world dominated by zombies: she is caught between an inability to see the very real loss of her husband and an almost mystical belief that, if turned herself, she will be able to share his state.[22] Mary wonders, later, whether the Unconsecrated have anything left of themselves, but the trilogy makes it clear that they do not (except for someone like Catcher). Mary's mother's decision pushes the trilogy towards its resolution in a series of happy romantic endings, but is itself a consequence of a dangerous despair also rooted in romantic ideals. At the same time, the trilogy is relentless in its pursuit of a particular zombie motif, the family composed of broken parts. Robert Kirkman's graphic novel series *The Walking Dead* (2003–) is probably the best-known example of this, as the group led by Rick Grimes includes families composed of parents and children unrelated to each other. After Mary, we have a succession of orphans, people who believe they are orphans (Catcher and Cira, Annah and Abigail), and children raised by people who are not their parents: Jacob, an orphaned boy in the first book, is raised by Harry and Cass; Abigail/Gabrielle, by Mary. Further, Elias and Annah pretend to be siblings for no particularly compelling reason, beyond the echoes of the biblical Abraham and Sarah. This deceit provides them with no apparent protection, although it may be connected to the mechanism by which Elias can become a citizen of the Dark City through service as a Recruiter. The point is that biological conception has been largely replaced by quilted-together families, which (along with *The Walking Dead*) indicates a new interest not only in what happens after the apocalypse, but also in how traditional family structures can be rebuilt and even reinvigorated in the face of continuing catastrophe. Ryan inherits her version of this from the Gothic: Radcliffe's Adeline is given a happy ending precisely because she is welcomed into new families, which, in turn, help her reclaim elements of her original family.

Ryan's engagement with the idea of motherhood is, however, a deviation from earlier Gothic material. The broad outlines of this deviation will already be apparent: Abigail and Annah's mother dies in childbirth, and Harry and Cass adopt them when they cannot conceive children.[23] Mary adopts a baby that she finds in the Forest but never marries or has children of her own, and Annah is effectively raised by a childhood friend posing as her brother. But the rejection of mothers and motherhood is most acute in *The Forest of Hands and Teeth*. Mary's mother is, for children's literature, a troubling figure. Her love of an ocean she has never seen is passed on to Mary, despite the latter's skepticism about its existence. The mother's knowledge of the ocean echoes the Gothic, located in stories "passed down from her many-greats-grandmother" and glimpsed only in a photo that has itself been destroyed by fire long before the novel's events.[24] When Mary finds another photo of the ocean late in the first novel, she breaks into weeping for all the lost possibilities of her life and momentarily observes and then rejects a physical similarity between a child in the picture and herself, a moment where doubling is evoked only to be rejected.[25] But Mary's mother longs for something besides the ocean: her husband has gone missing, and although months have passed, she is unable to accept that he is gone and has probably turned. Her vigil at the fences that keep the Unconsecrated out are dangerous enough that Mary is tasked, by her brother, with making certain she does not get too close to the zombies. Mary fails, and her mother chooses to turn and be allowed out into the Forest, a tradition grudgingly permitted by the Sisterhood as a matter of free will.[26] Late in the book, Mary's growing (if doomed) love for Travis prompts her to a realization about her mother. Young Mary could believe that her mother never went in search of the ocean because she had two children to raise; older Mary realizes her mother was always more concerned with her husband than with their children,[27] the first of four women in the trilogy whose pursuit of love stands in for and thus replaces a concern for the social until the final book in the trilogy. Only then does Annah manage to reconcile her love for Catcher with his humanitarian work of bringing supplies to people trapped in the zombie-besieged Dark City, something only he can do because of his immunity.

Mary's interaction with an earlier baby, well before she finds and adopts Abigail/Gabrielle, is particularly telling in light of her mother's failures. The group has discovered a village that appears to be the original Gabrielle's and that has suffered a recent zombie attack. In one of the village's platform tree houses, Mary finds a zombified baby, silently screaming, who had probably died after the village was overrun. She is overcome by an initial tenderness, holding the child gently and running her finger along its face in an automatic gesture intended to soothe the creature: "But this child will never sleep, will never dream, will never love," so she lets the child drop to the ground below, hoping that "its delicate head" doesn't survive the fall. When Travis, who has watched the scene, asks for comfort in the form of Mary's stories of the ocean, she is finally able to confess that she is afraid it is just a fiction even as she is filled with an unexpected hope for the present moment.[28]

Ryan's ruined world seems incapable of creating anything really new to replace the world that was lost, at least until the central characters are pushed into a need to innovate in the final book. The world is full of death tableaus, like the one Annah comes across near the end of the trilogy while she raids for supplies: a boarded-up room with two skeletons embracing, "as if they lay down one night to sleep and never woke up."[29] The village Mary and her companions find in *The Forest of Hands and Teeth* is simply the most elaborate of these, which exist in ever-proliferating numbers: these aren't ossified scenes from the original apocalypse, but new ones created as the descendants of the original survivors pass pathetically into the night. That this village appears to be the original Gabrielle's hints that any attempt to break the cycle of passive despair leads only to more brutal and quicker destruction. While contemplation of the remnants of lives formerly lived and brutally interrupted is an endemic zombie trope, mobilization of the trope here is almost always simultaneously pushing towards reconstitution of the nuclear family while also undermining that very possibility. The destruction of planned marriage alliances in *The Forest of Hands and Teeth* is matched in the next generation by the temporary loss of the survivors' children (Elias, Abigail/Gabry, Annah, and, to a lesser extent, Catcher).

In a sense, the trilogy turns the Gothic on its head, invoking the Gothic's nostalgic anxiety about the past and throwing it, instead, into the future. Ryan's books depict not the ancient world haunting the present, but a ruined present haunting the future. The last book emphasizes the literalized weight of history in the form of zombie hordes. Elias, a former Recruiter with access to their records, tells Annah that there were eight billion people in the world when the zombie apocalypse occurred, an overwhelming number of potential zombies. Gabry admits to Annah that she and Elias are responsible for waking up a horde during their escape from the Forest at the end of *The Dead-Tossed Waves*, one that Elias admits is "tiny compared to some of the others" but is nonetheless going to destroy the Dark City when it inexorably arrives there.[30] In this zombie text, the moment of transition between living and being undead is not the silent one it is in Romero's original films: "The dead sometimes scream when they return, a horrid eerie cry"[31]: even the moment of transformation, an inherently "historical" moment of personal change, is accompanied by a kind of sonic agony, a scream of despair. The commander of the Recruiters, Ox, shows Annah their war room, stuffed full of maps with colored pins denoting both existing and lost settlements and the location of the major hordes.[32] This knowledge later haunts Annah:

> And what of the rest of the world that's already fallen? Stars blinking away, their light slowly fading? ... The Earth will spin, the stars will rearrange themselves around one another and the world will crawl with the dead who one day will drop into nothingness: no humans left for them to scent, no flesh for them to crave. Everything—all of us—will simply cease to be.[33]

The only possible peace is also the end of history: no stories left to tell after the last, simplest one—about the flesh-eating zombies—ceases to be told.

The trilogy's end does suggest a way out, through another escape, one that suggests a happy ending through the fall of the Recruiters and the promise of passage to new places, away from the Forest, Vista, and the Dark City. Annah, imprisoned on the Recruiter island, is doing laundry, washing old blankets and quilts, which fall apart as she does so. Her first instinct is to lament, as Ryan's characters often do, for the world that has been lost: "All the half-finished products of people's lives."[34] Only when she gives up and starts trying to repair a picture that she has drawn of Catcher, a picture that includes balloons, does she put two different things together: the old fabric and the idea of a balloon-based escape from the Recruiter island.[35] It is here that the tropes of romance take over from those of the zombie and move the text closer to its Gothic forebears. Both Annah and Gabry end up with the love interest whom they have come to prefer, the trilogy's relentless doubling providing two men for two women in a happy ending that would not look out of place beside Shakespeare's *As You Like It* or *Twelfth Night* (or, for that matter, in Jane Austen's novels). While there is a growing subgenre of zombie comedy-romance, as in *Shaun of the Dead* (2004, directed by Edgar Wright) or *Warm Bodies* (2013, directed by Jonathan Levine), it is by no means a predominant one. It also seems to fly (literally) in the face of the utter ruin of Ryan's world. Where could they be going that might be better than where they've been? The trilogy does not have to answer this question because it chooses to end with the beginning of flight, not with the destination.

Ryan's The Forest of Hands and Teeth trilogy, taken as a zombie text, does a number of things that other contemporary zombie texts do. Faced with the rapid proliferation of the genre, creators have been encouraged or even forced into finding new narrative spaces: geographic (setting the story somewhere other than America, or in parts of America often neglected); chronological (setting the story well after an outbreak); generic (mashing the zombie with another, usually unlikely, genre); and, as is evident in the present volume, formal (writing about the apocalypse in a new form, even one as potentially unwelcoming as the novel). The Forest of Hands and Teeth trilogy gains something from being novels, which allow access to a character's inner thoughts much more extensively than any other medium. The novel has space in which to develop those thoughts, while also channeling events and other characters through that specific singular lens. In a film, the physically active zombies overwhelm the tropes borrowed from other genres; in a novel, the zombies are arguably subordinate to the other genre's features.

I began this essay by suggesting that The Forest of Hands and Teeth series is better seen as a romance than as a horror narrative. The trilogy's emphasis on Gothic elements such as crumbling ancient ruins and displaced or rearranged familial structures loom larger on the page than they would on screen, by sheer weight of the time taken to explore them. Zombie movies need to spend much of their time on zombies attacking, being killed, and feeding. These scenes take a mere few lines in novels; the rest of Ryan's books are taken up by female leads pining for boys, lamenting lost opportunities with boys, and trying to save or be saved by boys. As romances, Ryan's The Forest of Hands and Teeth trilogy participates in a significant trend within young adult fiction: the turn away from the active female heroine (a Buffy or a Katniss Everdeen) and towards more passive heroines (such as *Twilight*'s Bella Swan). Ryan's trilogy is an important intervention in both zombie texts and young adult texts, in that it repurposes the Gothic to create more modern versions of the traditional Radcliffean Adeline.

NOTES

1. Walpole, "Preface to the Second Edition," 65.
2. Hogle, "Introduction," 15; italics in the original.
3. Miles, "The 1790s," 45.
4. *Ibid.*, 45–46.
5. Radcliffe, *Romance of the Forest*, 15.
6. Ryan, *Forest of Hands and Teeth*, 28.
7. *Ibid.*, 31–32.
8. Ryan, *Dark and Hollow Places*, 268 & 240.
9. *Ibid.*, 257–59.
10. Ryan, *Dead-Tossed Waves*, 336–37.
11. Ryan, *Dark and Hollow Places*, 6 & 15.
12. Ryan, *Forest of Hands and Teeth*, 71.
13. Ryan, *Dead-Tossed Waves*, 336–37; Ryan, *Forest of Hands and Teeth*, 113.
14. Radcliffe, *Romance of the Forest*, 5.
15. Ryan, *Dead-Tossed Waves*, 365–70.
16. Ryan, *Forest of Hands and Teeth*, 269–73.
17. Ryan, *Dark and Hollow Places*, 93 & 196.
18. *Ibid.*, 32–33.
19. *Ibid.*, 16.
20. *Ibid.*, 131.
21. Ryan, *Dead-Tossed Waves*, 17.
22. Ryan, *Forest of Hands and Teeth*, 2–15.
23. *Ibid.*, 305–06.
24. Ryan, *Forest of Hands and Teeth*, 1.
25. *Ibid.*, 211.
26. *Ibid.*, 2–15.
27. *Ibid.*, 225.
28. *Ibid.*, 195–97.
29. Ryan, *Dark and Hollow Places*, 337–38.
30. *Ibid.*, 143 & 157.
31. *Ibid.*, 218.
32. *Ibid.*, 124–28.
33. *Ibid.*, 249.
34. *Ibid.*, 278.
35. *Ibid.*, 279.

Toward a Genealogy
of the American Zombie Novel
From Jack London to Colson Whitehead

Wylie Lenz

Something of a truism has emerged in the field of zombie studies. Scholars often repeat the claim that, unlike the vampire, the zombie—particularly in its contagious, flesh-eating form—lacks any true literary antecedent, as its origins lie wholly in cinema of the late twentieth century.[1] Most observers will point to George A. Romero's 1968 film *Night of the Living Dead* as the *Urtext* that birthed this seemingly ubiquitous pop culture figure. Book critics have made parallel claims about the unprecedented nature of Colson Whitehead's 2011 zombie novel *Zone One*. While we have seen the publication of numerous genre works centered on the figure, this book apparently serves as the first "serious literary treatment" of "zombie mythology."[2] We can rest assured of this novel's serious, literary qualities because its author possesses unassailable critical respectability, having won a MacArthur "genius" grant, while each of his novels has earned a range of prestigious accolades, nominations, and awards.

These intertwined assumptions ultimately impose artificial boundaries on the zombie genre and potentially limit our understanding of the cultural work the genre performs. Certainly, zombies have been mediated by a robust cinematic interlude—to which *Zone One* makes direct and repeated allusions—but so has virtually every cultural monster, no matter how undeniably literary its origins. Rather than construct the contagious-voracious zombie as a *sui generis* figure of relatively recent cinematic origin, we would more accurately situate that figure in a long-established literary tradition: the apocalyptic plague narrative. During its lengthy history, this tradition evolved a clear set of topoi that have since become familiar to viewers of *Night of the*

Living Dead and its myriad celluloid inheritors. Indeed, at least a few previous studies have pointed to various examples of such narratives as antecedents to the zombie genre.[3] Even these studies, however, tend to focus exclusively on medieval and early modern European texts as progenitors of zombie *cinema*, effectively ignoring both American literature's historical contributions to the corpus of plague narratives and the resonances of those contributions in the contemporary American zombie *novel*. In correcting this oversight, we see that *Zone One* represents a culmination of the plague narrative's sustained "serious literary treatment" in American fiction, rather than a radical break. Moreover, Whitehead's use of this genre's conventions and his exploration of its persistent themes do not merely replicate the cinematic and televisual versions of the zombie narrative, but rather offer an essentially written experience for the audience that could not be produced through visual media.

Zombie Taxonomy Revisited

Steven Zani and Kevin Meaux observe that "[n]o cinematic monster has experienced as many reinventions or taken as many forms as the zombie."[4] Such fungibility from text to text seems to invite critiques that catalogue the zombie's characteristics in order to arrive at a stable definition. Somewhat ironically, such taxonomic efforts illuminate the arbitrary and even contradictory nature of the boundaries of the zombie figure and, consequently, its genre. For instance, in a key article in the field, Kyle William Bishop notes that his analysis "is limited in scope to those films that openly embrace the genre conventions established by George A. Romero in his series of zombie movies," namely "stories that feature hordes of cannibalistic human corpses that relentlessly pursue an isolated group of survivors and can only be killed by a gunshot or blow to the head."[5] However, Bishop acknowledges the central role of Danny Boyle's 2002 movie *28 Days Later* in initiating the current zombie renaissance—although Boyle's "infected" figures are explicitly *not* reanimated corpses, but rather diseased humans who operate by the known rules of mortality, and therefore cannot be zombies. Nicole LaRose, meanwhile, seeks to acknowledge and accommodate this contradiction by designating Boyle's infected as "zombies that are not zombies," or "ZnZs."[6]

Scholars further argue that even the universally acknowledged creator of the contagious-voracious zombie apparently gets his own monsters wrong. Bishop observes that "Romero has been experimenting with the idea of zombie evolution, a concept progressing toward sentient ghouls," which "seems illogical."[7] It is true that both *Day of the Dead* (1985) and *Land of the Dead* (2005) feature zombies that exhibit emotional responses and demonstrate the ability to learn. Still, suggestions of zombie sentience appeared at least as early as Romero's second zombie film, *Dawn of the Dead* (1978).[8] Moreover, the film as a whole repeatedly and explicitly troubles the human/zombie oppositional binary, a point to which I will return. Carl Joseph Swanson goes even further than Bishop, almost paradoxically distinguishing between what he calls "Romeroesque zombies," which function as "antisubject anticharacters," and the *zombies Romero actually portrays in his films*, because "Romero's own zombies have evolved slowly into characters."[9] Finally, it seems as if zombie scholars have succeeded in generating no more stable boundaries for the figure than Supreme Court Justice Potter Stewart did for pornography when he offered only one criterion: "I know it when I see it."[10]

The problem with these attempts to establish some sort of Platonic zombie ideal in contrast to the representational content of existing (and even seminal) texts is that the specific ontological and epistemological ramifications of what we talk about when we talk about zombies have tremendous import in the theoretical-interpretive project of zombie studies as a whole. It matters greatly whether a zombie in a given text is actually dead or merely infected with a potentially curable contagion. It matters whether a zombie has been hollowed of all subjectivity or perhaps retains human memories and even possesses the ability to learn and make moral choices. It even matters whether a zombie shambles or sprints. If nothing else, these variations suggest potentially meaningful differences in the metaphorical deployment of the monster, possibly even undermining its presumed monstrosity.

If the zombie has few, if any, essential characteristics from text to text, perhaps the kinship most audiences intuitively perceive between, say, Romero's undead ghouls and Boyle's still-living infected derives less from what a zombie *is* than from what a zombie *does*. Here, I follow Swanson's emphasis on narrative, even while I argue that he ultimately formulates an unnecessarily constrictive definition of the figure. However unresolved the definition of the zombie's ontology remains, narratively the figure's power derives from its abilities to (1) act as an agent of contagion and (2) disrupt a host of categories reliant on presumed binaries, destabilizing oppositions such as human/nonhuman, subject/object, and—most obviously—living/dead. In turn, the zombie narrative becomes less a distinct genre than a subgenre of the apocalyptic plague narrative, which relies on unescapable epidemic to enact what René Girard describes as "a process of undifferentiation, a destruction of specificities."[11] Bishop actually hints at this approach when he notes that Stephen King's novel *The Stand* has "no zombies" even while containing "most of the other zombie motifs."[12] However, it makes more sense from a genealogical perspective to reverse this framing: whether discussing Romero's works, *28 Days Later*, or virtually any other zombie film, we are in fact dealing with apocalyptic plague narratives that just happen to contain zombies. This approach allows us to conceive of apocalyptic plague narratives as proto-zombie narratives—or, to alter slightly LaRose's phrasing of such taxonomical slippages, *zombie narratives without zombies*.

Consistent with this formulation, Zani and Meaux assert that "the messages and themes of zombie texts are quite compatible with [the] plague narratives" first appearing in medieval Europe, so much so that these narratives' "threatening elements ... have been absorbed into the zombie genre to the point where they have become its very conventions."[13] Similar to contemporary zombie films, texts as diverse as Giovanni Boccaccio's fourteenth-century collection of tales *The Decameron*, Thomas Dekker's pamphlet "The Wonderfull Yeare" (1603), and Daniel Defoe's *A Journal of the Plague Year* (1722) all give expression to anxieties attending the seemingly imminent collapse of social, religious, and governmental institutions.[14] While this analysis is convincing in identifying "loss of control, loss of meaning" as the sole unifying element of the zombie genre,[15] Zani and Meaux understate the essential roles both contagion itself and the mechanisms of contagion play in plague and zombie texts. Oddly, their critique gives no mention to the first truly *apocalyptic* plague novel, Mary Shelley's *The Last Man* (1826). While Boccaccio, Dekker, and Defoe responded to historical visitations of the plague after the fact—in other words, after humanity had recovered—Shelley imagines a future epidemic that results in total human extinction. Even if her twenty-first century setting looks a lot like the early nineteenth century technologically and politically, the author effectively modernizes the apocalypse by decoupling it from religion. Pamela Bickley explains that "[i]n *The Last Man* mankind will be destroyed but there will be no revelation of the Second Coming, no Last Judgment, no conventional *fin du monde*."[16] Instead, the revelations of Shelley's and subsequent apocalyptic plague narratives remain distinctly human and secular.

Zani and Meaux also pass over American literary contributions to the development of the plague narrative, instead referring to Albert Camus' *The Plague* (1947) as "the only major account written in the modern era."[17] Still, they and other scholars have not wholly ignored the American literary origins of the Romero (or "Romeroesque") zombie, calling particular attention to Richard Matheson's influential short novel *I Am Legend* (1954), which itself has been directly adapted for film several times.[18] John Edgar Browning builds on the pioneering work of Gregory A. Waller to demonstrate convincingly that almost all zombie texts of the last several decades owe to Matheson not only a monster figure that looks an awful lot like the modern zombie, but two crucial and persistent narrative-structural elements, namely the zombie as "threat en masse" and the plot centrality of the "survival space."[19] For his part, Romero has long acknowledged this debt, explaining, "I took the idea [for *Night of the Living Dead*] from Richard Matheson's novel *I Am Legend*.... I ripped off the siege and the central idea, which I thought was so powerful."

Romero goes on to present his creation of the zombie as almost accidental: "I didn't want to do vampires because [Matheson] had already done vampires. So.... I made them flesh-eaters instead of blood-drinkers. But I never thought of them as zombies.... They were 'ghouls' or 'those things.'"[20] In an interview following the publication of *Zone One*, Whitehead offers a similar lineage, saying that his own "idiosyncratic timeline" of the zombie in popular culture "begins with ... *I Am Legend*, which offered up an early viral apocalypse.... Then comes the George Romero 'Living Dead' trilogy, with its template for the slow-moving zombie."[21] Yet, as we will see, even this reverse timeline of specifically American literary predecessors to the zombie narrative terminates too recently and abruptly.

Jack London's Protozombie Plague

While not the first fictional epidemic narrative in American literature,[22] Jack London's short novel *The Scarlet Plague* effectively distills Shelley's apocalyptic plague scenario down to its narrative and thematic essence. Published in 1912, London's work provides a crucial step in the evolution of the plague narrative tradition because, unlike previous writings, "it reflected deeply the contemporary scientific discoveries on pathogens."[23] London drew on the insights of bacteriology, which, in coalescing as a field in the last decades of the nineteenth century, had "demonstrated how specific microbes caused communicable diseases and," as a result, "documented routes of transmission that had hitherto only been suspected."[24] Simultaneously, *The Scarlet Plague* serves as an early example by a canonical American author of the proto-zombie narrative, making use of what are now instantly recognizable conventions, motifs, and themes—present in Romero's work, *28 Days Later*, and numerous other zombie films, as well as Matheson's *I Am Legend* and Whitehead's *Zone One*—including the previously mentioned threat *en masse* and the survival space or barricade. The story opens in 2073, sixty years after the titular pandemic has killed all but a few hundred people in the United States. The futuristic setting would not have obscured for London's readers the relevance of epidemic fears, given that San Francisco had recently witnessed an outbreak of bubonic plague (1900–04); London also anticipates by only a few years the influenza pandemic of 1918–20, which would cause 20 million deaths worldwide.[25] With so few survivors in London's novel, industrial civilization has collapsed entirely, and, over the course of three generations, humanity has reverted to a tribal social structure and lost all its accumulated knowledge beyond primitive survival skills. Nature has reclaimed the domesticated world, revealing humanity's dominance as tentative and transitory.

The bulk of the narrative, however, consists of the account of "Granser," "the last man who was alive in the days of the plague and who knows the wonders of that far-off time,"[26] who describes the process of collapse to his mostly uninterested teenage grandchildren. Before the end of the world, he had been James Howard Smith, a literature professor at the University of California, Berkeley. In Smith's recounting, the scope of the plague and human progress are linked: "as men increased and lived closely together in great cities and civilizations, new diseases arose.... And the more thickly men packed together, the more terrible were the new diseases that came to be."[27] Modernity produces the very conditions that render its own apocalyptic destruction inevitable. The notion of a manufactured apocalypse similarly informs contemporary zombie films, from *Night of the Living Dead* (with radiation as the culprit) to *28 Days Later* (in which a medical experiment goes horribly awry).

The Scarlet Plague functions as a protozombie narrative in part by including, in LaRose's terms, zombies that are not zombies. Indeed, as Swanson argues, any zombie narrative "must have zombies—the sine qua non of the genre."[28] But ZnZs similarly have the power to move the basic zombie plot forward. The afflicted characters of apocalyptic plague novels performed the essential infectious and deconstructive narrative functions well in advance of Romero's or even Matheson's particular innovations. Because of the plague's one-hundred-percent mortality rate, London explicitly presents infection in terms of living death, more than forty years before Matheson created his bacterial vampires. Those with symptoms, or even those who have merely been exposed, remain living yet are "already dead."[29] People with the telltale scarlet visages inspire terror in their loved ones and neighbors, so that which was familiar and trusted now embodies an ever-widening existential threat.[30] Following the appearance of symptoms, death arrives in a matter of hours, at which point the infected become even more dangerous, due to "the rapidity of decomposition. No sooner was a person dead than the body seemed to fall to pieces, to fly apart, to melt away even as you looked at it. That was one of the reasons the plague spread so rapidly. All the millions of germs in a corpse were so immediately released."[31] The radical physical transformation upon death and that transformation's role in the accelerating rate of infection prefigure by almost six decades the reanimation of the infected and voracious corpse in zombie films.

However, just as in the Dead series, *28 Days Later*, or *The Walking Dead* (2010–, created by Frank Darabont), London's afflicted do not present the only, or even always the primary, narrative threat to survival. Rather, finding themselves free from enforcement of society's laws, many people begin looting, robbing, and murdering, either individually or in roving bands. Smith describes these marauders as "foul fiends" and, more strikingly, "ghouls,"[32] the very word survivors apply to the infectious flesh-eaters in *Night of the*

Living Dead. Romero articulates a similar troubling of the boundary between zombie and human most directly in a famous scene from *Dawn of the Dead.* After a small group has taken refuge in a mall, one of their number looks down at a mass of undead and asks, "What the hell are they?" to which another survivor responds, "They're us; that's all." The point becomes even more pronounced when a rival group of survivors violently invades the mall, demonstrating that while the threat of the infected apparently operates according to disinterested instinct—much as London's germs spread according to an amoral biological directive—humans who have retained the ability to think present a source of deliberate, willful terror.

Survivors, then, must protect themselves from these overlapping threats. Thus, the new reality of total collapse prompts the use of what Browning calls the "safe space" and Swanson calls the "barricade," one of "the most easily recognizable tropes of the zombie genre.... Barricades are crucial in that the preservation of the *narrative* part of the *zombie narrative* depends on maintaining living characters."[33] Moreover, the barricade provides the narrative mechanism by which "living characters can continue to function as if the categories *living* and *dead* were still stable."[34] This denial of the zombie figure's ability to rupture the living/dead binary will ultimately fail, because the barricade must fail to prevent narrative stasis. In *The Scarlet Plague,* the first such barricade is Smith's own home, which he defends against plague victims and violent looters alike through "a night of terror," during which social order collapses entirely.[35] The next day, lacking the resources for an extended siege, he joins a group of faculty members and their families, approximately four-hundred people total, who have taken refuge in the Chemistry Building on campus. They have brought along provisions and weapons and set about creating a semipermanent, defensible safe space by forming sanitation, food, and defense committees. Meanwhile, the city continues to burn, and eventually "a number of the plague-stricken prowlers [i.e., looters] ... drifted against our doors," prompting an extended gun battle.[36] While this defensive action succeeds, the ultimate collapse of the barricades begins from within when "a little nurse-girl in the family of Professor Stout" exhibits signs of infection.[37] Again, this episode prefigures a scene in Romero's *Night of the Living Dead,* when a young girl dies and reanimates as a zombie, then consumes her dead father and kills her mother.

Much like Matheson's vampires and Romero's zombies, London's ghoulish looters seem horrific from the perspective of the point-of-view characters behind the barricades, yet the implied author leaves room for at least a modicum of sympathy. In this way, London's plague functions apocalyptically not just in depopulating the world but also in prompting a revelation. As a picture of pre-plague society emerges from Smith's narration, it becomes clear that, far from protecting humanity, industrial civilization has enabled its self-inflicted brutality. In 2013, the year of the cataclysmic outbreak, American society resembled the dystopia London previously imagined in *The Iron Heel* (1908), having evolved into a sort of industrial oligarchy ruled by the President of the Board of Industrial Magnates. In this highly stratified society, "the ruling classes," of which Smith, as a member of the intellectual elite, was a part, "owned all the land, all the machines, everything," while the masses who labored to produce the material necessities of life "were our slaves."[38]

London's ghouls, then, are exploited and disenfranchised laborers, much as zombies in both their voodoo and viral iterations neatly symbolize workers under a capitalist regime. For this segment of the population, the plague opens up romantic-utopian possibilities by ensuring profound social leveling. With all their resources, the rich still cannot outrun or suppress infection; only a rare and randomly distributed natural immunity saves any particular individual. Such apocalyptic scenarios "represent everything we most fear and at the same time, perhaps, secretly desire: a depopulated world, escape from the constraints of a highly organized industrial society, the opportunity to prove one's ability as a survivor."[39] The postapocalyptic tableau enables "[t]he idea of destroying our crowded, bureaucratic world and then rebuilding afresh"[40] a new world in which a liberated humanity avoids all the perceived ills of contemporary civilization. One of the surviving ghouls, now known only as Chauffeur in reference to his former occupation, later tells Smith, "You had your day before the plague, but this is my day, and a damned good day it is. I wouldn't trade it back to the old times for anything."[41] He makes his utopic reasoning even more explicit when he explains that "we're up against a regular Garden-of-Eden proposition."[42] In the neo-tribal order that develops among scattered groups of survivors along the California coast after an anarchic interregnum, a former laboring ghoul might very well thrive. Indeed, "to this day, the tribe he founded is called the Chauffeur Tribe."[43] Were they articulate, zombies could no doubt make similar claims about the postapocalyptic settings in which they dominate.

Much as London's apocalyptic plague narrative forecasts the ways that the zombie would later be deployed metaphorically to interrogate alienated labor, it also anticipates the figure's racial implications, again in its voodoo and viral guises.[44] Smith cannot help reading socioeconomic difference, and its leveling, in racial terms. Class inequality had reached such proportions before the plague, he admits, that "[i]n the midst of our civilization, down in our slums and labor-ghettos, we had bred a race of barbarians, of savages."[45] Isiah Lavender III observes that anxieties regarding contagion and race are inextricably intertwined, particularly in speculative fiction that gives plagues even greater depopulating and mutative powers.[46] Just as historical contagions such as bubonic plague, smallpox, influenza, and AIDS "have had a lasting catastrophic bearing on the world, scarring our memories with cultural, social, political, and religious consequences," what Lavender calls "[a]ilments of race, such as miscegenation, the one-drop rule, passing, and racism, have done the same," in that fears surrounding both contagion and race "creat[e] otherhoods."[47] In this way, as a metaphor for race, "contagion is unmistakably connected to the master narratives of social Darwinism, change, and acceleration."[48]

Consistent with this analysis, the language of natural selection appears throughout those passages in *The Scarlet Plague* detailing the interregnum, during which the humans, fauna, and flora best suited to survival in a state of nature thrive while the rest—the most domesticated and cultivated— mostly die away. Steadfast in his nostalgia for a lost civilization, Smith can only understand these changes in terms of racial degeneration, as this new world favors "savages." Moreover, he uses the same dehumanizing terminology often applied to nonwhites in the nineteenth and early twentieth centuries to describe Chauffeur: he is "a large, dark, hairy man, heavy-jawed, slant-browed, fierce-eyed," an "ape-like human brute."[49] Unsurprisingly, in Smith's eyes, Chauffeur provides a stark contrast to Vesta Van Warden, Chauffeur's postapocalyptic mate. Vesta (named for the virgin goddess of home and family in Roman mythology) is an embodiment of civilization's virtues, "born to the purple of the greatest baronage of wealth the world has ever known," "the perfect flower of generations of the highest culture this planet has ever produced."[50] The union represents nothing short of intolerable miscegenation for Smith, who explains to his grandsons that "in the days before the plague, the slightest contact with such as he would have been pollution."[51] As Lavender suggests, this metaphorical and metonymical strategy conflates racial "pollution" with epidemic contagion.[52] Such anxieties inform all subsequent contagious-voracious zombie narratives: fear of infection by the Other, fear of degrading transformation, fear of total subsumption.

Richard Matheson's Transitional Zombie Plague

With the evolution of the protozombie narrative over the century following *The Scarlet Plague*'s publication, variations on all London's themes have emerged again and again.[53] Seen from such an expanded perspective, Matheson's *I Am Legend* becomes less a foundational text and more of a transitional, albeit crucial, work. Indeed, Matheson takes the racial concerns implicit in the novel and brings them to the foreground in terms of both theme and plot.[54] For the bulk of the story, protagonist Robert Neville—the close-third narration always refers to him by his full name, keeping the character at a distance—adopts the same vantage point as Smith, mourning the loss of human civilization and resenting the triumph of an apparently non-human contagious-voracious Other. The novel begins in a depopulated world, in 1976, approximately a year after the plague appeared, and unfolds over the course of the next three years. Like Smith, Neville represents the last of his kind, the last to remember and yearn for the world that existed before the plague. He spends his days hunting slumbering vampires, and occasionally abducting them to perform experiments as he seeks to understand the scientific basis of vampirism and his own immunity. He spends his nights getting drunk and listening to classical music as vampires surround his barricaded house and their leader, Ben Cortman, calls out, taunting him.

On one such night, after a few drinks, Neville ironically imagines a mock-progressive speech delivered on behalf of the vampire "as a minority element."[55] If the reader considers that the book was published in the year of the *Brown v. Board of Education* decision, the allegorical ramifications for racism and segregation become impossible to ignore:

> Why, then, this unkind prejudice, this thoughtless bias? Why cannot the vampire live where he chooses? Why must he seek out hiding places where none can find him out? Why do you wish him destroyed? Ah, see, you have turned the poor guileless innocent into a haunted animal. He has no means of support, no measures for proper education, he has not the voting franchise. No wonder he is compelled to seek out a predatory nocturnal existence.[56]

To make the point even more explicitly, Neville then provides the likely reply that such an attempt to place race in a social context would elicit from an unconvinced listener, delivered as a *coup de grâce* to deflate liberal hypocrisy: "Sure, sure … but would you let your sister marry one?"[57] Once again, the threat of miscegenation preoccupies the protagonist, with Neville struggling to suppress his own troubling sexual attraction to vampire "women posing like lewd puppets" in an effort to lure him outside.[58]

Racialized language also crops up throughout the free indirect discourse representing Neville's thoughts about those Others he perceives as a threat. For instance, although the vampires are actually pale, Neville frequently refers to them as "black bastards."[59] These processes of creating an Otherhood are not merely reactionary; rather, they justify a moral structure essential to the actions he believes he must take to survive. Although he acknowledges that he makes no distinction between the true vampires—the truly dead—and those living humans merely infected with the bacterium, Neville continues to engage in brutal parallel campaigns of extermination and experimentation, targeting both populations. "In the years" during which he conducts these campaigns, "he had not once considered the possibility that he was wrong."[60] To continue his activities, he must suppress any empathetic inclination, at least as far as the living infected are concerned, that "but for some affliction he didn't understand, these people were the same as he."[61]

Matheson would go on to write more than a dozen episodes of *The Twilight Zone*, and the conclusion of *I Am Legend* anticipates the sort of ironic twist ending that became one of that program's signature devices. Similar to an episode of the television show, the novel is designed to provide a singular moment that facilitates for both Neville and the reader a simultaneous last-minute aspect change, in the Wittgensteinian sense: "I *see* that [the observed object] has not changed; and yet I see it differently."[62] Yet, for the observer, the shift is so profound, so revelatory, it is "quite as if the object had altered before my eyes."[63] For Neville, that change comes after he meets another survivor, the first he has seen in years.

The process of this aspect change begins when Neville discovers that Ruth, an apparently immune woman, turns out to be infected. Moreover, she is part of an organized community of infected who have found a way to live with the disease and plan to rebuild society. Neville comes to understand that the group he had viewed as wholly Other—as an existential threat devoid of humanity—in fact share his motives and interests. He had misapprehended all other occupants of this postapocalyptic world as an undifferentiated mass. Through his brutal actions, however, he has ensured the impossibility of reconciliation; instead, he has provided this new race with its own object of terror and hatred. Revising his earlier characterization of the vampire as a "minority element," Neville comes to understand that he has become "the abnormal one now. Normalcy was a majority concept, the standard of many and not the standard of just one man."[64] Indeed, this irony provides the meaning of the novel's title: from the perspective of this new race, "he was anathema," a "black terror to be destroyed.... I am legend."[65] Neville's final epiphany is itself as apocalyptic as the plague, inasmuch as "apocalypse" denotes revelation. While all three major direct adaptations of the novel ignore this revelation, the first four installments of Romero's Dead series in aggregate emphasize it to undermine the audience's initial sympathies and transfer them to the infected ghoulish figure; each successive film affords the zombies greater individuality, interiority, and agency, making it ever more difficult for the viewer to celebrate their killing by human survivors. In this sense, Romero provides the truest adaptation of Matheson's work.

Colson Whitehead's Traditionalist Zombie Plague

With *Zone One*, Whitehead embraces the apocalyptic plague tradition that London, Matheson, and Romero refined over the previous century.

Certainly, the novel's infectious monsters and the apocalyptic scenario that their appearance precipitates look familiar in the broad strokes. Even if none of the characters ever uses the word "zombie," these infected fit the Romeroesque schema. Like his forerunners, Whitehead does not present his monsters uniformly, instead allowing for differentiation and even sympathy. While most of the undead "skels" conform to the contagious-voracious model, a tiny minority of unaggressive "stragglers" seem relatively innocuous, "[a]n army of mannequins" posed in significant places from their pre-plague lives— as often as not places of employment.[66] If, in the mundanity of their former roles as workers and consumers, "[t]heir lives had been an interminable loop of repeated gestures," then following infection "their existences were winnowed to this discrete and eternal moment."[67] Many scholars and book reviewers alike have regarded these "stragglers" as Whitehead's unique contribution to the subgenre, arguing that "what makes these zombies different from other treatments is the level of humanization that" the protagonist "ascribes to them."[68] To reach this conclusion, however, a reader must ignore the ways Whitehead's description echoes the complex portrayal of zombies in Romero's *oeuvre*, which often highlights the similarities, rather than the differences, between zombies and humans.

The close-third narration places the reader in the perspective of a survivor known only by the nickname "Mark Spitz"; as with Robert Neville, the narrative voice consistently uses this full appellation, in this case drawing attention to its artifice, especially for those readers who recognize its origins. The story takes place over the course of three days—Friday through Sunday—and follows Mark Spitz's three-person "sweeper" team on its task of systematically clearing any remaining stragglers from lower Manhattan after the Marines have built an island-wide barricade along Canal Street. In conjunction with the armed services, the American Phoenix project has reconstructed a bureaucratic apparatus to direct this effort and rally the nation by returning this symbolically loaded municipal sliver, the titular "Zone One," to its erstwhile glory. Having led a directionless life before the plague, Mark Spitz discovers his exceptional talent for survival once zombies eliminate all the complications and nuances of contemporary postindustrial life.

Given Whitehead's significance to the contemporary American literary scene and the explosive growth of zombie-based entertainment, the attention that scholars have paid to this novel is hardly surprising. Similar to most important zombie texts, *Zone One* tends to elicit allegorical readings. Sven Cvek offers a convincing if familiar claim that the zombie narrative generally operates as a critique of late capitalism and that Whitehead's novel fits squarely within this tradition.[69] Anne Canavan, meanwhile, situates the novel as a critical post–9/11 text that pushes back against the "avalanche of narratives designed to other a faceless enemy and bind the nation together in a tidal wave of fear."[70] Again, this familiar reading argues that Whitehead deploys his zombies to well-rehearsed symbolic ends. In contrast, Leif Sorensen argues that "the import of Whitehead's critical reworking of the contemporary zombie narrative arises from [the] moment in which the apocalyptic and pre-apocalyptic worlds collapse into one another, suggesting that the death-world has already arrived."[71] However, given the consensus that speculative fiction about the future serves to defamiliarize and thus critique the present, it seems like a stretch to make such a claim. Whether it's economic inequality in *The Scarlet Plague*, racial tension in *I Am Legend*, or empty consumerism in *Dawn of the Dead*, zombie and protozombie narratives alike have always tended to blur the boundaries between the preapocalyptic and apocalyptic worlds. More convincingly, Swanson posits that *Zone One* "derives its most powerful figures and motifs from variations on the formal conventions of the zombie genre" and therefore serves as an exemplar of the genre, rather than a deviation.[72]

Still, while Whitehead's portrayal of zombies does not vary significantly from the existing models, and his story employs the generic narrative beats of earlier apocalyptic plagues, *Zone One* finds innovative uses for the zombie story, particularly as a vehicle for exploring racial themes. Like Matheson, Whitehead deploys the plague narrative in service of an apocalyptic racial revelation—but one that occurs only on an extratextual level, exclusively for the reader, not the characters. This revelation emerges slowly, in conjunction with the gradual explanation for the protagonist's nickname. Initially, the reader learns only that "[t]hey started calling him Mark Spitz after … the incident on I-95," and that "[t]he name stuck. No harm."[73] The full story behind that renaming incident begins at the novel's midpoint and resolves over a hundred pages later, delivered largely via free indirect discourse in response to a question from Gary, a bitten (and therefore doomed) member of the sweeper team. Before his relocation to Zone One, Mark Spitz had been helping to clear a section of I-95 in Connecticut when his crew was trapped by a horde on a bridge. Rather than following his companions in jumping into the river below and swimming to safety, Mark Spitz overcomes impossible odds and manages to shoot down every single attacking zombie. To justify this reckless action, he later lies to his companions and claims he did not jump because he cannot swim. In response, "they laughed. It was perfect: From now on he was Mark Spitz."[74] The conclusion of this anecdote arrives much later, when the nonlinear narration finally circles back to it, picking up again with Gary asking, "Why do they call you Mark Spitz?"[75] The narrator quickly recaps the earlier explanation and then completes the apocalyptic revelation through the casual evocation of a racial stereotype: "Plus the black-people-can't-swim thing."[76] This moment, thirty-five pages before the book's conclusion, is the first explicit mention of the protagonist's racial identity.

Book critics have had a variety of responses to this revelation, much as they have presented a variety of responses to the representations of race in all of Whitehead's writing. Some of them appear to have missed its narrative and thematic significance, or even its existence. One book reviewer complains that "Mark is also a young black man, but strangely that element of his identity is bleached away in this novel."[77] Terri Gross seems not to have finished the book, asking Whitehead during an interview, "So what's going on racially in your new novel? Is your character African-American? Is he white? Is race an issue?"[78] Whitehead pointedly avoids answering the question.

Meanwhile, some scholars have discussed the moment within a larger argument for Whitehead as a "postracial" writer. In doing so, however, Kimberly Fain understates the centrality of race in *Zone One* and Whitehead's other novels. While it is true that Whitehead's various protagonists "are defined by more than their race," it does not necessarily follow that in these texts "a character or society can attain the quality of *racial irrelevance* due to their talents, passing, education, economics, and/or color blindness of characters toward one another."[79] In none of Whitehead's novels—not even *Zone One*—does race ever become irrelevant for either the characters or the reader. Ramón Saldívar also uses the term "postrace," albeit to support a more nuanced claim, applying it to Whitehead's writing "under erasure and with full ironic force,"[80] ultimately concluding that the relatively limited space devoted to race in *Zone One* implies that "only a complete and total destruction of contemporary life will allow for the end of the color line."[81] Even this reading, though, undervalues the potential impact of the moment of belated revelation and the protagonist's experience as a racialized subject—precisely because the apocalypse manages merely to suppress, but not end, the color line.

In fact, Whitehead's delaying strategy takes on additional significance when compared to the author's identification of a protagonist's race in his four previous novels. Three of them are identified as black in the jacket copy, and the narration addresses their race explicitly within the first several pages of the text, usually with the characters noting their difference with respect to others. In *The Intuitionist*, Whitehead's first novel, the protagonist Lila Mae perceives a building superintendent reacting to both her race and her gender even before he remarks, "I haven't ever seen a woman elevator inspector before, let alone a colored one."[82] Sutter, the main character in *John Henry Days*, "possesses the standard amount of black Yankee scorn for the South."[83] Benji, Whitehead's only first-person narrator, lets the reader of *Sag Harbor* know early on that he "was used to being the only black kid in the room."[84] The jacket description of *Apex Hides the Hurt* does not mention race, but the unnamed protagonist constructs his racial identity through his repeated observations regarding the whiteness of the other characters he encounters. So it comes as no surprise when, about a third of the way through the novel, he recalls attending "the African American Leaders of Tomorrow conference" as a high school student.[85]

Zone One's representation of its protagonist's race, then, markedly differs from that of all Whitehead's previous work. Yet the novel is not a "passing" narrative in the manner of, say, James Weldon Johnson's *The Autobiography of an Ex-Colored Man* (1912) or Nella Larsen's *Passing* (1929). Instead, the novel's treatment of its characters' racial identities finds its closest antecedent in Toni Morrison's one published short story, "Recitatif," which the author describes elsewhere as "an experiment in the removal of all racial codes from a narrative about two characters of different races for whom racial identity is crucial."[86] The narrator, Twyla, recounts the few months she shared a room at a children's shelter with Roberta, "a girl from a whole other race."[87] While Twyla makes clear of these two characters that one is "[a] black girl" and one "a white girl," she fails to designate which is which—not because she deliberately withholds that information, or because the characters' racial identities have no significance, but rather because they are so obvious *within* the story that they require no further clarification.[88] Yet even as familiar racial signifiers and stereotypes (e.g., physical traits, food preferences, religious expressions, sexual mores) accumulate and initially appear to provide direction, each detail calls into question the interpretive value of the one before it. Additionally, as adults recalling their shared childhood, Twyla and Roberta cannot come to a consensus reading of yet a third character's race, thereby replicating within the story the experience of the reader of the story.[89]

Similarly, while Mark Spitz's race may remain unacknowledged by the narrative until the novel's final pages, it is nonetheless unambiguous within the story. Given his understanding of his nickname's irony, his race clearly informs his interactions with other characters. Indeed, a filmed version could not replicate the revelatory moment's potential impact, in that Mark Spitz passes for white only if the reader has actively imagined him as such. In this regard, the novel exploits what Wolfgang Iser calls "the elements of indeterminacy, the gaps in the text" central to the reading experience: "with a literary text we can only picture things which are not there; the written part of the text gives us the knowledge, but it is the unwritten part that gives us the opportunity to picture things."[90] Both Whitehead and Morrison understand and exploit the fact that not to announce a character's race in a written text is to prompt the reader to take the imaginative step of filling in this gap.

Any discussion of how a given reader might do just that necessarily depends to a degree on speculation, but neither the text nor its generic context is wholly neutral on the matter. Here, it would be useful to dust off another concept associated with reader-response criticism, specifically Hans Robert Jauss' notion that an audience will formulate a horizon of expectations "that arises for each work in the historical moment of its appearance, from a pre-understanding of the genre, from the form and themes of already familiar works, and from the opposition between poetic and practical language."[91] Specifically in the case of *Zone One*, these expectations stem in part from the audience's pre-existing grasp of the apocalyptic plague narrative's well-established conventions. Of course, consumers of apocalyptic stories may have no genre-specific reason to assume a white protagonist—Romero's *Night of the Living Dead* and *Dawn of the Dead* both feature black actors as heroic lead characters, after all, while *Day of the Dead* and *Land of the Dead* have racially diverse casts—but in *Zone One* Whitehead makes use of a specific permutation of the apocalyptic genre, wherein a slacker finds meaning, purpose, and previously untapped talents in the simplified conditions of the apocalypse. Before the plague, Mark Spitz "was bereft of attractive propositions, constitutionally unaccustomed to enthusiasm, and … adrift on that gentle upper-middle-class current that kept its charges cheerfully bobbing far from the shoals of responsibility."[92] He appears to possess a special talent for the sort of mediocrity that results in neither "exceptionality [n]or failure," so that he always gets by, "never shining, never flunking."[93] Following the simplifying impact of the plague, however, he "effortlessly … grasped and mastered the new rules, as if he had waited for the introduction of hell his whole life."[94] The horizon of expectations for this subgenre has a definite racial tinge, given that the slacker character in popular culture is generally coded young, educated, middle class, and white.[95] Meanwhile, black characters who don't work are generally portrayed as either criminal or tragically victimized by a racist socioeconomic structure. In other words, Mark Spitz is not constructed with the typical pop cultural signifiers of blackness. Nor does he represent blackness as constructed from a white perspective, not only because of his middle class, suburban background, but also because of his geeky preoccupation with horror movies.[96]

Knowledge of the themes embedded in the author's prior work and the author's race might also play a role in shaping reader expectations, yet with this novel Whitehead has reached a new audience beyond the literary crowd by writing in an immensely popular genre; the cover of the paperback edition, unlike his previous novel covers, announces *Zone One* as a "national bestseller." Many people reading this novel would therefore be unfamiliar with the themes embedded in the author's other books. Such a reader looking for a good zombie yarn might ignore any postmodern literary devices, consuming *Zone One* as pure genre. And even readers invested in "literary" fiction might recall that black authors have long written about white characters—particularly white characters who have the cultural capital and privilege of being adrift—as James Baldwin did in *Giovanni's Room* (1956). If nothing else, a reader is likely to notice that the text omits clarification.

It is especially significant that the racial revelation comes about through an explanation of Mark Spitz's nickname. Literary scholars have long interrogated the ways that naming—or renaming—plays a central role in African American cultural and literary traditions. Kimberly Benston argues that "naming is inevitably genealogical revisionism," and "[a]ll of Afro-American literature may be seen as one vast genealogical poem that attempts to restore continuity to the ruptures or discontinuities imposed by the history of black presence in America."[97] In Ralph Ellison's *Invisible Man* (1952), the protagonist's name is entirely suppressed as he seeks to create a self. Malcolm Little deliberately reinvents himself when he exchanges his last name with "X." Slave narratives often incorporate a scene in which the self-emancipated narrator replaces the surname received from his or her former master with a new appellation associated with freedom. In contrast to "these highly self-conscious (re)baptisms,"[98] the protagonist of *Zone One* has passively accepted an externally imposed name and its manifold implications: "Mark Spitz is fine," he says when asked what he prefers to be called.[99] Given that the nickname's origin story hinges on a refusal to leap into the water, this act of renaming appears as the inverse of a liberatory rebaptism. The reader instead knows the protagonist solely by the name of a famous white Olympic swimmer—a name ironically bestowed on him by white characters in perpetuation of a racial stereotype. Following the revelation, each use of the sobriquet "Mark Spitz" in the text must now be understood retroactively as a reinforcement of the character's racialized identity. It is more subtle than Huck Finn's repeated use of the epithet "nigger" to refer to his companion Jim, perhaps, but nonetheless an insistence by other characters that Mark Spitz cannot fully transcend his race.

Narratively, the zombie plague facilitates this renaming and justifies the delayed explanation of its racial implications. While it would be implausible to withhold mention of a character's blackness in a contemporary American realist novel, in a zombie-filled world, race wouldn't be foremost in anyone's mind. As much as Whitehead has pushed back against the notion that the United States has somehow become a "postracial" society that has "eradicated racism forever" in electing a black president,[100] he acknowledges that survivors of the apocalypse would likely "have more things on their mind than skin color."[101] Finally, however, the point is not that plague has eliminated all perceptions of racial difference, as Saldívar somewhat facetiously suggests, but that it hasn't. Even if race matters less during the apocalypse, it ultimately still matters. In contrast to London and Matheson, who use the protozombie figure to interrogate pre-plague racial anxieties of a dominant white culture, Whitehead uses the figure to facilitate representation of experience from a racialized subject position.

The racial revelation in *Zone One* also adds a layer to the zombie narrative's exploration of nostalgia. In *The Scarlet Plague*, Smith's inability to let go of the past signals his failure to adapt. In *I Am Legend*, Neville struggles "desperately to accept the present on its own terms and not yearn with his very flesh for the past," lest he become distracted from his singular objective of survival.[102] Similarly, for Mark Spitz nostalgia for the pre-apocalyptic world presents an ongoing danger: the undead always "came for you when you had one foot in the past, recollecting a dead notion of safety."[103] The problem is so prevalent that survivors have been universally diagnosed with Post-Apocalyptic Stress Disorder, or PASD, a homonym for *past*.[104] Indeed, yearning for the past almost always creates problems in apocalyptic narratives, but Whitehead reveals the particular complications attendant to nostalgia when race is involved. Nostalgia is an expression of privilege, in that it cannot be divorced from the racist structure of the fallen society, just as romanticizing the 1950s in contemporary political discourse necessarily entails a yearning for the pre–Civil Rights era of segregation. Mark Spitz's nickname demonstrates the tenuous nature of any postracial apocalyptic developments. While it is true that "[t]here was a single Us now, reviling a single Them," Mark Spitz knows full well that "[i]f they could bring back paperwork, they could certainly reanimate prejudice."[105] The hope implied by the entire American Phoenix reconstruction project is necessarily tempered. How can a black man feel unambiguously supportive of efforts to return to the way things were?

This foreboding sense that society's most egregious ills will see inevitable replication informs the apocalyptic plague genre in its written and cinematic iterations. In thinking about the enduring appeal of this narrative tradition generally and the zombie narrative specifically, we might benefit from broadening our analytical perspective even further. We might consider the ways in which ancient conceptions of history as cyclical have continued to persist well beyond all the Enlightenment's efforts to straighten out historical and social development into a linear and ever-progressive upward movement. While Mark Spitz anticipates the return of racism, in *The Scarlet Plague*, Smith offers a eulogy for the inevitable future repetition of past mistakes:

> Nothing can stop it—the same old story over and over. Men will increase, and men will fight.... [G]unpowder will enable men to kill millions of men, and in this way only, by fire and blood, will a new civilization, in some remote day, be evolved. And what profit will it be? Just as the old civilization passed, so will the new. It may take fifty thousand years to build, but it will pass. All things pass.[106]

Neville similarly foresees the way that divisive fear and hate have come "[f]ull circle"; through his actions, he has provided the emerging society with "[a] new terror" to undermine rationality, "a new superstition entering the unassailable fortress of forever."[107] Perhaps the appeal of infectious ghouls created by London, Matheson, Romero, Boyle, and now Whitehead stems from our need to acknowledge, however tangentially, the suspicion that despite our progress, we are condemned to apocalyptic visitations by familiar literal and figurative plagues.

NOTES

1. The introduction of this collection reiterates this assertion, and I have similarly made this claim elsewhere. See Bishop and Tenga, "Introduction: The Rise of the Written Dead," 3; Boluk and Lenz, "Generation Z, the Age of Apocalypse," 3.

2. Fassler, "How Zombies and Superheroes Conquered Highbrow Fiction."

3. See, for example, Cooke, *Legacies of the Plague in Literature, Theory and Film*, especially 163–84; Boluk and Lenz, "Infection, Media, and Capitalism," 126–47; and Zani and Meaux, "Lucio Fulci and the Decaying Definition of Zombie Narratives," 98–115.

4. Zani and Meaux, "Lucio Fulci and the Decaying Definition of Zombie Narratives," 98.

5. Bishop, "Dead Man *Still* Walking," 25n1.

6. LaRose, "Zombies in a 'Deep, Dark Ocean of History,'" 166.

7. Bishop, "Dead Man *Still* Walking," 25n8.

8. In this film, one of the main characters, after succumbing to infection, retains enough human memory to lead a group of fellow zombies to the survivors' fortified hiding place. One could even argue that *Night of the Living Dead* (1968) allows the ghouls a certain level of agency, or at least personality; for instance, the zombified Johnny (Russell Streiner) seems to recognize and target his sister, Barbra (Judith O'Dea).

9. Swanson, "'Only Metaphor Left,'" 389n12.

10. *Jacobellis v. Ohio*, 378 U.S. 184 (1964).

11. Girard, "Plague in Literature and Myth," 833.

12. Bishop, "Dead Man *Still* Walking," 21.

13. Zani and Meaux, "Lucio Fulci and the Decaying Definition of Zombie Narratives," 100–01.

14. As Zani and Meaux would likely acknowledge, the medieval plague narrative in turn has ancient antecedents, so any attempt to claim a particular text as the sole protozombie narrative could be countered with a host of other candidates. The endeavor remains finally unresolvable, similar to debates over which particular text serves as the first modern novel, a discussion that in turn depends on blurry generic distinctions between the realist novel and the fantastical romance.

15. *Ibid.*, 114.

16. Bickley, Introduction, xviii.

17. Zani and Meaux, "Lucio Fulci and the Decaying Definition of Zombie Narratives," 107.

18. Official adaptations include *The Last Man on Earth* (1964, directed by Ubaldo Ragona and Sidney Salkow), *The Omega Man* (1971, directed by Boris Sagal), and *I Am Legend* (2007, directed by Francis Lawrence).

19. Browning, "Survival Horrors, Survival Spaces," 44.

20. Biodrowski, "George Romero Documents the Dead."

21. Pappademas and Whitehead, "When Zombies Attack!"

22. The 1793 Philadelphia yellow fever epidemic provides the backdrop for much of Charles Brockden Brown's *Arthur Mervyn* (1799); Lionel Verney, the narrator of Shelley's *The Last Man*, directly invokes both Brown's and Defoe's novels of contagion (Shelley, *Last Man*, 206). Of course, Edgar Allan Poe's 1842 short story "The Masque of the Red Death" also deserves note. Indeed, in terms of symptoms the eponymous contagion apparently prefigures that of London's novel: "The scarlet stains upon the body and especially upon the face of the victim, were the pest ban which shut him out from the aid and from the sympathy of his fellow-men" (Poe, "Masque," 43–44). However, Poe's treatment of the disease is otherwise fantastical, in contrast to the realism of the other texts discussed in this chapter.

23. Riva, Benedetti, and Cesana, "Pandemic Fear and Literature."

24. Wald, *Contagious*, 13.
25. *Ibid.*
26. London, *Scarlet Plague*, 170.
27. *Ibid.*, 62.
28. Swanson, "'Only Metaphor Left,'" 386.
29. London, *Scarlet Plague*, 81.
30. The infected thus exploit the sensation of the uncanny, which, as formulated by Freud, "is that class of the frightening which leads back to what is known of old and long familiar" (Freud, "Uncanny," 220). Zombies generate a similar response.
31. London, *Scarlet Plague*, 75.
32. *Ibid.*, 115, 137.
33. Swanson, "'Only Metaphor Left,'" 386.
34. *Ibid.*, 390.
35. London, *Scarlet Plague*, 95.
36. *Ibid.*, 114–15.
37. *Ibid.*, 117.
38. *Ibid.*, 53.
39. "Disaster," *Encyclopedia of Science Fiction*.
40. "Post-Holocaust," *Encyclopedia of Science Fiction*.
41. London, *Scarlet Plague*, 156.
42. *Ibid.*, 159.
43. *Ibid.*, 144.
44. See, for example, Moreman and Rushton, *Race, Oppression and the Zombie*.
45. London, *Scarlet Plague*, 105.
46. Lavender, *Race in American Science Fiction*, 120.
47. *Ibid.*, 119.
48. *Ibid.*, 122.
49. London, *Scarlet Plague*, 143, 158.
50. *Ibid.*, 146–47.
51. *Ibid.*, 152.
52. Lavender, *Race in American Science Fiction*, 120.
53. Several works of depopulating apocalyptic fiction published between 1912 and 1954 address racial concerns directly. For example, George R. Stewart's *Earth Abides* (1949) finds its white male protagonist, Ish, repopulating the world with a black woman, Em. The end of civilization has brought about the end of racial prejudice, Ish assures Em upon learning that she is pregnant: "[T]he Jew-baiters and the Negro-baiters" are all dead, he insists. "Maybe a thousand years from now people can afford the luxury of wondering and worrying about that kind of thing again. But I doubt it" (Stewart, *Earth Abides*, 120). When this novel was published, twenty-nine states had antimiscegenation laws on the books; sixteen of these states would maintain such laws until 1967, when the U.S. Supreme Court ruled them unconstitutional. Even earlier, and more radically, W.E.B. Du Bois' 1920 short story "The Comet" posits a postapocalyptic world apparently populated only by Jim, a black man, and Julia, a white woman. Gradually recognizing the implications of their new circumstances, they come to see "how foolish our human distinctions seem—now" that mass death has served as both "the leveler" and "the revealer" (Du Bois, "The Comet," 268). The prevailing racial order is restored, however, when a band of survivors finds the couple and nearly lynches Jim.
54. Because the influence of Matheson's novel on the contemporary zombie narrative has been explored in detail by previous studies, I do not replicate the scope of that work here. For in-depth discussions, see Browning, "Survival Horrors, Survival Spaces," and Waller, *Living and the Undead*, 233–328.
55. Matheson, *I Am Legend*, 20.
56. *Ibid.*, 21.
57. *Ibid.*
58. *Ibid.*, 7.
59. *Ibid.*, 23.
60. *Ibid.*, 135.

61. *Ibid.*, 28.
62. Wittgenstein, *Philosophical Investigations*, 193.
63. *Ibid.*, 195.
64. Matheson, *I Am Legend*, 159.
65. *Ibid.*
66. Whitehead, *Zone One*, 60.
67. *Ibid.*, 62.
68. Canavan, "Which Came First," 45.
69. Cvek, "Surviving Utopia."
70. Canavan, "Which Came First," 41.
71. Sorensen, "Against the Post-Apocalyptic," 587.
72. Swanson, "'Only Metaphor Left,'" 381. Swanson's article provides a nearly exhaustive catalogue of the allusions to previous zombie media in *Zone One*.
73. Whitehead, *Zone One*, 26.
74. *Ibid.*, 182.
75. *Ibid.*, 286.
76. *Ibid.*, 287. Significantly, Mark Spitz remains silently skeptical when Gary pleads ignorance of this particular racial stereotype: "They can't? You can't? ... I hadn't heard that" (*Ibid.*). Here, Gary essentially offers a variant of more common white denials of racism, such as "some of my best friends are black" or, even more pertinently, "I don't see race." Mark Spitz's skepticism pertains not just to Gary in this particular case, but also to the notion that society generally could achieve a postracial perspective.
77. Charles, "'Zone One.'"
78. "When Zombies Attack Lower Manhattan."
79. Fain, "Colson Whitehead" (emphasis added).
80. Saldívar, "Second Elevation," 2.
81. *Ibid.*, 13.
82. Whitehead, *Intuitionist*, 8.
83. Whitehead, *John Henry Days*, 14.
84. Whitehead, *Sag Harbor*, 7.
85. Whitehead, *Apex Hides the Hurt*, 70.
86. Morrison, *Playing in the Dark*, xi. Thanks to Lars Schmeink for pointing out the resonances between Morrison's story and *Zone One*.
87. Morrison, "Recitatif," 1403.
88. *Ibid.*, 1410.
89. In her critical study *Playing in the Dark*, Morrison illuminates the ways in which she and Whitehead approach racial identity in "Recitatif" and *Zone One*, respectively: "What does positing one's writerly self, in the wholly racialized society that is the United States, as unraced and all others as raced entail? What happens to the writerly imagination of a black author who is at some level *always* conscious of representing one's own race to, or in spite of, a race of readers that understands itself to be 'universal' or race-free? In other words, how is 'literary whiteness' and 'literary blackness' made, and what is the consequence of that construction?" (Morrison, *Playing in the Dark*, xxi).
90. Iser, "Reading Process," 288.
91. Jauss, *Toward an Aesthetic of Reception*, 22.
92. Whitehead, *Zone One*, 8.
93. *Ibid.*, 10, 11.
94. *Ibid.*, 31.
95. The characters in Richard Linklater's film *Slacker* (1991) are almost all white, and white protagonists abound in the slacker apocalypse subgenre: *28 Days Later* features a bike courier as its lead; *The World's End* (2013, directed by Edgar Wright) revolves around a manchild alcoholic; and the recent Fox sitcom *The Last Man on Earth* (2015–, created by Will Forte) follows a character who is "[j]ust your average middle-age white guy who likes *Star Wars*, Twinkies, and sex" (Jensen, "Last Man on Earth").
96. Whitehead has addressed this issue explicitly in his previous work. For example, in *Sag Harbor*, his narrator recounts his announcement that "I can't wait for Master of Horror

George A. Romero to make another film. *Fangoria* magazine—still the best horror and sci-fi magazine around if you ask me—says he has trouble raising funding, but I think Hollywood is just scared of what he has to say" (Whitehead, *Sag Harbor*, 24) as yet another misfire in "the long war over what white culture was acceptable and what was not" (*Ibid.*, 63). Such rigid racial boundaries in the production and consumption of popular culture are still reinforced within fan communities. For example, such "demographic anxiety" informed the controversy surrounding the 2015 Hugo Award nomination process: "right-wing fans who say they've been marginalized by affirmative action gone mad … organized a successful nomination campaign to undo … [recent] gains in diversity, creating an unprecedented party-line slate which has led to the stacking of this year's Hugo ballot largely with white men once again" (Heer, "Science Fiction's White Boys' Club Strikes Back").

97. Benston, "I Yam What I Am," 152.
98. *Ibid.*
99. Whitehead, *Zone One*, 114.
100. Whitehead, "Year of Living Postracially."
101. "When Zombies Attack Lower Manhattan."
102. Matheson, *I Am Legend*, 47–48.
103. Whitehead, *Zone One*, 108.
104. *Ibid.*, 69.
105. *Ibid.*, 288.
106. London, *Scarlet Plague*, 178–79.
107. Matheson, *I Am Legend*, 159.

"Systems Die Hard"
Resistance and Reanimation
in Colson Whitehead's Zone One

KELLI SHERMEYER

How do we maintain distinctive identities when we live within a system of institutions that turns us into bytes of demographic data? What forms of hierarchy and social arrangement reemerge after a natural disaster decimates cultural or political institutions? What bodies are acceptable targets for physical, social, or linguistic violence? These are the kinds of questions that fiction set in the apocalypse or postapocalypse is particularly poised to examine. The recent reappearance of doomsday narratives that Paul Cantor calls the "apocalyptic strain" in popular culture[1] allows us to rethink the values of an American dream that is inextricably fettered to American political or financial institutions. Contemporary readers and viewers have a complicated relationship with these narratives because they force them to imagine a world without the institutions that they have come to rely on to achieve success and stability, but that they also blame for their lack of fulfillment.[2] These narratives indulge a fantasy that an apocalyptic event can cleanse society of corrupt or inept bureaucracies: "perhaps a plague or cosmic catastrophe can do some real budget-cutting for a change."[3] We imagine pressing a "reset button" that, by returning us to a state of being that is free from the distractions and manipulations of large-scale institutions, frees us to rebuild human society, reclaiming agency over our own governance. Yet in this moment of proliferating doomsday narratives, we can take comfort (or terror) in the fact that our alien, zombie, disaster, or plague story is just the next in a series of narratives of global destruction stretching across geography, culture, and history: evidence that our social and political concerns always return to plague us. As many of these narratives show, the problems of the pre-apocalypse remain because we rebuild our new world in the image of our dead one.

The zombie story has become a key subcategory of apocalyptic narrative, and the filmic canon is filled with bodies kept unnaturally alive by plague or magic that prey on human beings. This volume draws attention to the way that the zombie has emerged as a literary figure in novels such as Max Brooks' *World War Z* (2006), Seanan McGuire's (as Mira Grant) *Feed* (2010), and the subject of this essay, Colson Whitehead's *Zone One* (2011). Despite the relative newness of the zombie as a cultural phenomenon, the undead or resurrected human corpse is not an entirely new literary figure: Dante conjures the image of a shambling horde, "so long a file of people—I should never have believed that death could have unmade so many," whose "blind life is so abject that they are envious of every other fate."[4] The undead also feature, at least metaphorically, in the first section of *The Waste Land* ("The Burial of the Dead"), where Eliot both borrows Dante's image and envisions his own undead: "'The corpse you planted last year in your garden,/ 'Has it begun to sprout? Will it bloom this year?"[5] According to Andrew Hoberek, the contemporary literary zombie is a kind of "anti-character" whose "very flatness allegorizes the breakdown of the ethos of individual autonomy central to the realist novel."[6] Because it maintains the body—in some state—of the human it once was, the debate over the zombie's status as a human being or a disposable body creates much of the tension in zombie narratives. Human characters strive, but often fail, to differentiate themselves from the horde of resurrected corpses. Mark McGurl argues that "zombies represent a plague of suspended agency" and give us the sense that we are "witnessing a slow, compulsive, collective movement toward Malthusian self-destruction."[7] The zombie that is presented as our inverse or opposite often reveals to us our own capacity for self-consumptive destruction alongside our habits of self-destructive consumption.

But even within this general frame, zombies come in many shapes and shambles, and each can represent a whole host of human behaviors and conditions, many of which Sarah Juliet Lauro and Karen Embry catalog in "A Zombie Manifesto." The authors describe the zombie as

> *animal laborans*, the reified laborer of capitalist production, and the zombie as threatening body, the zombie as brain-dead, the zombie as brain eater, the zombie blindly following its own primal urges; the zombie that is pure necessity, the zombie that is anti-productive, the zombie that is female, the zombie that is avid consumer … the zombie as cyborg, the zombie as postcyborg, the zombie as posthuman, the zombie as slave, and as slave rebellion.[8]

As this list suggests, zombies can be maligned as figures of capitalist consumption and deindividualization, monstrous representations of disease and disability, or figures for various marginalized people—zombification is rarely a liberating condition. They conclude instead that the swarm-singularity called a "zombii" offers humans the potential for freedom from the strictures of late capitalism, wherein the notion of people as individual subjects has been replaced by the notion of people as a single-minded swarm of consumers. However, this potential freedom is realized only through the inauguration of a posthuman condition. If zombie narratives agree on anything, it's that humans are faced with problems that were generated by their actions. Therefore, the fantasy of "apocalypse as reset" is never fully realized as we continue to replicate the problems that led to the apocalypse in the first place.

In *Zone One*, Whitehead applies the figure of the undead to the aesthetic problem of modernist (or postmodernist) deindividualization.[9] Littered with flashbacks and digressions, *Zone One* is a jumbled autobiography that reveals that the protagonist's particular mediocrity in the old world is what makes him the ideal apocalyptic citizen in the new one. The novel imagines earth not at the very moment of crisis and fall, but after society has been in the process of reconstruction for a significant, yet undisclosed, amount of time. Some characters refer to the era as the "interregnum,"[10] which implies a time between two mountainous empires but still not a time when society "could again afford the indulgence of democracy."[11] The main narrative, which fills comparatively few pages compared with the flashbacks, takes place on a weekend as the ironically nicknamed protagonist Mark Spitz[12] and his teammates Kaitlyn and Gary are working as sweepers—citizens tasked with clearing Zone One (Manhattan) from any remaining skels (one of the novel's terms for zombies).

This essay examines the way that *Zone One* constructs the relationship between a citizen and the state through the tension that arises between the maintenance of individual identity and fantasies of a posthuman future. It looks at the possible futures for human survivors offered by the novel, both of which essentially entail becoming part of a horde: survivors can join the citizenry of the new American Phoenix and face deindividualization and commodification by this new bureaucratic biopower, or they can die and become one of the plagued undead terrorizing what's left of the human race. In the face of this inevitable "zombification," Mark Spitz improvises two forms of resistance: the reclamation of individual identity through storytelling and the recapturing of personal agency through suicide. The end of this essay weighs the recuperative possibilities of these improvisations while positing that the solution to the apocalyptic problems that the narrator describes is, however tentatively, the reassessment of "human" as a productive category.

Reanimated Systems and the Commodification of the Citizen

We meet our protagonist in the midst of a fairly hopeless situation. Ninety-five percent of the world's population is dead, the government-run safe zones are experiencing a series of skel incursions, and an undead horde is poised to break through existing barriers and storm Manhattan, reminding all that the survivor population is still incredibly vulnerable to zombie attack. The government of the new "American Phoenix" nation (nicknamed "Buffalo" for its capital) must find ways to organize labor to support the country's infrastructure and boost its global reputation, so it offers an ideology of optimism and American industriousness as an alternative to the bleak realities of the postapocalyptic situation. Buffalo offers supplies, shelter, and hope to survivors at the cost of a buy-in to the ideology of mandatory participation in various forms of reconstructive labor. The Buffalo motto, "We Make Tomorrow," encourages citizens to look towards the future and invites them to imagine their own role in the construction of a new nation-state from the ashes of catastrophe. Once citizens have bought in to the American Phoenix's vision of communal responsibility, they are assigned to one of a variety of tasks. Mark Spitz and his fellow sweepers are charged with clearing Zone One of its remaining skel threats in order to return New York to its former ideological glory. To the authorities in Buffalo, a reclaimed Zone One would symbolize power both to the citizens whom they must continually employ in useful labor and to an international audience that they will host during an upcoming diplomatic summit. Although publicly optimistic, Buffalo is not blind to statistics: one of the public relations directors acknowledges that the reclamation of Zone One is primarily a publicity stunt and that it will take years to make the territory safe enough for official reoccupation.[13] Despite these realities, Buffalo continues to insist on progress and survival in an attempt to unite survivors under the ideological banner of hope and industrious laboring.

Human life, in Buffalo's model, means the survival of the species rather than the flourishing of individualism; therefore, government agents are primarily concerned with administering and organizing their population in ways that consolidate people into one demographic. Buffalo has sweepers collect statistics that account for losses to its labor force and infrastructure more than they account for the loss of human life. When the sweeper teams encounter skels, Buffalo is "keen for the sweepers to record demographic data: the ages of the targets, the density at the specific location, structure type, number of floors."[14] The only human data collected here are the ages of the deceased, usually found on ID cards present at the scene. As the voice of individualism in the novel, Mark Spitz sees ID collection as an unbearable duty and refers to the cards as "[t]he detritus that passed for identity, the particulate remains of twenty-first-century existence."[15] However, his comment about the practices of human resource departments before the apocalypse, when "human beings were paraphrased into numbers, components of bundled data to be shot out through fiber-optic cable toward meaning,"[16] indicates that summarizing human lives into bits of data is not entirely a postapocalyptic phenomenon. As Laura Hubner observes in her essay in this volume, the change in nomenclature from "personnel" to "human resources" in many workplaces demonstrates the increasingly prolific conceptualization of the human as primarily an economic resource.[17] The institutions that arise after an apocalypse still engage in many of the same activities for organizing and consolidating its population, showing that the scarcity of human beings does not necessarily lead to a greater degree of individualism.

Although Buffalo's statistical collection practices may reveal interest in managing its population, it's the Buffalo version of psychological diagnostics that actively consolidates the survivor population into one homogenous demographic. By the estimate of the head physician Dr. Neil Herkimer,[18] virtually all of the survivors manifest a so-called disorder that Buffalo has christened PASD—Post Apocalyptic Stress Disorder. The acronym echoes the real-life PTSD (posttraumatic stress disorder) that haunts so many of our own survivors: the substitution of the A for the T in the acronym suggests a rough equality between apocalypse and trauma. Disease or disorder is a key part of the contemporary zombie narrative—the canon is filled with the "infected" who join the undead horde after their deaths.[19] But a disorder that affects an entire population creates a homogenous horde of another type: one composed of sufferers who are all in need of Buffalo's training seminars and medical aid in order to keep living as productive citizens of the new American Phoenix. By coding various behaviors and emotions under the rubric of PASD, Buffalo can provide "treatments" to everyone, encouraging citizens to believe that their feelings of hopelessness, depression, or anxiety are abnormal and therefore should literally be worked through.

At first, it appears as though PASD could be viewed as an individualizing force as Mark Spitz explains how the disorder's expression varies considerably in each person. Unlike real-life PTSD, which has a very specific set of symptom qualifications for diagnosis,[20] PASD's list of symptoms is massive:

> feelings of sadness or unhappiness; irritability or frustration, even over small matters; loss of interest or pleasure in normal activities; reduced sex drive; insomnia or excessive sleeping; changes in appetite leading to weight loss, or increased cravings for food and weight gain; reliving traumatic events through hallucinations or flashbacks; agitation or restlessness; being "jumpy" or easily startled; slowed thinking, speaking, or body movements; indecisiveness, distractibility, and decreased concentration; fatigue, tiredness and loss of energy so that even small tasks seem to require a lot of effort; feelings of worthlessness or guilt; trouble thinking, concentrating, making decisions, and remembering things; frequent thoughts of death, dying, or suicide; crying spells for no apparent reason, as opposed to those triggered by memories of the fallen world; unexplained physical problems, such as back pain, increased blood pressure and heart rate, nausea, diarrhea, and headaches. Nightmares, goes without saying.[21]

With a list this expansive, it is no wonder that Mark Spitz describes it as "[a] meticulous inventory with a wide embrace. Not so much criteria for diagnosis but an abstract of existence itself."[22] The list of PASD symptoms—a fairly negative abstract of existence, indeed—accommodates people who react to the apocalypse through extreme lethargy and paranoia, insomnia and excessive sleeping, fatigue and agitation. Further examples of PASD in the novel increase the scope of the disorder even further, registering symptoms that range from an average citizen's feeling moderately unhappy to Mark Spitz's low-level hallucinations[23] and to the guy in Rainbow Village writing Bible verses on the wall "in his own shit."[24] Though it may have appeared to have individualizing potential, in practice, a PASD diagnosis functions as a leveling mechanism by refusing to acknowledge individual responses to trauma, treating all survivors as if they are suffering from the same basic disease, regardless of the severity of their symptoms or preexisting psychological conditions. Even the pronunciation of PASD as "past"[25] suggests that PASD is a universal disorder even before the apocalypse. Mark Spitz still insists that "[e]veryone was fucked up in their own way; as before, it was a mark of one's individuality,"[26] encouraging us to read PASD, as Hoberek does, much like trauma: "trauma is the thing that makes everyone at once unique (because everyone's is different) and the same (because everyone has one)."[27] This apparent contradiction exemplifies the tension between individualism and collectivity in the novel. Consolidating such a wide range of activities and feelings into one massive psychological disorder denies the effects of pre-apocalyptic events on people's behaviors; in this form of psychological homogenization, the human psyche can be entirely explained by the trauma of apocalypse, rather than by unique and individual past experiences.

Despite this breadth of symptoms, Buffalo is silent about some behaviors that we may actually consider pathological: specifically, acts of extreme or excessive violence towards skel bodies. Although the authorities strictly warn sweepers against "brutalizing, vandalizing, or even extending the odd negative vibe toward the properties"[28] that they are clearing, the rules for debasing skel bodies are more flexible. Mark Spitz's teammate Gary is permitted "one unnecessary act of carnage per floor"[29] as a form of healthy release or occupational therapy, and Mark Spitz remarks that the defacement of zombie corpses is not a subject typically mentioned in PASD seminars. By refusing to incorporate behaviors that would otherwise seem psychopathic into a larger constellation of PASD symptoms, Buffalo reveals its value system: all behavior is normal as long as it does not interfere with reconstructive labor. Despite being disturbingly violent, Gary is a very effective sweeper.

As the mandate against brutalizing buildings suggests, Buffalo is concerned with maintaining infrastructure and setting the foundations for a return to pre-apocalyptic economic systems. For example, Buffalo "created an entire division dedicated to pursuing official sponsors ... in exchange for tax breaks once the reaper laid down his scythe."[30] The new authorities attempt to orchestrate a return to state capitalism, under which the illusion of freedom and choice masks the strict management of the citizen population. *Zone One* illustrates how the zombie apocalypse does not successfully dissolve the possibility for hegemonic economic or social structures. Buffalo's diagnostic practices reveal the self-serving principles that structure its action; although its agents seem bent on preserving life, they are actually more concerned with promoting an ideology of collective participation while working to extend forms of pre-apocalyptic power. Mark Spitz describes arriving at his work detail as an entry into a "reanimated system,"[31] and he explains how early in the "reboot" Buffalo realized the importance of language in "rebranding survival": specialists were "hard at work crafting the new language ... the enemy they faced would not succumb to psychological warfare, but that didn't mean that the principles needed to remain unutilized."[32] Buffalo aims its linguistic weaponry against the survivor population to manipulate people into believing that their response to the trauma surrounding them is a pathological rather than logical reaction. Buffalo can continue to manipulate its people into believing there is a cure—even if this cure comes in a cheap form of optimism requiring "a marketing rollout, hope, psychopharmacology, a rigorous policing of bad thinking, anything to stoke the delusion that we'll make it through."[33] Thus the apocalyptic scenario in *Zone One* does not liberate humans from controlling structures as we may hope, but enables the eventual return of "zombie systems," reanimated prejudices, and culturally and politically hegemonic institutions.

As for Buffalo's insistence on hope and the human potential for restoration, "Resist," advises the narrator. He claims that he must "get all that crap out of his head or else it would turn out bad for him."[34]

Improvisations of Resistance

Survivors crystallize their traumatic memory of the zombie apocalypse in unique "Last Night stories" shared with those whom they meet along their journeys through the skel-infested wastelands. Mark Spitz has three different versions, curated for specific audiences: the Anecdote, the Silhouette, and the Obituary.[35] The choice to tell a shorter or longer tale seems to depend on the perceived emotional investment in his audience, generally expressed in how long Mark Spitz anticipates spending with a particular group of people. Notably, the only person (besides the reader) who gets his "Obituary" version is Mark Spitz's only romantic interest in the novel. Thus, identity is configured through storytelling, and narrative becomes, as Hoberek claims, "a form of defensive individualization."[36] Mark Spitz represents his identity through a series of scattered small anecdotes weaving in and out of each other; his dissociative third-person narration compounds apocalyptic trauma with personal voice, and the novel itself functions as Mark Spitz's Last Night story. The genre of the Last Night story, which a character *has* and can *give* (in various forms) to others, insists on reclaiming the apocalyptic experience as deeply individual and particular, rather than experienced ubiquitously as the PASD diagnosis would suggest.

But the irony of narrative individuation is that, as Mark Spitz tells us, "[a]t their core, Last Night stories were all the same: They came, we died, I started running."[37] Yet narrative still sorts people into a set of homogenized categories: the "they" and "we" inscribe them into the systems and institutions that eradicate various forms of difference. Perhaps then, a narrative rebellion must always be incomplete as it does not completely sever the ties between people and institutions. By illustrating how a rebellion against Buffalo's biopolitical practices begins with an acknowledgment of an inscription within established governmental categories, the novel plays with Giorgio Agamben's observation that "the spaces, the liberties, and the rights won by individuals in their conflicts with central powers always simultaneously prepared a tacit but increasing inscription of individuals' lives within the state order."[38] However, Mark Spitz's separation of "I" from "we" in the above passage still adamantly insists on a distinction between self and others made possible through storytelling—he carefully maintains the category of the individual even as he claims that all narratives are ultimately the same.

Furthermore, Mark Spitz insists on connecting the skels he confronts to experiences he's had and people he knew before the apocalypse. He recognizes eighth-grade lab partners, old girlfriends, and TV actresses in the bodies he is tasked with eliminating. By explicitly allowing the creatures to remind him of people he used to know, Mark Spitz conflates the skels with human beings. The act of recollection becomes a way of recapturing parts of certain individual lives that cannot be accounted for by the ID collection routine that he so despises. Instead of seeing this conflation as threatening Mark Spitz's ability to clear skel threats effectively, his boss from Buffalo views this practice as a "successful adaptation" that allows Mark Spitz to see himself as "an angel of death" rather than "a mere exterminator."[39] Whereas many zombie narratives ultimately insist on the inhumanity of the zombie monster (and consequently, the right of the living to kill it violently and with impunity), the line between man and monster remains blurry in *Zone One*. By imagining skels in human terms, Mark Spitz attempts to rebel against Buffalo's consolidation of human life into statistics and challenges the division that marks zombies as nonhuman bodies, or even more saliently, humans as nonzombie bodies.

In contrast to Mark Spitz's imaginative rebellion, some citizens stage their revolt in another, more bodily way: "One of the snipers observed the Lieutenant walk out to the helipad atop the bank. It was a quiet evening, sparse with the dead all day, one of the last quiet evenings before the devils started accumulating in their recent density. The sniper waved at the Lieutenant. The Lieutenant waved back and jammed a grenade in his mouth."[40] The Lieutenant, a plucky and admirable figure in the novel, appears to be an unlikely candidate for suicide as his status in Buffalo protects his material conditions and bodily safety—he has every apparent reason to be hopeful about his future. Perhaps his suicide stems from an increased degree of realism about the prospects for the future gained from the vantage point of his supervisory position. Mark Spitz presents suicide as the purest form of realism about the horror that the new world offers the human subject: "[t]he suicides accepted, finally, what the world had become and acted logically," even if, or especially if, a new level of bodily safety allowed for contemplation of the extent of the horrors of the apocalypse and the "semblance of normalcy" that survivor camps offered.[41] However, Buffalo considers suicide "the forbidden thought," and immediately orders new training units to be added to the PASD modules, treating suicide as an unallowable action rather than one tragic but normal symptom of PASD. Part of Buffalo's strategy, as we have seen with the PASD diagnosis, is the regulation of behaviors that compromise a person's labor potential. While Buffalo is perfectly willing to accept Gary's skel mutilation as occupational therapy, suicide reasserts individual agency over the body and threatens official efforts to maintain the larger population. Seen as an escape from a hopeless world, suicide is potentially the ultimate act of agency in the novel precisely because it represents the one true rebellion available to Buffalo's citizens—a near-complete removal from the system.

Suicide is more than just a challenge to the commodification of human life as potential units of labor; it also represents a deep loss of hope and therefore Buffalo's failure at fully consolidating its population into an ideologically unified mass. As Mark Spitz explains, "[k]illing yourself in the age of the American Phoenix was a rebuke to its principles."[42] In order to get people to contribute to reconstructive efforts, Buffalo must seduce them into a hopeful sense of responsibility towards their future, which easily translates into a responsibility to the state. Empires, after all, need citizens. When life becomes commodified and then becomes scarcer, Buffalo becomes less able to provide the material and ideological resources that serve as the glue holding its regime together. Furthermore, suicide may betray hopelessness but also indicates fearlessness, both equally dangerous to Buffalo's reconstructive efforts. And it is this fearlessness that can undo the workings of institutions in power: as Breckinridge Scott reminds us in World War Z, "fear is the most valuable commodity in the universe."[43] If Buffalo's leaders cannot continue to manufacture a certain degree of fear and the solution to that fear, they may find themselves without the bodies that they need to complete reconstruction.

Mark Spitz's end demonstrates the merger between human and horde in his own extempore rebellion by "immersion," which he describes as "swimming" in an ocean of other bodies, releasing into the future, melding with the horde of skels as it storms Manhattan. Although he characterizes this action as giving in to his own forbidden thought because "we cannot delude ourselves that we will make it out alive,"[44] Mark Spitz describes his suicide by skel as "learning how to swim," which is a positively connoted metaphor for growth and maturity. The first two forms of resistance offered—narrative individuation in the face of mass homogenization and suicide as a way to escape full inscription into the state—both insist on individuated identity as an important category for freedom and agency. In his deliberate, but almost desperate, final choice, Mark Spitz seems to eschew this individuality altogether. Lauro and Embry have provided the term "zombii" to describe the posthuman swarm-singularity that spells the end for late capitalism, and we can easily imagine Mark Spitz's inauguration in this type of horde at the end of the novel. The zombii is the "potential of the posthuman subject" that "exists in its collectivity (and in its multiplicity and its hybridity)," which "forfeits consciousness as we know it—embracing a singular, swarm experience."[45] This language—forfeiture, embrace, swarm—echoes the language Mark Spitz uses to describe his own entry into posthuman subjectivity: "Fuck it, he thought. You have to learn how to swim sometime. He opened the door and walked into the sea of the dead."[46]

But a key difference between the zombii and *Zone One*'s zombie swarm is that the latter maintains the tension between the individual and the collective through playfully imagining two different types of undead. The usual zombie ("the ruthless chaos of existence made flesh"[47]) is represented by the "skel" that infects the living with its bite, but Whitehead also creates the "straggler," a zombie that is stuck in endless repetition of a single moment in its past life. The skel is a monster we know well as the frenzied, violent embodiment of late capitalism's consumptive impulses. The stragglers, however, are perhaps even more deeply familiar: individuals so defined by a moment in their past that they are stuck repeating, reliving, or re-processing it for the remainder of their existence. In *Zone One*, zombies are seen as a swarm of monsters that threaten the future of the human race, but also as pathetic individuals who continue to let their pasts dictate their futures, much as we do. The line between human and straggler is so exceptionally thin that Gary jokingly interacts with a straggler stuck in the act of fortune-telling, undaunted by the fact that she is one of the undead—a mistake that costs him his life. By presenting us with kinds of undead whose main traits are also recognizable in the living, *Zone One* asks us to consider: What does it mean to be human? Or are we already zombies?

Even if we are not willing to agree that Lauro and Embry's swarm organism postsubject "zombii" is the ideal posthuman future, or that willful zombification is a viable rebellion, something in the zombie narrative asks us to assess the value of humanity as a category when we perpetuate systems of power that disenfranchise other beings. *Zone One* insists that the bad practices of the pre-apocalyptic state are maintained rather than revised after catastrophe. As in many other doomsday narratives, survival here does not equal evolution, so the new world orders of the postapocalypse end up replicating the practices and prejudices that led to disaster in the first place. In McGurl's words, "only zombies make this fundamentally social and self-accusatory charge: we the people are the problem we cannot solve. We outnumber ourselves."[48] Novels like *Zone One* show that humans are the problematic category and that wherever there are humans, there is the potential for all of the ugliness that we associate with cultural or political hegemony. Thus, the apocalyptic narrative often just confirms the inevitability of humanity's self-destruction—eventually we'll create an end of the world so large that we do not survive it, and then finally the systems of power and disenfranchisement that we so despise will fall, taking us with them. Mark Spitz's merger with a skel horde may activate "the other, utopian side of the zombie story ... that sees the breakdown of our categories of individual and even the human not as tragedy but as a form of release."[49] This breakdown will eradicate the "zombie systems,"[50] old networks of prejudice that remain constants in human society. But because the novel continually conflates human and skel bodies, we can see its solution to these zombie systems not as an eradication of humanity but as a transformation, a new posthumanity where individual subjectivity is no longer a valued or necessary category.

Mark Spitz is not the only character who improvises resistance. In the final section of the novel, he recounts his experience with the Quiet Storm, a woman who arranges vehicles on the now-defunct I-95 corridor into massive and yet-unreadable texts. Mark Spitz saw "her mosaic, in its immense tonnage, outlasting all of Buffalo's schemes, the operations under way and the ones yet to be articulated. What readership did she address? Gods and aliens, anyone who looks down at the right time, from the right perspective."[51] Even the Quiet Storm admits to Mark Spitz that she did not have access to the meaning of her giant inscriptions; she relies on an interpreter to come from afar and reconstruct her meaning. Perhaps, then, despite its suggestion of zombification and loss of human subjectivity as the ways to eradicate zombie systems, the novel quietly authorizes the written word to bring humanity into the future. Though yet unreadable, the Quiet Storm's language will one day be the key to reclaiming humanity's identity, even if that identity is only restored to the realm of narrative—the story of a long-lost race, an almost-forgotten collective. Thus to answer Mark Spitz's defiant call to resist the siren song of Buffalo's hope, we must persist in giving voice to humanity's inner scream through composing and reading texts: we the human species must write our way into the future.

NOTES

1. Cantor, "Apocalyptic Strain in Popular Culture," 23.
2. *Ibid.*, 26.
3. *Ibid.*
4. Dante, *Inferno*, lines 55–57 and 47–48.
5. Eliot, *Waste Land*, lines 62–63, 71–73. Eliot's poem has resonance in *Zone One*; the word "wasteland" or "wastelanders" echoes throughout the novel.
6. Hoberek, "Living with PASD," 408.
7. McGurl, "Zombie Renaissance," 168–69.
8. Lauro and Embry, "Zombie Manifesto," 105–06.
9. Hoberek, "Living with PASD," 409–10.
10. Whitehead, *Zone One*, 202.
11. *Ibid.*, 23.
12. We never learn our protagonist's pre-doomsday name, but we do learn how he earned his moniker Mark Spitz. Instead of jumping into the river with his comrades to escape a zombie horde, he vaults from car to car shooting skels, all the while believing that in the logic of this new world, his supreme mediocracy made him invincible. After killing all of the skels, he tells his companions that he didn't jump because he couldn't swim—they laugh and name him after the Olympic swimmer Mark Spitz, an ironic but fitting nickname because the protagonist sees his mediocrity as rendering him in peak condition to thrive in the newly mediocre world. See *Ibid.*, 147–48.
13. *Ibid.*, 250.
14. *Ibid.*, 30.
15. *Ibid.*, 50–51.
16. *Ibid.*, 17.
17. Hubner, "Love, Connection, and Intimacy," 43.
18. Incidentally, Herkimer is a city located about a three-hour drive from Buffalo, which could suggest that this "expert" doctor has been invented by Buffalo to justify its diagnosis.
19. Not only does the presence of the zombie often result from some sort of virus or disease, but survivors can also develop physical or psychological disorders. For example, in the novel *World War Z*, people can get ADS (either Asymptomatic Demise Syndrome or Apocalyptic Despair Syndrome "depending on who you were talking to"), which is a psychological disorder resulting from feelings of helplessness and the loss of will to endure. But unlike PASD, suicide was separated out from the disorder as a separate phenomenon, and the list of symptoms was less stable—people died in perfect health. However, as in *Zone One*, the solution to the disorder involved a media publicity scheme (Roy Elliot's movies in *WWZ*). See Brooks, *World War Z*, 159.
20. The symptom criteria for posttraumatic stress disorder is quite narrow in comparison, though there is a good deal of overlap. Diagnostic criteria for PTSD can be found under 309.81 (F43.10) in the *DSM-V*, the standard guide used by clinicians to assess mental illness.
21. Whitehead, *Zone One*, 54–55.
22. *Ibid.*, 55.
23. *Ibid.*, 187.
24. *Ibid.*, 233.
25. *Ibid.*, 55.
26. *Ibid.*, 30.
27. Hoberek, "Living with PASD," 412.
28. Whitehead, *Zone One*, 12.

29. *Ibid.*, 13.
30. *Ibid.*, 39.
31. *Ibid.*, 89.
32. *Ibid.*, 79.
33. *Ibid.*, 202.
34. *Ibid.*, 24.
35. *Ibid.* 112–13.
36. Hoberek, "Living with PASD," 411.
37. Whitehead, *Zone One*, 112.
38. Agamben, *Homo Sacer*, 121.
39. Whitehead, *Zone One*, 16.
40. *Ibid.*, 202.
41. *Ibid.*, 201.
42. *Ibid.*, 202.
43. Brooks, *World War Z*, 55.
44. Whitehead, *Zone One*. 255.
45. Lauro and Embry, "Zombie Manifesto," 106.
46. Whitehead, *Zone One*, 259.
47. *Ibid.*, 258.
48. McGurl, "Zombie Renaissance," 169.
49. Hoberek, "Living with PASD," 412.
50. *Ibid.*, 412–13.
51. Whitehead, *Zone One*, 233.

"Condemned to history by the Hate"

David J. Moody's Hater and Postmillennial Rage

DAWN KEETLEY

Published in 2006 by Thomas Dunne Books, British writer David J. Moody's *Hater* is the first of a trilogy, followed by *Dog Blood* (2010) and *Them or Us* (2011). Although Moody has written several other novels that are more explicitly about zombies (notably the Autumn series [2001–12]) and runs a publishing company called Infected Books, his Hater novels are not quite as clearly about zombies. In this essay, I argue not only that the first novel in the trilogy is indeed a zombie novel, but also that it constitutes an important development in the collective zombie narrative.[1] *Hater* draws on the "rage zombies" of *28 Days Later* (2002, directed by Danny Boyle), although its "zombies" are not the result of infection: instead, they are incarnations of affect—of overwhelming rage. *Hater* is narrated, moreover, by one of these embodiments of rage, adding to the scant literature that attempts to voice the perspective of the zombie. Through the central conceit of an overwhelming rage, in which subjectivity drops out and "zombie" sweeps in, *Hater* explores both ontology and politics, disclosing a deep malcontent with postmillennial modernity.

Hater is set in an unremarkable British city, and events unfold through the eyes of Danny McCoyne, a distinctly ordinary character, who (like most of us) has no ready aptitude for the apocalypse that confronts him. Danny is perennially shiftless, shuffling through life expending as little effort as possible. In his late twenties, he has had a series of jobs for the local town council, being demoted from one to the next, and, when the novel opens, he "works" (although he tries hard not to) in the Parking Fine Processing office, mostly dealing (ineptly) with irate people who have been issued parking tickets or had their cars clamped. Danny and his wife, Lizzie, have three small children, Ed, Ellis, and Josh, and they all live in a cramped council flat in a condemned building. Integral to the novel, Danny's ordinary and yet distinctly deadening existence echoes another iconic British zombie narrative, *Shaun of the Dead* (2004, directed by Edgar Wright), a film that exploits to humorous effect the fact that distinguishing zombie from human has become difficult in contemporary urban life. *Hater* turns this around to horrific effect, showing that the impoverished conditions of modernity may be less effect than cause—may actually *precipitate* a cataclysmic zombie outbreak.[2]

Danny starts getting shaken out of his rut after he sees a violent and seemingly unmotivated attack as he is trudging to work one day. But even after witnessing several more such assaults—at a club, in a pub—it takes him a while to grasp the enormity of what is happening. The TV news reports the outbreaks as anomalies at first—sporadic riots, perhaps. Soon, however, the media register the scale of the "pandemic," trying to diagnose it: mass hysteria, emotional contagion, a virus, perhaps. Most ominously, all channels finally go off the air, broadcasting simply a warning that everyone should stay calm, stay alert, stay where they are. The government apparently has things under control, which does little to reassure anyone. Before total media silence, Danny and his family learn that the affected (possibly infected) people are being dubbed "Haters," not least because they turn on others without discernible cause and display a single-minded intent to kill them, no matter what the cost. About one-third of the population, it seems, is suddenly given over to the driving force of an overwhelming rage.

The Haters are zombies of a very particular kind—"affective zombies," hijacked by rage and thus on a continuum with the infected rage zombies introduced in Boyle's groundbreaking *28 Days Later*. In their becoming pure "rage," moreover, the Haters mark a political subtext for the trilogy, uncannily anticipating the riots that broke out in several cities in England in the summer of 2011. The Hater uprising, through its protagonist Danny McCoyne, both limns the conditions that produced these riots and also offers a violent fantasy of escape for the utterly disenfranchised.

Haters as Zombies

The trilogy makes many allusions to zombie narratives, as well as overtly suggesting that the Haters are akin to zombies. In *Hater*, in the confusion of the initial outbreak, references are oblique. Discussing the initial media coverage of the bursts of violence, for instance, Danny questions how much the news presenters actually know, whether the coverage is based in fact: "The whole setup reminds me," he says, "of the start of that film *Dawn of the Dead* where the views of another so-called expert are ripped apart by a nonbelieving TV presenter. I know we're not dealing with a zombie apocalypse here but the way these people are talking to each other makes it feel eerily similar."[3] The "eerie" similarity seems more fully realized once Danny becomes a Hater—after which he analogizes himself and other Haters more than once to zombies. As he says in *Dog Blood*, to someone who is trying to figure out what kind of "monster" they most resemble: "We drag ourselves around constantly, looking for Unchanged to kill. It's almost like we're feeding off them." When they're not killing, Danny continues, "[I]t's like you're in limbo. Just existing. Not really living, but not dead either." Danny concludes that "we're like zombies, [like] one of the undead."[4] Such paradoxical self-awareness comes later, however, and the first novel of the trilogy represents a more capacious and less familiar definition of the zombie, illustrating Stephanie Boluk and Wylie Lenz's claim that the zombie "resists generic and taxonomic containment; it is remarkably capable of adapting to a changing cultural and medial imaginary." This "fungibility of the zombie" is one reason it has persisted for so long—mutating and spreading.[5] Persisting through all of its many incarnations, however, is the notion of the death of self, its reanimation in different form. Most obviously, this death is actual, and the return is as the living dead. A more expansive definition doesn't take "death" so literally, though. A zombie can be the result of a catastrophic loss of self through some other means than death. The "viral zombies" inaugurated in *28 Days Later*—and which feature in *28 Weeks Later* (2007, directed by Juan Carlos Fresnadillo), *Dawn of the Dead* (2004, directed by Zack Snyder), and *Rammbock* (2010, directed by Marvin Kren), for instance—are not people who have died and become reanimated (unless the process happens in a split second); rather, infection triggers an absolute transformation. The self has vanished, and in its place is a contagious and ravening drive, a single-minded and unreasoning urge to kill and consume.

The Haters are not the risen dead, nor are they viral zombies (although there's a suggestion for a while that they might be). Instead, they are a variant I call the "affective zombie." In *Hater*, the particular form of affect that initiates the loss of self is rage. The "rage zombies" of *Hater* are not the same as those infected by the "rage virus" in *28 Days Later*, however; while *Hater* at first leaves the source of the "contagion" open and (like *28 Days Later*) suggests a virus as its origin, it later becomes clear that the Haters are actually not afflicted by a virus. What incites their all-consuming affect, their rage, is something already immanent in their bodies. As an emerging leader of the Haters (Chris Ankin) puts it at the end of the novel, "there is a fundamental *genetic* difference between us and them. A fundamental and basic difference, which, until now, has remained dormant." The "change," he continues, "seems almost to amplify our instincts." It strips away many of "the layers of conditioning and control imposed upon us by society."[6] The Haters, it seems, are simply human—and the "Hate" has been there all along, buried instinct.

What the rage zombies of *Hater* usefully do, then, is explore the ways in which people who are neither literally dead nor infected can nonetheless experience a complete and catastrophic death of "self," a death that is due to an emotion *inherent to human nature.* In *Hater*, rage is not (and perhaps by its nature never can be) a permanent state: it sweeps over Haters periodically. When they come into the presence of what they call the Unchanged, they become pure ravening fury, unable to control themselves. Even at other times, though, they are still not who they once were: they remember their former lives with an utter detachment, even shame and contempt. At such times, they translate their rage into a lifelong project—desiring more consciously to destroy every one of the Unchanged, their lives centered on the next transformation (when they see an Unchanged) when "self" completely disappears and they become all "zombie."

Moody's rage zombies have a literary genealogy that exceeds the zombie tradition, one illuminated by Peter Sloterdijk's discussion of epic poetry in *Rage and Time.* Sloterdijk argues that the epic (his example is Homer) manifests a notion of both character and action as consumed by passion: humans don't have passions, he writes; rather, "it is the passions that have their human beings." Sloterdijk focuses in particular on rage, a primary emotion animating epic heroes, and he argues that when rage "has" a character, it leaves behind "no complex inner life, no hidden psychic world." He goes on to describe the epic character consumed by rage in ways that echo perfectly Moody's Haters, themselves filled (only) with rage: "It is typical of the surging rage that it fully becomes one with its own lavish expression."[7] "[S]hapes become more determinate," he continues. "Now clear lines lead to the object. The enraged attack knows where it wants to hit."[8] Rage forms a subject, then, that is nothing but the expression of its particular passion. It suffers no hesitation, no self-doubt—no (hidden) interiority at all, in fact. Interiority is extinguished in its own externalized "lavish expression." While Sloterdijk is in part defining a literary genre of a past era, he argues that the characteristics of rage-filled epic heroes offer a utopian alternative, in the present, for those suffering from the conditions of modernity. For those who have "settle[d] down" and for whom the "virtues of hesitations have become authoritative," the metamorphosis into a being utterly lacking "reflective inwardness, intimate conversations with themselves, and the ability to make conscientious attempts to control their affects" is a form of fantasy.[9] The Haters are precisely this kind of utopian, rage-filled subject—a response to the numbing, mindless, postmillennial existence. Not ruled by hesitation or plagued by self-doubt, or even self-consciousness at all when they are in the throes of the "Hate," they are given over wholly to single-minded action, to the unequivocal and liberating manifestation of a single affect.[10]

That the Haters' all-consuming rage may serve a utopian purpose in the complex and often deadening contemporary world is suggested by the fact that it is possible to read Danny's metamorphosis into Hater as anticipated in the simmering anger that defines his character—and thus to read his transformation as a solution, of sorts, to his marginalized existence. Danny's perpetual state of being "pissed-off" suggests a link between anger and the Hate, grounding Moody's Hater allegory in the conditions of a postmillennial life that is boring, barren, sordid—a constant struggle. Certainly Danny is always aggravated—with his boss, his wife, his father-in-law, his kids (who seem to do nothing but wake him up, demand food, and insist that they be allowed to watch TV), and, indeed, with virtually everyone he meets.

That mundane anger suffuses Danny's world is clear right from the opening scene of Danny at work, in which his "sneering" and "scowling" boss demands that he make up the five minutes of work he lost because he was late; a conversation with two of his fellow employees leads in short order to Danny's "beginning to get annoyed"; and in an encounter with a furious woman whose car has been clamped, everyone—Danny, his boss, the woman with the clamped car—becomes enraged.[11] On the train home, Danny is surrounded by "pissed-off travelers"; his first moments with his wife when he gets home make him think that *she's* "really beginning to piss me off."[12] Every moment with his three children is filled with intense frustration and rage—and Danny thinks darkly, about his father-in-law, that he is "beginning to piss me off" such that "it's getting to the point where I can see us coming to blows."[13] The anger that pervades Danny's dealings with others is fueled by *everyone's* misery and malcontent.

When the Hate erupts, then, it seems an explosion of something that's been lurking all along, which fits Ankin's explanation that the Hate is produced by an inherent "genetic difference" that "has remained dormant."[14] While the all-consuming enragement of the Hate might well be an extension of everyday anger, it also serves as a solution to that same pervasive malcontent. When the Hate kills the "person" in the moment of metamorphosis, the bored, angry, and resentful person becomes an embodiment of pure rage, driven only to kill. And in the moment when the newly transformed Haters attack any and all Unchanged near them (even loved ones), they not only rid themselves of the dystopian burden of contemporary life, but also save those whom they kill—for the Haters look upon the lives of the Unchanged as unequivocally miserable. The dyad of Hater and Unchanged, then, each locked in the struggle to kill the other, represents a fantasy of escape from a destitute modernity.

Hater thus dramatizes Sloterdijk's theory of rage: the death of the "self" in all-consuming rage, he argues, creates a subject "safe from suffering problems of meaning." A "persistent will excludes boredom," he continues. "The deep simplicity of rage satisfies the all-too-human desire for strong motivations. One motive, one agent, one necessary deal: this is the formula for a complete project." Thanks to rage, he concludes, "the utopia of motivated life realizes itself in a domain in which an increasing amount of people feel empty."[15] This emptiness, which vies with anger in the world of *Hater*—and, indeed, which produces it—is remediated once the Hate erupts. Danny describes one of his first battles with the Unchanged: "Faced with death I actually feel more alive! ... All around me this animal instinct is taking over and we are killing to keep ourselves alive. This is what I was born to do."[16] Danny explicitly thinks (in words that resonate uncannily with Sloterdijk's), "All of the confusion and uncertainty has gone. The pain has disappeared" as they engage in a battle that is "brutal and relentless, basic and almost medieval."[17] Danny's sense that his single-minded passion is "almost medieval" echoes Sloterdijk's discussion of epic characters, possessed by "surging rage," bereft of any contemplative inner life, transported to a state where all that matters is the object of fury, where the "enraged attack knows where it wants to hit."[18] His former self is erased in the affective zombie state of rage, and when Danny's "self" does drop away—when it "dies" in rage, when he becomes rage "zombie"—he feels, paradoxically, "more alive."[19]

Rioters Without a Cause

Like most zombie narratives, *Hater* explores not only ontology but also politics—and, indeed, the two are interrelated, as the death of the marginalized, "pissed off" self in the state of "Hate" forms a politics as well as a subject. As Boluk and Lenz have pointed out, "With each new historical iteration of the zombie, the figure gives expression to the anxieties of that particular cultural moment."[20] Just as the subjectivity of the Haters is similar to that of the "infected" in *28 Days Later*—in that they are afflicted, wholly taken over, by "rage" (as virus in the film and as affective state in the novel)—their politics have much in common as well. Both *28 Days Later* and *Hater* evoke a particular kind of late twentieth- and early twenty-first-century politics that is predicated on social identity, but only to mark the politics of identity as *in and of the past* and then to shape a new politics that is defined by rage and that is strictly divided between the "zombie" and everyone else.

The "rage virus" of *28 Days Later* is not merely organic matter: it begins in a primate research center, where scientists are giving chimpanzees an "inhibitor" and then force-feeding them a steady stream of violent media images. The chimpanzees are literally "infected" with "rage," as one of the researchers puts it. The film opens on a scene of riot, which, as the camera pulls back, blossoms into many scenes of beatings and burnings from around the globe. As the camera retracts still further, we see that the riots are all captured on TV screens at which a chimpanzee is forced to stare. The images do not, moreover, represent random acts of violence: most seem to be political protests involving clashes with authorities, thus hinting at the way in which the rage virus, when it ultimately blossoms, cannibalizes how politics *used to be*. It is from this scene of horror that animal rights activists seek to liberate the chimpanzees, but the instant they free one of the animals, it attacks them, and the "rage" epidemic is unleashed. The shots of actual protest glimpsed at the beginning of the film are soon swallowed up by hordes of rampaging "infected," who have no will, no reason, only the drive to kill whoever remains uninfected. The multiple global conflicts over such things as ideology, land, race, and religion (seen only in the videos streaming in the lab) mutate into a clear-cut, present-time battle of "us" against "them." What might, in pre-apocalyptic days, have been meaningful protest grounded in history and identity, in other words, mutates into violence starkly unmoored from such meanings and translated into the present time of rage. It is perhaps no coincidence that this once-meaningful protest, now consigned to the past, includes the animal rights activists who inadvertently caused the apocalypse in the first place. Their well-intentioned act of protesting injustice, their advocacy for a particular oppressed group, extinguished the very notions of both justice and dichotomized oppressive and oppressed groups: their political act is fully self-annihilating.

Like *28 Days Later*, *Hater* explicitly consigns familiar politics predicated on social identity to the past: all the complex, historically rooted reasons for rioting before the "Hate" are rendered anachronistic, and in their place erupts the stark and very present divide between Hater and non–Hater. In explaining his initial theory of the Hater riots, for instance, when they are just beginning, Danny reminds Lizzie of the riots *"last summer"*—a "string of race-motivated disturbances in a few major cities."[21] And Haters leader Chris Ankin later proclaims, *"Until now* we've discriminated against each other according to race, religion, age, gender, and just about every other differentiation imaginable. Look around you tonight and you'll see that *those differences are gone.* Now," Ankin continues, "to put things as simplistically as possible, there is just 'us' and 'them,' and it is impossible for us to coexist." Ankin makes the point still clearer when he tells his audience, *"Forget your past."*[22] In the second book in the trilogy, Danny thinks, "Equality, diversity, and political correctness *are all things of the past now*, condemned to History by the Hate—the great leveler."[23] Even the publisher's blurb on the back of *Hater* points out that the typical divisions of social identity no longer apply: "[E]veryone, irrespective of race, class, or any other difference, has the potential to become a victim—or a Hater." Both the personal and the collective past—history and memory—are now consigned to oblivion, along with all the social affiliations of place, religion, race, gender, and class that constituted that history. Even kinship, the most fundamental of social bonds, no longer matters, as Haters and non–Haters turn on each other no matter what ties of blood and marriage bind them: the climax of *Hater* is Danny's murder of his father-in-law and attempt to kill his wife and two of his children.

As the *Hater* novels explicitly represent all divisions based on social identity (gender, age, class, race, religion, nation) as "condemned to History by the Hate," they leave a perpetual present in which there is only the apparently timeless division of "us" and "them." Terry Harpold has aptly described "zombie time," which is also Hater time, as not only without a past but as the "absolute menace of that perpetual present with no possibility of founding an actual future."[24] *Hater*, in other words, represents the evisceration of traditional grounds of political action and protest—and, in this way, it maps what Simon Winlow and Steve Hall have called the "post-political present," thus presciently anticipating, I suggest, the riots of the summer of 2011.[25] As does *Hater*, these strangely apolitical riots made dramatically manifest the rage of the marginalized. *Hater*, however, *also* offers rage as a kind of solution—perhaps only, pessimistically, because there is no other.

"Inarticulate Rage" and Consumerism

In early August 2011, an estimated 13,000 to 15,000 people rioted (and looted) in several UK cities (including London, Birmingham, Liverpool, Manchester, and Nottingham). The ostensible cause of the riots was the fatal shooting of Mark Duggan by the police, but, in the end, many commentators agreed that they appeared to be apolitical manifestations of the simmering anger of the disenfranchised.[26] The rioters for the most part made no demands on those in power, and Winlow and Hall argue that "[c]onsciously they wanted to change nothing." They were, however, "subsumed by the *experiential adventure* of the riot," suggesting a subconscious desire to change *something* about their state.[27] Above all, it was the rioters' "inarticulate rage" that seemed most on display—and Winlow and Hall argue that "occasional outbursts of collective rage" go along with the "development of contemporary advanced marginality," and that "objectless and unconscious rage" emerges "in the absence of alternative political narratives of the present."[28] Bereft of a "genuine politics," then, the riots "took the form of a blind, impotent, and aggressive outburst."[29] It is precisely this pure rage that Moody's *Hater* so presciently captures, a rage that is indeed inarticulate and inchoate, not symbolized in or through any familiar political forms. Those who become Haters are divested of all self-consciousness; their self "drops away,"[30] along with all politics predicated on it—and all they experience is the drive to destroy.

Just as commentators agreed, however, that even while it was not being given conventional political expression, marginalization and poverty lay behind the rage of the 2011 riots, so too in *Hater*. For if Danny's eventual metamorphosis into Hater is prefigured in his perpetual pre–Hate anger, it is also potentially rooted in the major causes of his being "pissed off"—that is, poverty and what Winlow and Hall call the reaction "against humiliation and the suffocation of hope."[31] Danny and his family live a life undeniably defined by poverty and hopelessness. Danny says of his house that "it's not much but it's all we've got at the moment and it will have to do for now"— and they find it hard "to put food on the table."[32] Danny got into an unspecified "mess with my bank a year or so ago and they canceled everything on my account"—obviously a sign he had tried (and failed) to live beyond his means. Now, he pays bills and then gets by on what's left of his pay for the month; toward the end, there's not much—and even buying food becomes difficult.[33] The McCoynes fight because the apartment they live in is too small for the five of them; on one occasion, he and Lizzie fight because he was late and didn't have the credit on his cell phone to call her,[34] and he gets supremely angry at her when she repeatedly asks him to buy them all lunch at a pub after they've taken one of their children to a birthday party. Danny keeps snapping at her that he doesn't have the money, but she keeps pushing it.[35] The constant humiliations and deprivations that define Danny's life, and precipitate his pre–Hate anger, seem to have something to do, at least, with the eventual eruption of the Hate.

Besides the "objectless and unconscious rage"[36] of the rioters—expression of a thoroughgoing marginalization—what was most striking about the riots of 2011 was the fact that the rage of those who joined in was expressed through looting. Numerous commentators have located the difference of these riots precisely in this desire for consumer goods, which seemed to go hand in hand with the absence of a clear political agenda. Winlow and Hall claim that "the focus upon the looting of consumer goods indicates the huge power of consumer imagery."[37] And they are not alone in this assessment. By almost all accounts, the riots of 2011 demonstrated the incredible ability of consumerism to shape identity in the early twenty-first century, co-opting traditional politics and demonstrating the "centrality of a consumerist way of life and its grip on contemporary English society."[38] In separate commentaries in the aftermath of the riots, Zygmunt Bauman, Slavoj Žižek, and Stuart Hall all pointed out how those who participated seemed enthralled by the ideology of consumerism. As Bauman wrote, "We are all consumers now, consumers first and foremost, consumers by right and by duty."[39] Consumerism, as Hall succinctly put it, "has got to them too."[40]

What commentators found distinctive about the 2011 riots, in short, defined as they were by pervasive looting, is the way in which consumerism seemed so thoroughly to have pervaded them, giving form to an "impotent rage and despair" that was channeled through and as "shopping."[41] The riots may well have been about more than acquiring things, but those reasons were nonetheless crucially expressed through looting. The riots became an inchoate expression of how consumerism strives to create for all of us a *singular* identity. Bauman claims that the 2011 riots were "riots of defective and disqualified consumers," arguing that the *sole* measure of success is now consumption: "It is the level of our shopping activity and the ease with which we dispose of one object of consumption in order to replace it with a 'new and improved' one which serves as the prime measure of our social standing and the score in the life-success competition."[42] Consumerism almost completely constitutes the postmillennial subject. As Hall puts it, "Consumerism puts everyone in a single channel,"[43] an idea of course (to return to zombies) that George A. Romero presciently imagined in his 1978 film *Dawn of the Dead*.

Like the 2011 riots, *Hater* certainly suggests that lurking beneath Danny's anger could be his failure as a consumer, the *raison d'être* of contemporary life; he did, after all, get in "a mess with [his] bank." While the same consumerist ideology may shadow Moody's subtext, though, it is telling that the singular identity shaped for its characters is not "shopper" but pure, corporeal rage. The consumerism on display in the 2011 riots and the "Hate" may be similar, then, to the extent that each shapes a singular all-consuming identity (markedly different from the multiple identity politics of the past), but the Hate is utterly unmediated, born of the body, experienced as liberating and enlivening. It offers a "genuine truth,"[44] a moment of transformation that feels authentic. As Danny thinks, "All around me this animal instinct is taking over and we are killing to keep ourselves alive. This is what I was born to do."[45] *Hater* expresses a singular all-encompassing identity that is markedly *not* consumerism: it is rage rooted in the bedrock of the body, providing a vivifying *real* experience. Indeed, *Hater* suggests that all political protest may have only ever been, in the end, an epiphenomenon of innate human aggression, dividing the world into those who fight and survive and those who don't, a stark either-or division only subsequently co-opted by consumerism.

While Danny compares himself and other Haters more than once to zombies, then, they do not represent, figuratively, the deadening state of late modernity. The zombies of *Dawn of the Dead* did famously allegorize precisely those encroaching effects of consumerism: its zombies were akin to mindless shoppers wandering the mall, driven by urges they didn't understand, not least because they weren't authentic.[46] The affective zombie state of rage—the Hate—*frees* Danny and all other Haters from precisely this kind of deadening existence. He feels "alive," as a liberating rage wipes away subjectivity, politics, and ideology.

In articulating a stark rage that annihilates the complications of identity politics grounded in history and eviscerates consumerism as the measure of a successful self, *Hater* serves as a fantasy of escape, cutting through what is represented as a superficial identity politics, revealing—allowing—the clearcut and stark division between "us" and those who threaten "us." There's a clarity about the Hater/non–Hater binary that expresses a desire to transcend the increasingly complex and tangled webs of social identity. *Hater* offers a world of two powerful opposed forces—not a world of "microaggressions." It presents a world divided into "Them or Us" (the title of the third novel in the trilogy). And, indeed, when Danny realizes he is a Hater, his world becomes much simpler: "It's us against them. There's not going to be a tie or a ceasefire or any political negotiations to resolve this. There won't be an end to this fighting until one side has prevailed and the enemy lies dead at their feet. It's kill or be killed. Hate or be hated."[47] Haters are driven by a single instinctual affect, not hemmed in by rules, hesitation, and self-doubt. *Hater* revels in the real freedom of an apocalypse that wipes away the weight of history, borne individually and collectively. *Hater* offers the truth of the affective zombie, the rage zombie—what John Protevi has called a "corporeal agent,"[48] in which modern subjectivity is absent, and the authentic experience of the body, and only that, remains.

NOTES

1. The second and third novels in the trilogy, *Dog Blood* and *Them or Us*, which are certainly themselves interesting interventions in the zombie tradition, are quite different from *Hater*, which charts the beginnings of the outbreak. While *Hater* concerns its protagonist's dawning recognition that he is a Hater, *Dog Blood* and *Them or Us* track his struggle with what he has (already) become. What these two novels mean to the zombie tradition warrants a separate study.

2. Thanks to Angela Tenga for pointing out this relationship between *Hater* and *Shaun of the Dead*.

3. Moody, *Hater*, 106. There's a more indirect reference to another of George A. Romero's films, *Night of the Living Dead* (1968), in *Hater*, when Danny sees a young girl bludgeon her mother to death with a tin of food in a grocery store (*Ibid.*, 161–62), replaying the infamous scene in which young Karen Cooper stabs her mother with a trowel in the cellar of the farmhouse.

4. Moody, *Dog Blood*, 25. Still later in the series, Danny thinks, again, that "the monsters he and the rest of his kind had come to resemble most of all were zombies." Their fate was to drag themselves "through what was left of their world until their physical bodies finally failed them, all of them desperate to satisfy an insatiable craving that would never be silenced. Nothing else mattered anymore. Their lives were empty but for the hunt and the kill" (Moody, *Them or Us*, 8). Glimpses of the Haters from the perspective of the non-Haters, the Unchanged, also ratify their similarity to zombies: they engage in "frantic, unpredictable movements," their behavior is "uncoordinated, nomadic"—and they manifest an "apparently insatiable desire to kill" (Moody, *Dog Blood*, 11).

5. Boluk and Lenz, "Introduction," 9.

6. Moody, *Hater*, 275; emphasis mine.

7. Sloterdijk, *Rage and Time*, 9.

8. *Ibid.*, 10.

9. *Ibid.*

10. As the trilogy continues and, perhaps by narrative necessity, the Haters become more developed as characters, the unambiguity of being possessed wholly by rage gets passed to what are called the Brutes, an extreme form of Hater, unable to hold back from attacking the Unchanged even when their own death is certain: "[A] Brute wouldn't have held back. They can't. They catch a scent of Unchanged and they'll hunt them down and attack, no matter what the odds are" (Moody, *Dog Blood*, 42).

11. Moody, *Hater*, 7, 13, 20–22.

12. *Ibid.*, 24, 27.

13. *Ibid.*, 36.

14. *Ibid.*, 275.

15. Sloterdijk, *Rage and Time*, 61.

16. Moody, *Hater*, 269.

17. *Ibid.*, 270.

18. Sloterdijk, *Rage and Time*, 9–10.

19. *Hater* thus joins the very few zombie narratives that consider the zombie state as potentially positive. One notable character from the zombie canon who expresses the desire to be a zombie is Cholo (John Leguizamo) in Romero's *Land of the Dead* (2005), saying he wants to "see how the other half lives." Most characters, when confronted with the impending zombie state, prefer extinction.

20. Boluk and Lenz, "Introduction," 9.

21. Moody, *Hater*, 105.

22. *Ibid.*, 275–76; emphasis mine.

23. Moody, *Dog Blood*, 58; emphasis mine.

24. Harpold, "End Begins," 161.

25. Winlow and Hall, "Gone Shopping," 164.

26. For a description of and context for the riots, see Briggs, Introduction, 9–25; Briggs, "Frustrations, Urban Relations and Temptations," 27–41; and Winlow and Hall, "Gone Shopping," 163.

27. Winlow and Hall, "Gone Shopping," 153; emphasis mine.

28. *Ibid.*, 149, 154.

29. *Ibid.*, 156.

30. In the notion of the self "dropping away," I'm drawing on John Protevi: "in a blind rage the subject drops out" (Protevi, *Political Affect*, 145).

31. Winlow and Hall, "Gone Shopping," 162.

32. Moody, *Hater*, 25.

33. *Ibid.*, 159.

34. *Ibid.*, 26.

35. *Ibid.*, 56–57.

36. Winlow and Hall, "Gone Shopping," 154.

37. *Ibid.*, 153.

38. *Ibid.*; see also Briggs, "Concluding Remarks," 386.

39. Bauman, "London Riots."

40. Hall, "Saturday Interview."

41. Žižek, "Shoplifters of the World Unite."

42. Bauman, "London Riots."

43. Hall, "Saturday Interview."

44. Winlow and Hall, "Gone Shopping," 164.

45. Moody, *Hater*, 269.

46. For a discussion of consumer ideology in Romero's *Dawn of the Dead*, see Harper, "Zombies, Malls, and the Consumerism Debate"; Loudermilk, "Eating 'Dawn' in the Dark," 83–108; and Bishop, "The Idle Proletariat," 234–48.

47. Moody, *Hater*, 217.

48. Protevi, *Political Affect*, 149.

The Psychosomatic Zombie Man

The Postmodern Subject in Warm Bodies

Steven Holmes

The leitmotif of contemporary criticism on postapocalyptic narratives essentially comes down to Fredric Jameson's claim that "it is easier to imagine the end of the world than the end of capitalism."[1] George A. Romero's *Dawn of the Dead* (1978) is widely regarded as a critique of consumer culture,[2] so it makes sense that many subsequent postapocalyptic narratives have followed along similar lines. In the spirit of Romero, Isaac Marion's *Warm Bodies* (2010) seems to literalize Jameson's claim with an added degree of specificity: it is easier to imagine the end of the world than it is to imagine the end of personal property. Beyond strictly consumerist themes, Marion also explores the ends of marriage and love by playing on Shakespeare's *Romeo and Juliet*. Even among the undead, there is still wealth in brains.

Shifting the emphasis of the postapocalyptic narrative from the human survivors to the zombies means retaining much of the theoretical groundwork on postapocalyptic narratives. For example, Gerry Canavan characterizes necrofuturism as a way of describing narratives in which the future destroyed by capitalism seems to be the only possible future.[3] Marion actively avoids giving any indication of how or why the zombie outbreak in his narrative emerged, but the subtext of several passages suggests that indifference played a large role in it: "How did this start?" asks R, Marion's narrator, but he then accepts that no one knows—in fact, "No one talks about it much. We are here, and this is the way it is. We don't complain. We don't ask questions. We go about our business."[4] While this passage serves as a way of deflecting any hard and fast answer, the subtext reinforces the role of the indifferent accept-ance of change by impassive subjects.

Whereas necrofuturism characterizes the subtexts of *Warm Bodies*, Evan Calder Williams' concept of salvagepunk is appropriate for this text. Sal-vagepunk refers to narratives wherein production is no longer possible due to environmental collapse and life persists only through the salvaging of rem-nants of civilization.[5] This concept is appropriate for films like those in the Mad Max (1979–2015) franchise, in which heroes strap together whatever they can to keep their cars and lives together. Although *Warm Bodies* loses the phenomenal appeal of trying to maintain a car on deserted highways, it strips down this subgenre to its essence by considering the (un)life of a zom-bie. What more appropriate characterization of salvagepunk than to embody the narrative from the perspective of zombies, creatures who seem to subsist purely on scavenging for human brains and whose pure entertainment comes from salvaging the brains of humans as a kind of memory drug? Both necro-futurism and salvagepunk characterize narratives that present a futureless world.

Each of these theoretical frameworks characterizes a sort of multiva-lence, not quite indifference, toward the conditions of life in postmodern America. The hopelessness of the narratives risks doing nothing but numbing the audience, mitigating any reasonable concerns the narratives should evoke. If all the audience members are left with is despair, they probably will not be inclined to be proactive in changing the conditions of their lives. Multivalence means presenting the challenges at hand while avoiding the representation of total hopelessness. As a zombie Gothic romance, *Warm Bodies* captures these multivalent attitudes in an awkward synthesis of common metaphors. R is multivalent about being a zombie, since the implication is that he met many of the conditions of being a zombie before he died. The joke becomes pointed as R speculates on the cause of the end of the world: "War? Social collapse? Or was it just us? The Dead replacing the Living?"[6] Marion frames the zombies' consciousness around the sense that they "recognize civiliza-tion—buildings, cars, a general overview—but [they] have no personal role in it. No history."[7] R continues, "It's not that different from before."[8] That is, the undead experience of a zombie is not that different from the lived expe-rience of a modern subject. Both are detached from the means of production, architecture, and civilization itself. Just as the zombie has forgotten its identity, so has the living subject forgotten its place in history.

Marion's novel echoes the first sentence of Jameson's introduction to postmodernism, that it "is safest to grasp the concept of the postmodern as an attempt to think the present historically in an age that has forgotten how to think historically in the first place."[9] For Jameson, the cause of this inability to think historically is more clearly articulated than in Marion's fiction: it is a symptom of the age of late capitalism, when the expansion of the state sector and increasing bureaucratization "[seem] a simple, 'natural' fact of life."[10] The facts of life in postmodernity include an international division of labor (hence R's detachment from the means of production of cars and other products which he passively consumes), the emergence of changing banking and stock exchanges (R presumes he worked in a bank), computers and automation, and with these "the emergence of yuppies, and gentrification on a now-global scale."[11] R is the embodiment of this gentrified yuppie.

R has no memory of his life before undeath, but he recognizes enough to see that he is coded as a yuppie: "I must have been a businessman, a banker or broker or some young temp learning the ropes, because I'm wearing fairly nice clothes. Black slacks, gray shirt, red tie."[12] Audiences familiar with *Shaun of the Dead* (2004, directed by Edgar Wright) would have been well familiar with the idea that zombies can be largely indistinguishable from workers in supermarkets, bus riders, customers, and alcoholics—indeed, in that film, Shaun manages to go to the market and return home without even noticing the outbreak around him. Marion's novel builds on the themes of films such as *Shaun of the Dead* to suggest that the zombie state is preferable to the ahistorical banality of postmodern life and work: "Before, when I was alive, I could never have done this. Standing still, watching the world pass by me, thinking about nearly nothing. I remember effort. I remember targets and deadlines, goals and ambitions. I remember being *purposeful*, always everywhere all the time."[13] In contrast to this, R feels that after he becomes a zombie, the "world has been distilled. Being dead is easy."[14] This sentiment is the complicated converse to multivalence; Marion succeeds in avoiding a narrative so depressing that it breeds apathetic hopelessness. In doing so, he risks sending the message that the zombie existence is almost desirable and that the threat of complacency is minimal.

Warm Bodies is, like *Dawn of the Dead* before it, a critique of consumerism. But it lacks bite. It is a critique that never escapes the register of bland generality. At the beginning of the novel, R's home is the airport. R's zombie unlife is built around collecting scraps of detritus on a 747, material goods that he enjoys in isolation, detached from the history of those items, their production, and their meanings. Are his current circumstances (being a zombie) a consequence of his disconnection from more intimate and local social bonds? Perhaps, like architect and artist Rem Koolhaas, Marion is suggesting that the zombie infestation that has robbed R of his identity is a product (or byproduct) of the "junkspace" of the airport. Koolhaas partly defines junkspace (the concept is somewhat expansive) as the airports, the escalators, and endless buildings united by air conditioning. Junkspace is what is left in salvagepunk worlds. In characterizing the meretricious beauty of airports, Koolhaas argues that "[j]unkspace is overripe and undernourishing at the same time, a colossal security blanket that covers the earth in a stranglehold of seduction."[15] Being dead is easy in the same way that living in an airport, going through transit, is: distilled, and detached from history. Despite the elegance of the initial metaphor, Marion never develops the critique. Instead, the airport becomes just one more token of disaster porn. R observes how the "runways are turning green, overrun with grass and brush. Jets lie motionless on the concrete like beached whales, white and monumental. Moby Dick, conquered at last."[16] The allusion to Melville further reinforces the multivalence of the narrative. Not only does Marion play with the possibility that the threat of complacency is minimal, but he shows that there can be a kind of joy in seeing modernity collapsed. Insofar as the immensity of modern life can make individual subjects feel as though their individuality is irrelevant, the destruction of the conditions of modern life can be as jubilant as it is terrifying.

While the critique of consumer culture is clearly meant to be the main thread of Marion's novel, the driving force that led the narrative to commercial success was indubitably its exploration of heteronormative libidinal desire, although the novel is much more refracted in its commentary than the film adaptation (2013, directed by Jonathan Levine). One of the most perplexing elements of Marion's novel is the role of marriage. Between the Boneys—undead that have lost all semblance of humanity—and the Dead— the more traditional zombies—a set of rituals emerges to inscribe undead marriage. R, after meeting a zombie receptionist, has a nonsexual relationship with her but still has no qualms about characterizing her as his girlfriend despite admitting how their "new love is simpler. Easier. But small."[17] The nonsexual nature of R's relationship with his wife becomes even more apparent when R is compared to M.[18] M is R's best friend, his *only* friend, in undeath. M continues to attempt sex with various girlfriends, despite R's emphasizing that "[e]rotica is meaningless for us now. The blood doesn't pump, the urges don't stir."[19] The Boneys marry R and his wife, and the next day the Boneys deliver zombie children (this event is as mystifying to R as it is to the reader). After watching the zombie children play in a way that seems to reclaim some of the airport, R expresses a new feeling: "Deep inside me, in some dark and cobwebbed chamber, I feel something twitch."[20] R feels the first sparks of life infuse his body in the attempt to raise undead children. The reanimation of R is the crux of the novel's plot, and these children initiate that process. The transformation of the banal junkspace airport into a place of play and life marks the beginning of the rejection of undeath as R begins to see the means by which he can return to life.[21]

Despite the banality, explicit superficiality, and nonsexual nature— and even apparent infidelity—in R's marriage, by the end of the novel R continues to think of the secretary-zombie as his wife. His growing humanity is accompanied by his recovery of the ability to read and form words out of let-ters. As a consequence, he realizes, "If I ever see my wife again…. I'll at least be able to read her nametag."[22] That he thinks of her still as "my wife" is worth emphasizing. After R has abducted Julie and is holding her at the airport, she sees R's wife with another zombie, their hands woven together. Although this does not seem particularly sexual, handholding appears to be almost the entire basis of R and his wife's marriage. R, who continues his tryst with Julie, expects a rebuke from his wife but receives none. In his elliptical fashion, R explains that he wants the discovery of this infidelity to hurt, but it does not. *Warm Bodies* creates a satirical joke without a punchline, unless the premise itself is the punchline. Instead of developing the critique of consumerism that the opening of the novel seems to be leading into, Marion antagonizes modernist romance and marriage. He does this primarily through an antag-onistic, hypertextual relationship with William Shakespeare's *Romeo and Juliet*.[23]

Although the initial level of hypertextual relationships between *Romeo and Juliet* and *Warm Bodies* is undeniable, the connections are not wholly systematic. Some are unclear: Are the Montagues zombies? Are the humans Capulets? Others are undeniable: R is Romeo and Julie is Juliet. Some reject so much of the character that the analogy can feel purely nominal. For exam-ple, Perry is Julie's former boyfriend, a characteristic closer to Rosalind than Paris. He also serves as a foil for Romeo, and has the favor of Juliet's father, somewhat like Paris. Despite this similarity, R's dream-vision form of Perry eventually gives his blessing to R, so that their rivalry instead becomes a kind of collusion, a full flip from the murderous duel at the end of Shakespeare's text. M, as a confidant of Romeo, is somewhat similar to Mercutio. Like Ben-volio, M is a faithful and well-meaning supporter of R. Unlike Mercutio, M does not advocate for greater violence, one of Mercutio's definitive traits. Likewise, Grigio, who as Julie's father sometimes functions as Capulet, also picks up the role of Tybalt as instigator of violent conflict. No doubt Marion actively avoids characterizing his work as an adaptation in part because his novel favors a character economy that makes one-to-one parallels with Shake-speare's text messy. Yet he retains enough allusions to reinforce the themes of love and nostalgia.

The concept of love is at the center of Marion's climax in addition to being the point where Marion's novel most emphatically rejects Shakespeare's play: namely, the tragic ending. Marion's novel appears to be a classical com-edy, with the reconstitution of civilization and the rehabilitation of the zom-bies. The love of Romeo and Juliet leads to violence and death. At the end of Marion's novel, it seems as though R and Julie's love is what allows R's heart to begin beating again. Julie is not the sole driving force in the rehabilitation of R, and to dismiss the ending of *Warm Bodies* as hokey sentimentalism is to miss a few key points. R, in the final scene of the novel, insists that he is choosing to build his future on a new history; however, it is not totally clear that this means he intends to continue a sexual relationship with Julie. First, there is R's wife. While wandering the sterile, junkspace halls of the airport, she finds that the children have begun posting photos on the glass walls. She sees pictures of "[a] girl climbing an apple tree. A kid spraying his brother with a hose. A woman playing a cello."[24] These photos, or the rehabilitation of junkspace that their existence coincides with, free her from the curse.

Moreover, R's apparent love for Julie is also interrogated as a kind of nostalgic drug. R's love for Julie is first and foremost experienced as nostalgic love through the proxy of Perry. When R eats Perry's brains, he experiences Perry's memories and life. Before R ever sees Julie as a person, he experiences Perry's love for her. The experience is so visceral that it prompts R to reconstitute a sense of personal property. When M attempts to join R in consuming Perry's brains, R chooses to "shove M aside and snarl, 'No. Mine.'"[25] In the group hunting system that the zombies exhibit, resources such as brains seem to be first-come, first-served, although R and M also partake in brain gift-exchange later on.[26] R chooses to hoard some of Perry's brain so that he can return to his fix later on. In doing so, R effectively treats Perry's brains as a sort of drug, which he must keep safe in a hidden stash.

Brains for R and M are indeed a kind of drug, one that serves to simulate nostalgia. R's appropriation of Perry's memory cannot be called nostalgia in and of itself. R is not Perry. Instead, R's consumption simulates nostalgia for a life and time that R has never lived or at least cannot remember. To this extent, R's consumption of Perry's brain and the usurpation of his memories are closer, in a sense, to Jameson's figuration of the "nostalgia film" within postmodernity. According to Jameson, a nostalgia film evades the present and avoids the details of history by "losing itself in mesmerized fascination in lavish images of specific generational pasts."[27] Jameson does not exactly condemn nostalgia films for their displacement of the present. Rather, he sees them as a symptom of the postmodern subject's failure to understand its own identity. Whereas Jameson characterized nostalgia for the present, the simulation of nostalgia that R feels actually is more abstract and more parasitic than the nostalgia films that Jameson characterized. This is the point where the logic of Marion's narrative begins to come into conflict with most theoretical paradigms. R escapes his zombie state precisely because of his consumption of an addictive substance, the brain. R realizes some level of kinship with Julie because of the theft and destruction of Perry's memories. R's salvaging of brains most embodies the principles of salvagepunk and highlights the messiness of salvagepunk as a framework.

Williams describes salvagepunk as the "simple recognition that the world is now irrevocably structured as apocalyptic wasteland."[28] The world of *Warm*

Bodies is already lost, and, in recognizing that all conventional wisdom of ethicality is moot, R ironically manages to regain his humanity and hope. Yes, R killed Perry. Unlike Romeo, though, who simply moves on from the corpse of Paris toward his own doom, R salvages the corpse of Perry. R consumes Perry's brain, and, in doing so, R can forget the abject hopelessness of his situation and pretend to be Perry, and it is this admission to proxy, simulated nostalgia for a life he did not live, that allows R to escape the bounds of undeath. If the novel followed conventional wisdom, R would realize his own identity to gain some sort of relationship with Julie. Yet R is a parasite, an undead man with no personality. To say that R should realize his own identity is to misunderstand the extent to which his identity has been annihilated by the conditions of postmodernity. R has no identity to realize or recover. What Jameson presents as the symptom, Marion presents as the cure: nostalgia.

If Marion presents nostalgia as not merely a symptom, but as a site of opportunity and exploration, then the hypertextual relationship his text explores with Shakespeare's *Romeo and Juliet* becomes greater in significance. In particular, Marion explores the multivalence of nostalgia in the balcony scene. While Marion remarks in interviews that the relationship with Shakespeare is supposed to be "another layer, not really the central theme of the story,"[29] Jonathan Levine, the director of the film, insists that the "Romeo and Juliet thing was central to Isaac Marion's book."[30] The connection to *Romeo and Juliet* is most notable in the balcony scene, which remains one of the most iconic theatrical images. With Julie leaning on a balcony overlooking an out-of-sight R below, Julie apparently monologues: "What's in a name, right?"[31] Her contemplation parallels Shakespeare's Juliet's:

> O Romeo, Romeo, wherefore art thou Romeo?
> Deny thy father and refuse thy name …
> *What's in a name?* That which we call a rose
> By any other name would smell as sweet.[32]

In Shakespeare's text, Juliet is just as willing to abandon her name as she is demanding that Romeo abandon his: she would forsake being a Capulet as well. Julie in Marion's text is not asking that R reject being a zombie, but rather interrogating the usefulness of "zombie" as a descriptor for R when he exhibits cognizance and the capacity for language. Julie and R are constrained by a language that cannot express their being, emotions, or relationship.

While stripping Shakespeare's language is inevitable with the still mostly monosyllabic R, Marion further draws attention to the absurdity of monologue in modernity. Julie appears to be partaking in a monologue when she reflects on the balcony, but it is not a monologue. It is a recording, a way of journaling orally. The framing device for her thoughts, the recorder, is soon discarded: "'Fuck this thing,' she mumbles to herself. 'Tape journaling ... not for me.' She fast-pitches it off the balcony."[33] Julie's recognition of the awkwardness of the tape recorder highlights some tongue-in-cheek play with the idea of a Shakespearean monologue, but it also serves as a transition to R's reaction. R collects the tape recorder as a souvenir, indicating that he will return it to his home among his other miscellaneous possessions: at his 747. Whereas Julie felt that the artifice of oral personal reflection made her performance seem inauthentic, R extols oral language precisely because he cannot speak it. On the other hand, despite Julie's rejection of the artifice of tape journaling and the quasimonologue that the technology enabled, once again R buys into simulated nostalgia. His only regard for this object is that it once belonged to Julie. As a hypertext to Shakespeare's balcony scene, R and Julie's performance remains one-sided. R is incapable of the rhetorical and verbal wooing that characterizes Romeo in the balcony scene. The only contribution to the conversation that R can manage at this point is once again in the mode of nostalgia, in this case an allusion to the Beatles' "Hello, Goodbye." A system of hypertextual allusion creates multivalence in presentation and interpretation. Is Marion critiquing Shakespeare's script when his Julie rejects the idea of a soliloquy? Or is Marion critiquing contemporary subjectivity through the monosyllabic inability of R to communicate anything but his most basic desires? Hypertextual play allows Marion to seem to do both and neither.

The transformation of theoretical breakages is even more apparent in the hypertextual play of the nurse. In Shakespeare's text, the nurse has a complicated relationship with Juliet. At first, she enables and supports Juliet's relationship with Romeo. To the extent that the audience supports this relationship (as is generally the case), the nurse is an affable character—until Act 3, that is, after Romeo is banished. At this point, the nurse sides with the Capulets against Juliet, arguing that "I think it best you married with the County."[34] Since Romeo is indeed banished, some modern audiences might arguably see the nurse as practical, but within the context of early modern England, the nurse's about-shift on this matter results in her advising Juliet on a matter that would condemn her body and soul: engaging in bigamy. In Marion's text, the ambivalence in the nurse-character is gone. Instead of an older nurse, Nora is an aspiring nurse that is more friend than elder. In one scene, Julie attempts to convince her father, Grigio, of R's humanity. When Grigio rejects R's humanity and attempts to kill him, Nora turns her gun on Grigio.[35] Instead of proposing bigamy and therefore betraying Romeo, as Shakespeare's nurse does, Nora betrays Grigio (or Capulet) in defense of both Julie and R. Nora's reversal in character role here reinforces the thematic and generic shift that Marion works toward—a move away from tragedy and toward comedy. Whereas the nurse's abrupt transformation in Shakespeare's text reinforces the sense that Juliet truly has no remaining allies to turn to, heightening her paranoia, Nora's steadfast support in Marion's text reinforces the possibility of homosocial friendship to overcome the obstacles presented by familial and military authority, a common theme in comedy. So long as the audience accepts that R will indeed recover his humanity, as the comic tone of the novel suggests he will, then Nora is a sympathetic and loyal ally in protecting R against Grigio.

R, as a locus for the postmodern subject, is embodied in nostalgia and multivalence. This multivalence is realized in R's 747 airplane home. In the midst of the apparent balcony scene, R takes Julie's tape recorder and deigns to return it to his 747.[36] When R initially captures Julie, he introduces her to his home: "a 747 commercial jet. It's not very spacious, the floor plan is impractical, but it's the most isolated place in the airport and I enjoy the privacy."[37] The commercial jet remains R's home regardless of whether he gets married or has a tryst with Julie. R feels ambivalent about life at the airport and living on the plane. His memory is tingled by the nausea of packaged sandwiches; he also has faint recollections of "the fresh lemon zing of *poisson* in Paris. The burn of *tajine* in Morocco."[38] While R may feel disconnected from humanity on the 747, in the airport, as a zombie, he does not always experience this disconnection as reprehensible: being alone on the 747 also highlights the privacy of the emptied world.

It is not surprising that *Warm Bodies* is generally read as a supernatural romance hinging on erotic love between Julie and R, given that the climax of the narrative hinges on their magic, life-restoring kiss. This point evokes the archetypal logic of what Nathan Rabin has apologized for characterizing as the "manic pixie dream girl," wherein a female character swoops in to rescue a male character from depression and ennui.[39] Yet this framework is not wholly applicable to Julie. She is not particularly quirky. R is a psychosomatic zombie man: someone who needs any sort of libidinal recognition to transform from a monosyllabic brute to an idealistic hero. As R and Julie kiss in the climactic scene of the novel, "Our tongues taste each other, our saliva flows, and Julie bites my lip. I feel the death in me stirring, the anti-life surging toward her glowing cells to darken them. But as it reaches the threshold, I *halt* it."[40] Within Marion's narrative world, the detachment from modernity and history can be simply willed away by wanting to live more. The climax robs the narrative of the strength of its central metaphors.

The problems with the narrative are not with the premise or with the elegantly written opening chapters. What begins as a novel satirizing bourgeois ennui simply begins to capitalize on archetypal "princess and the frog" wish-fulfillment fantasy with the patronizing resolution that the zombie curse will be solved because the protagonists want it enough. Despite these issues, some characteristics of R and his road to recovery are worth considering. R does learn: he learns to be active and proactive as a result of participating in a simulated nostalgia. So while Marion's novel may be criticized for not presenting a more elegant or elaborate climax that builds organically off the framework of the opening chapters, Marion does recognize the power of hope. Dealing with fractured identities and ahistorical subjectivities, moving past salvagepunk, and avoiding a necrofuturistic future hinge on the belief that the world and the future do not always have to be so apocalyptic.

NOTES

1. Jameson, *Archaeologies of the Future*, 199. An earlier form of the claim appeared in Jameson's article "Future City" in 2003, but both cite the original phrase as being attributable to an anonymous and apocryphal "someone."

2. For instance, see Bishop, *American Zombie Gothic*, 130.

3. Canavan, "*Snowpiercer* and Necrofuturism," 48.

4. Marion, *Warm Bodies*, 8.

5. Williams, *Combined and Uneven Apocalypse,* 22–34.

6. Marion, *Warm Bodies*, 6.

7. *Ibid.*, 4.

8. *Ibid.*

9. Jameson, *Postmodernism*, ix.

10. *Ibid.*, xviii.

11. *Ibid.*, xix.

12. Marion, *Warm Bodies*, 4. In the film adaptation, R is unemployed—a change in his appearance and coding.

13. *Ibid.*, 9.

14. *Ibid.*

15. Koolhaas, "Junkspace," 176.

16. Marion, *Warm Bodies*, 9.

17. *Ibid.*, 10.

18. M introduces himself as Marcus at the end of the novel, but I will continue to refer to him as M for the sake of consistency.

19. Marion, *Warm Bodies*, 23.

20. *Ibid.*, 12.

21. This entire sequence is cut in the film adaptation, thrusting the hinge of the plot on the desire of R for Julie.

22. Marion, *Warm Bodies*, 189.

23. Gérard Genette characterizes hypertextuality as "any relationship uniting a text B to an earlier text A, upon which it is grafted in a manner that is not that of commentary." I use these terms in lieu of "appropriation" because appropriation has connotations of intellectual property that is immaterial to this discussion, and because "adaptation" connotes a greater degree of similarity than is pertinent here. Genette, *Palimpsests*, 5.

24. Marion, *Warm Bodies*, 237.

25. *Ibid.*, 19.

26. *Ibid.*, 24.

27. Jameson, *Postmodernism*, 296.

28. Williams, *Combined and Uneven Apocalypse*, 36.

29. Smith, "Interview with 'Warm Bodies' Author."

30. Woerner, "You're the Real Zombie."

31. Marion, *Warm Bodies*, 127.

32. Shakespeare, *Romeo and Juliet*, 2.1.76–87; emphasis mine.

33. Marion, *Warm Bodies*, 127.

34. Shakespeare, *Romeo and Juliet*, 3.5.217. The "County" refers to Paris.

35. Marion, *Warm Bodies*, 200.

36. R continues to regard the 747 as his home, despite having at this point begun to recover his humanity.
37. Marion, *Warm Bodies*, 22.
38. *Ibid.*
39. Rabin, "I'm Sorry for Coining the Phrase."
40. Marion, *Warm Bodies*, 223.

Feeding the Frenzy
Mira Grant's Feed

ARNOLD T. BLUMBERG

As most zombie genre aficionados know, we are witnessing the most sustained surge in popularity ever experienced by the various incarnations of the living dead, and that popularity has taken the zombie fully mainstream. From the dawn of the pop culture zombie in films that built on the creature's Haitian roots (including 1932's *White Zombie* [directed by Victor Halperin] and 1943's *I Walked with a Zombie* [directed by Jacques Tourneur]) and through Romero and Russo's reinvention of the monster as the now-familiar modern ghoul, zombies remained on the fringes of entertainment, favored by horror fanatics and susceptible to a cyclical rise and fall in exposure throughout the latter half of the twentieth century. Apart from a notable spike in awareness following the 1983 debut of Michael Jackson's *Thriller* video (directed by John Landis), zombie films were usually found only in the shadowy corner of the local video rental store, tucked away shamefully in a "Horror" section often placed adjacent to pornography. By the 1990s, things were particularly quiet in the graveyard, and it almost seemed as if the zombie might pass into history as a seldom-recycled figure akin to the mummy.

And then America was attacked by terrorists on September 11, 2001.

In quick succession, the perfect metaphor for fear, that reliable zombie and its myriad cousins, came roaring and running—yes, *running*—back into view via *28 Days Later* (2002, directed by Danny Boyle), cinematic video game adaptation *Resident Evil* (2002, directed by Paul W.S. Anderson), Robert Kirkman's *The Walking Dead* comic book series (2003–), and a remake of *Dawn of the Dead* (2004, directed by Zack Snyder). There was even an early indication of a future move toward domestication via *Shaun of the Dead* (2004, directed by Edgar Wright). By the time a major movie studio, Universal Pictures, decided to give the Father of the Modern Zombie his biggest budget to date, leading to the release of Romero's *Land of the Dead* (2005)—itself a relentlessly unsubtle commentary on the unbridgeable economic gulf in modern American society—zombies were an unstoppable horde marching ever closer to mainstream dominance. It would take one more major debut to tip things over and fully establish the Zombie Media Apocalypse in which we now live.

After the airing of the six episodes that constituted its first season in the fall of 2010, AMC's *The Walking Dead* television series adaptation (created by Frank Darabont) provided the last surge that the horde needed to establish itself as mainstream entertainment. More than six years later, the zombie continues to pop up in just about every form imaginable, unstoppable and endlessly fascinating to all who seek meaning in media. Back then, though, a few months before the show that would become the zombie genre's de facto "brand" for many consumers, Mira Grant's novel *Feed* (the first volume in the Newsflesh series) had already surpassed *The Walking Dead* in its ingenious metaphorical uses of the ubiquitous flesh-eating corpses when it hit bookshelves the previous April.[1]

Feed is ultimately a sharp study of early twenty-first-century American fear with the zombie, as ever, as our humanoid symbol of everything stalking us in our hearts and minds. Through her postmodern soapbox approach via the fictional construct of Georgina Mason's blog in the *Feed* universe, Grant reshapes the zombie narrative to engage the reader on current issues, equating the oncoming horde with fear fueled by terrorism and political rhetoric, the frontiers of modern news media, and the clash between radical religious faith and scientific fact.[2]

Long Live the Newsflesh

Grant[3] built her novel's world on a combined research effort that mixed equal amounts zombie cinema history with audited courses in epidemiology; in addition, the fight sequences that Grant presents as narrative were staged to guarantee a higher level of accuracy.[4] The cover of Grant's *Feed* throws down the gauntlet with a brilliant twist on what has become a common term and its associated icon. The blogging culture that serves as the underpinning for the novel's entire plot is reflected in the use of the RSS feed logo—two curved lines emanating upward and to the right from a dot-shaped origin point—but here rendered as if smeared in blood by the fingers of an undead monster or perhaps its dying victim. The title itself, *Feed*, plays on the obvious, convenient, but still satisfying double meaning of an RSS feed and the way we now send, receive, and consume vital information via Internet feeds, versus the more literal consumption of flesh that defines the post–1968

Romeroesque reanimated corpse. Consumption as a central metaphorical conceit of the zombie genre remains a powerful one here; Grant has merely traded the conspicuous consumption of the 1970s American mall shopper, enshrined by Romero's *Dawn of the Dead* (1978), for that of the similarly conspicuous and ubiquitous 24/7 screen-staring multimedia and Information Age consumers of the early twenty-first century.

Blending the tropes of a political techno-thriller with those of a post–Romero zombie world, Grant makes the most of both genres with sharp satirical jabs at much of our modern American media system and its inseparable interweaving with our increasingly laughable, commercially driven electoral process. In addition, *Feed* was initially a rare narrative (though there are now many others) that was actually set within a variant of our own reality, one that had a history of zombie pop culture and therefore a general awareness of what some of the rules of survival *might* be should the dead ever get it in their heads to rise up and chew on the living. Indeed, the world of *Feed* has a parallel version of Romero—Georgina was named after him—and Romero's sometimes flexible rules provide the most reliable template for survival after that world's Rising, or as Georgina refers to it, "the day Romero movies stopped being trashy horror and started being guides to staying alive."[5]

In the book, Georgina and Shaun Mason are adopted twin bloggers living in the post–Rising world of 2040. Everyone carries the Kellis-Amberlee virus—an accidental combined mutation of attempts to cure both the common cold and cancer—and although the zombie apocalypse has come and gone to a certain extent, society now abides by very specific rules in order to avoid another full-scale attack of the living dead. Almost anyone might "amplify" at any time and become a threat to family and friends, and medical testing kits and other equipment have become commonplace in order to monitor everyone's viral load. The blogosphere has experienced its own concurrent Rising, since bloggers were the outlets that reported on the initial outbreaks while the traditional press was caught in a delaying cycle of doubt and debate fueled by the need to adhere to internal rules.[6] The Masons are at the top of that heap, delighting their spotlight-seeking adoptive parents but maintaining a palpable level of pressure to preserve the integrity and quality of their content.

Despite their success, the Masons are somewhat surprised when Presidential hopeful and moderate Republican Senator Peter Ryman handpicks their team at the *After the End Times* website to follow him during his campaign, a journey that will lead to the death of Ryman's daughter, an escalation in zombie outbreaks deliberately engineered by a clandestine terrorist group with ties to surprisingly high levels of authority in multiple areas of the government, and the revelation of a right-wing religious conspiracy hoping to take down Ryman and force the country down a more theocratic path.

Fear Is a Powerful Motivator

From the outset, Grant meticulously shapes the world of *Feed,* eschewing subtlety in order to immerse the reader in that world and lay bare her thematic objectives. In an interview, Grant explains the distinction that she draws between fear—"Do not actually put your hand in the alligator"—and terror—"Avoid Florida entirely because alligators exist."[7] Throughout *Feed,* it is terror that Grant addresses most often, especially as it is employed in a specific political context by certain United States powers in the postapocalyptic world to utilize the zombie threat against their own fellow citizens. Grant's point is that the zombies are mere backdrop, with the "War on Terror"—more accurately called a "War *of* Terror"—and its proponents serving as the true enemy. The world of *Feed* may be one that lives in constant fear of another zombie surge, but of course it is *our* world, trained by government and media in sync with one another to perpetuate a culture of terror: "Fear makes people stupid.... From blood tests to gated communities, we have embraced the cult of fear, and now we don't seem to know how to put it back where it belongs."[8] It is through Georgina's blog posts that Grant clarifies the media's role in that atmosphere and makes use of her created world to instruct the reader about the one right outside their door:

> The people who have the power want you scared. They want you walking around paralyzed by the notion that you could die at any moment. There's always something to be afraid of. It used to be terrorists. Now it's zombies.... The truth is only scary when you think part of it might be missing ... so they do their best to sit on the truth, to sensationalize the truth, to filter the truth in ways that make it something you can be afraid of.[9]

All of this of course perfectly captures the experience of following twenty-four-hour news stations that focus on ideology over accuracy; the predominance of such biased coverage also explains the rise of racist demagogues that capture millions of votes and inch their way toward the highest office in the land by stoking the fires of fear in those who are ignorant of a truth that they have never heard or refuse to hear.

As with all of her thematic points, Grant is passionately crusading against such forces by employing her original zombie mythos to enlighten readers about the threats that exist even in our very own pre-apocalyptic world. As before, Georgina's blog provides a summation of Grant's observations about the media-manipulated clash between truth and fear and the consequences of that conflict. In one notable blog post, Georgina discusses the ways we gladly give up our freedom for the illusion of security, something painfully real in the post–9/11 era of the Patriot Act and unfettered NSA surveillance of American citizens: "We are a nation accustomed to being afraid…. People crave fear. Fear justifies everything. Fear makes it okay to have surrendered freedom after freedom, until our every move is tracked and recorded in a dozen databases…. We limit our potential day after day in the name of a safety that we refuse to ever achieve."[10] These polemical passages may seem a bit jarring because they temporarily halt the forward motion of the narrative, but they're the primary forum through which Grant directly communicates with her reader—that virtual soapbox where she can step up between sections of plot in order to realign us as to themes of the novel and the intent of her work. Some readers may find that Grant's approach entails a bit more didacticism than they care for in their fiction, but the driving force of the story and the well-defined characters that inhabit it make up for the very few times that Grant brings down the curtain for an instructive intermission. Naturally, it also makes sense for Georgina to be our viewpoint character in more ways than one—her eyes *look* zombie-like, giving her the ability to intimidate through fear, but also occasionally hampering her freedom since a glimpse of her in the wrong circumstances might lead people to conclude that she's amplifying. But as our central figure, Georgina sees through the eyes of a zombie[11] and a human all at once; she sees a greater truth.

Given Grant's use of a double meaning for the word "rise" in the phrase aimed at readers via the Masons' website, *When Will You Rise*, we can also rely upon the fact that *Feed* is as much a fierce call to action as it is an allegory utilizing the zombie metaphor. Perhaps by employing the genre to frame the issues, Grant stands a better chance of getting through to those who would otherwise willfully or inadvertently miss the point and go on with their lives, oblivious to the maelstrom of media manipulation that has reduced them to cogs in the American machine and little more than zombies themselves.

Print Is Dead

Grant's dissection of the media via her envisioning of a new blog-centric hierarchy of reporters and outlets—one of many things that she constructs in her detailed world-building—involves the introduction of a new online paradigm in which the Masons and their competitors employ staffs of variously assigned writers to craft the American narrative of the mid-twenty-first century.

The different classes of writing that constitute a well-balanced blog team are labeled via euphemisms that occasionally incorporate a comical nod by Grant to obvious pop culture inspirations. On opposite sides of the spectrum are the fact-based "Newsies" and the "Fictionals." The "Newsies" attempt to do for their audience what Walter Cronkite did for his viewers for nineteen years from his anchor's desk at the *CBS Evening News*, telling it "the way it is." The "Fictionals" offer a wide variety of stories and poems and other styl-ized works that take the facts of post–Rising life and comment creatively on that experience. Between these two, the "Stewarts"[12] report via a more sophis-ticated presentation of editorial opinion that interprets the facts and puts them into a specific context, the "Irwins"[13] thrill audiences via death-defying hijinks in which they deliberately place themselves in harm's way to give everyone a front row seat to the apocalypse, and the "Aunties" are a source of recipes, anecdotes, and home-style comforts that balance out the dangerous antics of the Irwins. Grant's crafty use of pop culture references in some of these labels not only helps to key readers in to the thematic meaning behind these classifications and their role in the blogging hierarchy, but also throws a spotlight on the *Feed* world's equally familiar usage of iconic celebrities to signify the importance and function of individual bloggers for postapoca-lyptic media consumers.

Devoted fan followings build for many of these reporter/celebrities, the Masons among them, just as many of our current crop of online stars emerged from the realms of YouTube, Instagram, and beyond. The act of accessing the post–Rising blogosphere's endless mass of material—itself an unstoppable horde of digital words and images—is characterized as an addiction, putting a new twist on the common zombie genre tactic of blurring the line between "them" and "us." "We," in this case, are a society of consumer-zombies so tethered to our feeds that we can barely survive without checking them. As we all now live in a world of smartphone-staring zombies shuffling in the streets and running into things, quite literally precipitating injurious and perhaps even fatal situations by virtue of their single-minded attention to their devices rather than their environment,[14] this parallel is not at all a stretch on Grant's part but rather a relevant way of commenting on yet another mod-ern media-driven phenomenon. Even Senator Ryman expresses a distinctly strained feeling not just in the wake of a traumatic occurrence, but because the incident has delayed his access to information, thereby exacerbating his addiction. As he observes, "I haven't had a site feed since the outbreak bell rang."[15]

In our world, we have—as Marshall McLuhan once said—extended our nervous systems outside our own bodies via our interconnected technology,[16] but more than that, we have outsourced our own processes of memory and nearly all interpersonal communication, giving over all control of our minds to a series of social media platforms and devices that enable us to document the myriad mundane details of our lives and broadcast them to a world of similarly tethered and zombified sharers of kitten pictures and selfies. Many now even experience a regular disruption in their natural sleep cycle from staring into a bright blue-lit screen while in bed and ostensibly preparing to rest but unable to detach from their virtual world. Some apps have even been designed to address this issue by modifying the color balance of screen lighting, but the need for such correction just points to a more profound effect on us and our culture. The nearly inescapable need to check our feeds at all hours of the day and night has been called an addiction by many experts, although the jury is decidedly still out on the issue.[17] If that need were amplified by an apocalyptic fear, would it not eventually consume us all?

If the people of the *Feed* universe are in some sense Internet zombies, they do have a genuine reason to be connected, and those that provide vital information have become the heroes of the post–Rising era. As James L. Stewart observes in his article "Zombies V. Newsies: Novel Offers Post-Apocalyptic Critique of Journalism," Grant's decision to make her lead characters a new generation of bloggers who are as obsessed with their Internet traffic as they are with fending off the hordes of human *and* animal undead (a variation on the Romero model, in which only human beings come back to "life") gives *Feed* one of its most powerful sociopolitical and cultural focal points. Through Georgina and Shaun, as well as their team, we see a seismic shift in trust as traditional media outlets are not just lacking in accuracy but indicted as contributors to the downfall of humanity in the wake of Kellis-Amberlee, unable to inform the public fast enough to stay ahead of the apocalypse. At the same time, those who were screaming warnings were ignored as those crazy kids on the Internet. In the aftermath, however, bloggers are not just the New Media, but the New Gatekeepers of the Truth, enabling their consumers to "triangulate on the truth" via multiple fast-paced points of view or via a helpful aggregating blogger "who does your triangulation for you."[18]

While Stewart warns that this observed superiority of bloggers and their coverage is perhaps a simplistic view of the dynamic between new and old news journalism, it's certainly worth considering that in a world of corporate-owned outlets that are more concerned with their own agenda and their bottom line than with any responsibility to their consumers, the independent voices—the Masons of the world—may indeed be the only place to turn for a clearer view of reality. Even if one disagrees with that assessment, the importance of this theme in *Feed* is that it employs our zombie friends as the perfect backdrop against which to play out the debate, thus demonstrating how Grant has employed those versatile rotting metaphors to tackle the latest cultural issues, even those that may not seem to lend themselves as readily to symbolic representation as the shambling hordes.

Care for the Body and Soul

In addition to the issues of terrorism and public fear, as well as the transition to a decentralized form of information dissemination mediated by the

Internet and led by a younger generation of social-media-savvy gatekeepers, *Feed* also depicts a world in which the very management of our daily health in the wake of Kellis-Amberlee has transformed the corporate medical world. Apple, ever the innovator and design champion, now makes the most popular viral load testing kits, because of course the iPhone users of the world would naturally be quite comfortable trusting their bodies with the company's sleek combination of effortless usability and stylish plastic and metal lines. But as the people of the postapocalypse take advantage of medical and technological innovation, issues of trust in science, faith in a higher power, and the conflict between those two viewpoints serve as vital source material for Grant's thematic exploration.

Although the *Feed* universe's understandable obsession with the monitoring of everyone's viral load has genuine practical benefits in that world, the omnipresence of portable and easily accessible medical technology also nicely mirrors the similar explosion of hand sanitizer usage during the post–9/11 anthrax attacks in the United States. In that case, the sudden and widespread presence of gel-dispensing stations in so many public spaces constituted little more than a psychological panacea, since there was really no way the use of such products would truly control the impact of an actual attack.[19] In *Feed*, however, the fear and medical mania that developed have at least provided the people living in a post–Rising world with a means of warding off another massive amplification. Moreover, the urgent requirement for controlling the situation sidesteps decades of debate regarding the minutiae of medical health coverage and availability of treatment, at least in part; after all, even in the apocalypse not all zombies are equal. The need to contain the possibility of another Rising does, however, settle some arguments with utter finality.

If the practical aspects of caring for one's body have been dealt with logically and somewhat effectively by the inhabitants of the *Feed* universe, the issue of one's soul is still highly contentious. One of the things that I've always found intriguing about the more supernaturally based zombie stories is the suggestion that the dead are returning via some unnatural means beyond the realm of human technology and scientific principles. Such stories, while dark and frightening, also imply that the forces of light, like some form of a God who balances out the demonic powers at work in the apocalypse, must also exist. And of course, were we to experience a purely real-world, scientific phenomenon that led to the resurrection of the dead as Kellis-Amberlee does in *Feed,* we would still have to deal with many people whose religious convictions would force them to interpret the end of the world in line with their own mythology. And then, where would such misconceptions lead?

Grant gives us a potent example of just that kind of danger in misconstruing the origin of the zombie apocalypse via Governor David Tate, the man at the forefront of the conspiracy to steer America along more faith-based lines by reigniting the zombie threat and increasing the level of fear that already has the country in near total sociopolitical paralysis. Tate is a broadly sketched but recognizable rabid caricature of a far-right religious maniac that has perverted the concept of faith in a higher power in order to justify horrible actions toward his fellow human beings. In this case, the zombies become little more than pawns employed by living individuals seeking power over others by using their own fears against them, falling back into a slavish role not unlike early zombies at the dawn of their pop culture career.[20]

Beyond the Grave

As Brooks Landon notes, the need for zombies in our popular discourse is partly driven by the need for a visible target[21]; we may not be able to root out the terrorists that lurk in global shadows, or resolve the many other issues that make us afraid, but we can see the hordes of the undead marching toward us, and we can do something about it … as long as we know the rules. Zombies can serve to externalize, rationalize, and even heartily endorse hatreds deeply ingrained in our psyches—the "other" may be another race, nationality, or sexual orientation, but the zombie can stand in for every one of those and more. The satisfaction that we experience by capping a few in the head via a first-person-shooter video game, or vicariously in an action-packed feature film, provides an undeniable catharsis that has implications both good *and* bad. And for many, the very notion of the apocalypse itself is comforting—you won't need to worry about the rent when the world ends.

The twenty-first-century zombie is, like *The Avengers'* (2012, directed by Joss Whedon) Loki, "burdened with glorious purpose." Zombies carry with them a significant burden; perhaps that's why many (but not all) of them shuffle so laboriously. With every appearance, we expect them to drag in innumerable allegorical associations that allow them to reveal aspects of our own nature via their dark-carnival mirror reflections of us. Those unwavering expectations have led to countless zombie stories that desperately claw for meaning with little to no success, or worse, hammer away at a thematic point with no subtlety and less effect; even Romero himself is not immune to that failing. But there are occasions, rare though they may be after so much exploration in the genre, when an author manages to direct the horde in a new and enlightening direction. Mira Grant's *Feed* takes well-worn tropes and amplifies them into cogent, compelling cultural commentary that is as vital as it is relevant.

There's life in the old zombie yet.

NOTES

1. In fact, that very August, my University of Baltimore college course in "Zombies in Popular Media" launched, garnering worldwide press coverage as one of the first full-semester offerings at an American university that explored the sociopolitical and cultural themes of zombie narratives from a media literacy/critical thinking perspective. As far as can be determined, the only previous such course was one offered by Columbia College in Chicago, which had started in 2008.

2. The Newsflesh series continued with two additional volumes, *Deadline* (2011) and *Blackout* (2012)—all three were nominated for Best Novel Hugo Awards but lost to competitors—as well as supplementary stories and even *Fed* (2012), a far bleaker alternate ending to *Feed*. An anthology titled *Rise: A Newsflesh Collection* (2016), comprising two novellas and eight short stories, gathers all of the material not included in the three main volumes.

3. "Mira Grant" is a pseudonym for prolific fantasy author Seanan McGuire. As McGuire explains in the FAQ on her website: "I wanted a pseudonym for my science fiction because I wanted to create some 'distance' between it and my urban fantasy work. Mostly, I wanted people to judge the Mira Grant books on their own merits, not based on how much they read like something they'd expect me to write" (McGuire, "Writing FAQ"). Nevertheless, her identity did not remain secret for long, and since the success of the Newsflesh series, McGuire has maintained the use of the *nom de plume* with a knowing wink to her readership (I'll continue to use it here for purposes of clarity).

4. Grant, *Feed*, 580.

5. *Ibid.*, 538.

6. As Grant explains, "the 'real' media were bound by rules and regulations, while the bloggers were bound by nothing more than the speed of their typing" (*Ibid.*, 48).

7. *Ibid.*, 580.

8. *Ibid.*, 186.

9. *Ibid.*, 346.

10. *Ibid.*, 428.

11. Georgina has "retinal Kellis-Amberlee," a variation of the zombie-causing disease referred to as a "reservoir condition," in which the virus is contained in the eyeballs but does not necessarily spread to the rest of the body or turn the victim into a zombie. As a result of her condition, Georgina wears sunglasses to protect her extremely sensitive eyes from light, but she occasionally takes her glasses off to strike terror into the hearts of anyone who might see her "black, almost emotionless stare" and assume that she could be dangerous. Her eyes are thus zombie-*like* and useful as a tactical advantage; she doesn't truly see differently from how uninfected people see, but I refer here to her "seeing through the eyes of a zombie" in order to highlight Grant's decision to give her protagonist that condition as a clever metaphorical gambit.

12. The "Stewarts" are named after Jon Stewart, the longest-running host (1999–2015) of Comedy Central's political satire and commentary program, *The Daily Show*.

13. The "Irwins" are named after the late Stephen Robert "Steve" Irwin, otherwise known as "The Crocodile Hunter" (which was also the title of his television series). A conservationist and wildlife expert, Irwin frequently put himself in danger to educate and entertain; it eventually cost him his life.

14. For one of many examples of commentary on this psychological phenomenon, see Hyman, "Texting Zombies."

15. Grant, *Feed*, 554.

16. See McLuhan, *Understanding Media*.

17. The debate rages on, with some studies purporting to show addictive behavior akin to similar conditions caused by drug or alcohol usage, while others caution that this is overstating the case. One recent study by the PEW Research Center likened social media interactions to reward-based behavior that stimulates the brain's pleasure center. See Cohen, "New Study."

18. Grant, *Feed*, 50.

19. For some hard science on the issue, see "Show Me the Science."

20. In one of my favorite films, the 1971 adaptation of Richard Matheson's landmark 1954 novel *I Am Legend*, titled *The Omega Man* (directed by Boris Sagal), Charlton Heston's incarnation of the book's Robert Neville faces a particularly nasty form of religious zealotry via the infected horde known as the Family. Their leader Matthias (Anthony Zerbe) has taken on a traditional voodoo master's role in manipulating his zombie-like Family followers— little more than zombies—by encouraging their belief in themselves as anointed by God, charged with cleansing the world of humanity and its apocalyptic mistakes. There are parallels among Matthias, Tate, and other deranged leaders who use religion as a weapon on their own people in a war against another group and/or ideology.

21. Landon, "Is Dead the New Alive?" 8.

Teaching Zombies, Developing Students

Pedagogical Success in
The Girl with All the Gifts

KYLE WILLIAM BISHOP

With the ongoing popularity of AMC's *The Walking Dead* (2010–present) television series, few can question the zombie figure's continued mass appeal. In fact, these days, zombies can be found everywhere, transcending their once isolated place in obscure B-movies to appear not only on prime-time television, but also in the pages of books, in various apps and video games, down toy aisles, and even in the university classroom. It is not surprising that this popular proliferation has made fans both old and new hungry for zombie protagonists, updated versions of the monster that can think for themselves, make conscious choices, and even "live" sympathetic lives. While I find many manifestations of this so-called "agent zombie"[1] illogical and problematic—especially the unlikely zombie lotharios featured in recent paranormal romance novels[2]—some creative and inventive authors are finding more plausible ways to crack this elusive nut. Thanks to the first-person narration and free indirect discourse available to writers of literary fiction, agentic zombies appear with more frequency in short stories and novels than in movies and on television, and the most compelling zombie protagonist I've encountered can be found in the pages of M.R. Carey's captivating 2014 novel *The Girl with All the Gifts*.[3]

Carey's revisionist zombie tale takes place in a devastated postapocalyptic England, a country that has been all but decimated by the virulent spread of the *Ophiocordyceps* fungus. Taking marked liberties with the zombie monster codified (albeit inadvertently) by George A. Romero and his films, *The Girl with All the Gifts* imagines a scenario in which the now infamous "zombie ant" fungus has mutated to infect human beings, with most of the human population already long overpowered by this natural mycological agent by the opening of the novel. As seen in the real entomological world, the plague of Carey's narrative thus results in (re)animated "infected" zombies, not the traditional "walking dead."[4] The revenants of *The Girl with All the Gifts* continue to be driven by their instinctual biological programming, but, in an even more innovative twist, they not only consume human flesh, as in the Romero oeuvre, but also copulate and reproduce. The hybrid offspring of these infected "hungries," as they are known in Carey's novel, represent a new kind of zombie, living creatures that look human and have the capacity to think and learn and even love; yet as symbiotes forever partnered with the *Ophiocordyceps* fungus in their brains, they undeniably represent a new species, one that thirsts for blood and hungers for flesh. However, thanks to the tutelage of a dedicated schoolteacher, one of these "new zombies" comes to represent the "Eve" of her kin, a young girl whose unique subjective and intellectual development is central to the narrative course of the novel.

Carey's use of free indirect discourse, which shifts primary perspective from chapter to chapter, allows readers access into the minds of the protagonist characters, characters who regularly refer to the novel's titular "girl" in a variety of telling ways. For example, Caroline Caldwell, the myopically driven and even megalomaniacal scientist, hardly ever thinks of the young zombie girl as anything other than "test subject one," and Sergeant Eddie Parks, the soldier struggling to lead the group of survivors to safety, clinically calls her a "hungry" or "the hungry kid." Only Helen Justineau, a teacher enlisted by the military to instruct a cohort of infected children, consistently calls her by her given name: Melanie. While the first two, at least initially, use dismissive objectification in their attempts to render Melanie a thing, a monstrous Other, Helen Justineau—tellingly a *teacher*—recognizes the liminal girl's consciousness and her intellectual potential, allowing Melanie to recognize her subjective self in turn.

In other words, Carey has crafted a new zombie, an effective agent possessing self-consciousness because of the powerful force of an invested, student-centric pedagogy. Justineau's willingness to recognize Melanie as an individual, as more than just part of a mindless zombie horde, fulfills G.F.W. Hegel's dialectic process of establishing self-identity and subjectivity. Furthermore, through her efforts to instruct Melanie, Justineau guides her into Lacan's symbolic order, allowing her to complete a latent mirror stage and develop further into a self-perceived and actualized individual. Finally, by repeatedly and consistently defying the coarse stereotypes projected upon Melanie by the other human survivors in the novel, Justineau allows her young charge to overcome what psychologist Claude M. Steele calls "stereotype threat,"[5] a side effect of the unjust labeling of a group and its members proven to stifle intellectual development. In other words, *The Girl with All the Gifts* is more than just a zombie novel; I read it as a pedagogical cautionary tale that shows how teachers must recognize the subjectivity of their students while avoiding objectifying labeling and stereotyping for their students to learn, grow, and develop to the best of their natural abilities.

Subjective Development in the Agentic Zombie

It is quite telling that the first sentence in *The Girl with All the Gifts* is "Her name is Melanie."[6] Although the initial chapter goes on to describe Melanie in some detail, that description begins, first and foremost, with her name—or at least the name that has been assigned her. And while the literal meaning of the name Melanie, "the black girl,"[7] has little descriptive significance—at least not literally—the very act of giving a zombie a proper name begins the novel's gradual process of developing Melanie's identity beyond merely that of a ravenous monster. But Carey's Melanie is certainly not the first zombie protagonist, the first agentic zombie, or even the first zombie with a name—a name significantly used by the human characters as a form of subjective identification. One could trace Melanie's fictional lineage back to Bub (Sherman Howard) from Romero's *Day of the Dead* (1985), arguably the first zombie in the Romero tradition to show signs of cognition (but certainly not the last), a subjective cognition that results not just from his having a name, but also from the pedagogical efforts of a teacher who recognizes him dialectically as an individual being.

Bub's development as an individual zombie instead of just part of a mindless horde results from his dialectical engagement with Dr. "Frankenstein" Logan (Richard Liberty), a desperate man obsessed with the idea that zombies can be taught, trained, and conditioned to regain something of their humanity. He begins this process of domestication by naming his most promising test subject "Bub," the nickname by which his own father had once been known. Logan thus not only treats Bub as an individual subject, but also engages with the creature at the level of familial intimacy. In his *Phenomenology of the Spirit*, Hegel famously theorized the development of the individual—of the human "self-consciousness"—through the dialectical interactions of two distinct entities. He states, "Self-consciousness exists in and for itself when, and by the fact that, it so exists for another; that is, it exists only in being acknowledged."[8] Indeed, the individual *cannot* exist in isolation; only when one self-consciousness is confronted by another self-consciousness does subjective identification occur. The other thus acts somewhat like a Lacanian mirror, most effectively by mutual recognition: "They *recognize* themselves as *mutually recognizing* one another," a "moment of recognition" that arises from confrontation.[9]

Logan insistently allows Bub to recognize himself (or at least recognize who he once was) by encouraging him to recognize others, often via confrontation. In addition to interacting with Logan directly, without the interference of safety protocols, Bub recalls specific human behavior—such as throwing a salute and cocking, aiming, and firing an unloaded pistol—when he sees Captain Rhodes (Joe Pilato) in uniform. As the film progresses, Bub becomes even more of a self-motivated individual by pursuing the things he wants, including classical music, human flesh, and revenge for Logan's murder. Indeed, Bub's development as an agentic zombie arises largely from these kinds of subjective desires—he regains a sense of his human self because of what he *wants* (or, at least, what he *remembers* wanting). In his detailed analysis and commentary on Hegel, Alexandre Kojève describes the mutual recognition and confrontation of the human dialectic in terms of *desire*: "It is in and by—or better still, as—'his' Desire that man is formed and is revealed—to himself and to others—as an I, as the I that is essentially different from, and radically opposed to, the no-I. The (human) I is the I of a Desire or of Desire."[10] The dialectical process ensures, therefore, that "the human being is formed only in terms of a Desire directed towards another Desire, that is—finally—in terms of a desire for recognition."[11] Only through this mutually expressed desire can the self be recognized as an individual, actualizing one's self-conscious "I."

Logan's attempt to recondition Bub as an individual subject mirrors that of a desirous teacher, one who will go to great lengths—often with little confirmation of success—to achieve a desired pedagogical outcome. An even more overtly dedicated "zombie teacher," and one that clearly stands as an important antecedent for Carey's novel, can be found in the character of Ms. Geiss from Dan Simmons' progressive zombie short story, "This Year's Class Picture" (1992). Like Logan, Geiss comes across as more than a little mentally imbalanced, coping with the realities of a zombie apocalypse—what Simmons calls "the Tribulations"[12]—via an obsessive dedication to rehabilitative education. Geiss is an aging elementary school teacher, one who has survived the destruction of human society by converting her school building and its grounds into a well-protected and defensible fortress. Knowing little beyond her passion for educating fourth graders, apparently, she has risked everything to corral twenty-two dead children into her classroom, where she diligently and tirelessly strives to educate them as if they were living human children—after pulling their teeth and chaining them in place, of course. At the beginning of Simmons' story, Geiss welcomes a twenty-third child into her class, a young zombie boy whom she arbitrarily names "Michael," as she has given all of her dead charges unique names.[13] Like Logan, then, Geiss recognizes that the first, essential step to encouraging the development of a being's subjectivity is through naming, as naming defies the thing, defies the monster.

Beyond this recognitive act of naming, Geiss—again, like Logan before her—primarily approaches zombie education via conditioning, a series of repetitive acts designed to encourage cognitive development—or, at least, remembered human knowledge and behavior. Geiss somewhat stubbornly follows her established curriculum, conducting daily lessons in math and geography, and she reads to them in the hope that some spark of awareness will light up the dead children's eyes. Despite her best efforts with classic literature such as *Goodnight Moon*, the students "did not respond," for while they had ears, they "did not hear."[14] After miraculously defending the school from what appears to be a coordinated and organized attack by the walking dead, an attack that both evidences frightening new behavior on the part of the zombies and convinces Geiss that the adult dead are trying to "rescue" the dead children,[15] she decides her only course of action is letting her charges back out into the wild of the apocalypse. Simmons' zombies show no agentic traits or behaviors, and they certainly don't speak, but, in the unexpected conclusion to his short story, they do prove Geiss' efforts were *not* in vain after all, that the dead might indeed be taught, be reconditioned, be developed into autonomous subjects. The freed zombie children return to their classroom on their own volition, taking their seats and waiting, somewhat peacefully, for their lessons to begin.[16] A good teacher, Simmons seems to speculate, is all it takes to overcome the horrors of the zombie plague.

While *The Girl with All the Gifts* follows in the shambling footsteps of proto-sentient zombies such as Bub and Michael, the novel is far from a typical zombie narrative, be that one founded in appropriated Haitian Vaudou folklore or in the "living dead" scenarios devised by Romero. Nevertheless, Carey's book exists firmly in the postapocalyptic infection tradition. Set primarily in the "Region 6" division of England, which is somewhere just north of London, the narrative begins years after the deadly fungal pathogen has wiped out most of the human population of the island, and, implicitly, the rest of the planet, in what the survivors call "the Breakdown."[17] The myopic scientist Caldwell explains how a deadly pathogen mutated from the parasitic fungus *Ophiocordyceps unilateralis*, which "hot-wires" ants' neurological systems in the cause of the fungus' highly specialized reproductive cycle. Referencing an actual David Attenborough documentary,[18] Caldwell recounts the very real biological process through which the fungal spores infect an ant, force it to lock itself on the underside of a leaf with its own mandibles, and kill the host by forcing a "phallic sporangium" out the back of the ant's head to rain more spores on the unsuspecting ants below.[19] Luckily, the gestation and developmental cycle of this mutated *Cordyceps* is so long that the infected hosts have yet to form germinating structures, so the only way the infection can be transmitted is through "blood and sweat and spit and tears"[20]—in other words, through the bite of a "hungry," as in the more regularly recognized zombie narratives.

Yet, over time, the rough network of survivors—organized by the military around their holdout capital Beacon in the south of England—begin noticing infected *children*, and the behaviors of these children differ greatly from those of their adult kin. For starters, they can think and be taught to communicate, and while the infestation of the fungus can be found in every portion of their bodies, their behavior is remarkably similar to that of human children—with one notably dangerous difference: when confronted with pheromones from living animals, the children lose control of their higher cognitive functions, becoming ravenous monsters that bite and tear and rend. Their liminal state encourages scientists such as Caldwell to study them in hope of finding a cure, a way to reverse the fungal infection. And while Caldwell examines their physical structures, particularly their brains, Justineau, along with a team of other teachers, instructs the children in a remarkably normalized classroom setting, testing and exploring the hybrid zombies' cognitive abilities—with more direct interaction and visible success than Geiss ever enjoyed. In other words, the scientists cut them up, the teachers educate them, and the military keeps everything in check—at least initially.

Melanie is the top student in this unusual cohort of young pupils, which also makes her "test subject number one."[21] Like Bub, Melanie is a very special rat in a very special cage, but her humanity manifests through her obsession with naming things and learning names—indeed, she almost obsessively uses labeling to understand the world around her.[22] Like the mythological "Pandora," whose name she covets,[23] Melanie is driven largely by curiosity, a curiosity that is sated largely by knowing what things are called; she is particularly enamored of proper names. Her otherwise antagonistic relationship with Sergeant Parks changes, for example, when she learns he has a first name, "The same way the teachers do. The same way the children do. Up until now, Sergeant has been more like a god or a Titan to Melanie; now she knows that he's just like everyone else, even if he is scary. He's not just Sergeant, he's Sergeant Parks."[24] Names define a thing, define a *person*, and since Melanie has a name, she knows she has a subjective identity: "[W]henever she can manage it, she asks Miss Justineau questions, because what she most likes to hear, and to remember, is Miss Justineau's voice saying her name, Melanie, in the way that makes her feel like the most important person in the world."[25] When Justineau uses Melanie's name, she recognizes her in a Hegelian sense, an acknowledgment of self-consciousness apart from the collective.

While so many popular zombie narratives propose a course of action on the part of the surviving humans that consists almost exclusively of violence, destruction, and extermination, the alternative generic tradition developed from *Day of the Dead* to "This Year's Class Picture" to *The Girl with All the Gifts* presents fans with an alternate approach. These texts challenge the more popular notion that all zombies are mindless monsters, creatures that can only kill and feed and procreate through their deadly bites. Instead, these tales optimistically suggest that the best kind of hero in a zombie apocalypse is not a hardened soldier or an innovative scientist but a *teacher*, someone patient and dedicated enough to focus on the individual zombie and its individual potential. While training and conditioning are certainly key in these imagined approaches, the pedagogical efforts of these educators are founded on the relatively simple act of naming, an interactive, dialectical act that necessitates essential interactions between two individuals, desirous interactions that invariably lead to personal development and positive, nonviolent progress.

Stereotype Threat in the Zombie Apocalypse

Steele's theory of stereotype threat focuses on how "societal stereotypes about groups can influence the intellectual functioning and identity development of individual group members."[26] He and his fellow researchers were particularly interested in how stereotype threat affected success in school, and they sought connections between academic achievement, individual self-definition, and personal identity.[27] While Steele's studies and experiments focused primary on the academic performance of women and racial minorities, the theory also has value in a critical reading of *The Girl with All the Gifts*. For example, Melanie begins the novel as the "number one" academic performer in a group of similarly coded students, she spends the middle of the novel identifying (negatively) with the virulent hungries that plague humanity, and she finishes the novel having (rightly) identified herself as the leader of the new generation of human/fungus hybrids. Throughout her journey, then, Melanie wrestles with a variety of stereotype threats—both internal as well as external—which Steele formally defines as "a situational threat—a threat in the air—that, in general form, can affect the members of any group about whom a negative stereotype exists."[28] Because Melanie cannot help identifying herself with domains about which relevant stereotypes exist, as the humans with whom she interacts repeatedly emphasize, she finds herself in various self-threatening situations.[29]

During the course of the novel, Melanie engages directly with three humans who represent different castes of society and who all stereotype her differently because of her inclusion in the group of hungry children. These stereotypes are most commonly revealed by the ways in which those disparate characters refer to the infected humans, the other children, and Melanie herself. As I have said, names and naming are fundamentally important to the story of *The Girl with All the Gifts*, and most of the story is told from her perspective; but whenever the narrative shifts its free indirect discourse to the perspective of another character for the first time, that portion of the novel begins by clearly naming the person: the second paragraph of Chapter 4 begins with "Helen Justineau," the first sentence of Chapter 7 includes the identifying words "Caroline Caldwell," and Chapter 12 opens with "Eddie Parks."[30] Indeed, in most of the chapters in which the free indirect discourse focuses on a character *other* than Melanie, the full name of that character is restated on the first page.[31] By deploying this narrative style and strategy, Carey gives readers direct access to the different characters' psyches and insights into their particular stereotypical biases, particularly vis-à-vis Melanie.

Manifesting a scientific expectation for clinical distance, Caldwell unsurprisingly objectifies the hungries in terms of how they serve her research. She generally refers to the children only by their assigned numbers, calling Liam "Sixteen" and Marcia "Twenty-two," for example, although she does once refer to Melanie—"number one"—as "[o]ur little genius."[32] Indeed, Caldwell stringently rejects the idea of giving a hungry a name because "though it speaks and can even be christened with a boy's name or a girl's name, [it] is not the host. It's the parasite."[33] To her, the ability to look, speak, move, and even possess a beating heart does not constitute life; she sees the children only as corpses animated by the infesting fungus. While Caldwell generally does call Melanie by her given name to her face, she *thinks* of her as "a living sample," "the test subject," and a "specimen."[34] In other words, Caldwell coldly objectifies Melanie as nothing more than a thing: "The girl is part of my research," she tells Parks. "She belongs to me."[35] She never treats Melanie as a child; indeed, she doesn't even recognize her as a person—as her thwarted attempt at vivisection makes abundantly clear[36]—and her disparaging labeling results in a Melanie who understandably does not trust her.

After an organized gang of marauders overruns the Hotel Echo military base, the unlikely alliance of Parks, Gallagher, Justineau, Melanie, and Caldwell heads south towards Beacon. Traveling through London, they have a number of unexpected encounters with the hungries, and Caldwell must revise her understanding of the creatures they are dealing with, determining that the infected humans can exhibit three distinct states of being: a rest state, in which they stand stock still; a hunting state, in which they move quickly and relentlessly after their prey; and a "state that corresponds to a degraded version of normal consciousness" in which they can "interact with the world around them, fitfully and partially, in ways that echo their behavior before they were infected."[37] This third state recalls other zombie narratives, notably

Romero's *Land of the Dead* (2005), in which the living dead demonstrate a level of agentic consciousness based largely on remembered behavior. In *The Girl with All the Gifts*, of course, Melanie exhibits none of these three states, indicating from the very beginning of the novel that she is something more than a regular hungry, which explains Caldwell's near obsession with the girl. Once confronted by the infected children "in the wild," Caldwell refers to them variously as "monsters" and "creatures" as well as "hungries."[38] And when Melanie corners her near the end of the novel (and at the end of Caldwell's life), the doctor thinks of her as "this hectoring monster child" and, in self-aggrandizing scientific terms, as "*Ophiocordyceps caldwellia*."[39] To the end, in other words, she obstinately refuses to recognize Melanie's subjectivity.

In a similar fashion, Parks also thinks of the hungries only in negative terms, but, unlike Caldwell, he revises his attitude as his interactions with Melanie affect his understanding of her identity. He first calls Melanie "[l]ittle bitch" and later, sarcastically, "sugar plum"; when she challenges his authority concerning Justineau, he calls her "you little roach" in anger.[40] He refers to the collective group of children as "you little bastards" and "these frigging little abortions," but when referencing anyone else infected by the fungus, he usually uses the more official term of "hungry"—occasionally, though, the "don't-know-they're-dead."[41] He also thinks of the infected children as "the weird kids," "spooky little monsters," "kid-shaped monstrosities," or, most commonly, merely "the hungry kids."[42] Despite his misgivings, however, he *does* recognize that these child hungries are different: "the light inside their heads didn't go out, for some reason—or not all the way out … [t]he kids got stuck halfway."[43] As Caldwell will confirm at the end of the novel, these "hungry kids" are liminal creatures, both infected and human at the same time.

After fleeing Hotel Echo, even though Parks recognizes that Melanie is in Justineau's care, he generally continues to think of her in negative terms, such as "the nightmare-that-walks-like-a-girl" or "the monster."[44] However, when Melanie unthinkingly puts herself between Parks and a pair of menacing hungries midway through the novel, undoubtedly saving his life by misdirecting them with her scent,[45] his thoughts of the girl begin to change. As he reflects on the event, he wonders if "the kid" knew what she was doing and admits to himself that "he was screwed, and the kid unscrewed him," dropping the adjective "hungry" from his identifier—at least occasionally.[46] At one point, he even refers to Melanie as "a smart kid" to Justineau,[47] exhibiting more confidence in the girl's loyalty to the group than her former teacher does. He comes to trust Melanie—to a certain extent—and actually begins to respect her as a subjective being. Parks promises to protect the girl from Caldwell, for example, and Justineau realizes "he recognises Melanie as an ally, at least for now, and won't let her be hurt."[48] In other words, Parks puts Melanie to *work*, making her a contributing part of the team, thus strengthening her perception of her own subjectivity.[49]

Steele's research has produced a number of "wise strategies" to help combat stereotype threat, strategies that manifest variously in *The Girl with All the Gifts*. For example, he emphasizes the need to challenge stereotyped communities rather than remediate them. He claims that "giving challenging work to students conveys respect for their potential and thus shows them that they are not regarded through the lens of an ability-demeaning stereotype."[50] As Parks begins to realize—reluctantly—the kind of asset Melanie could be to the group, he agrees to let her off her preventative leash so she can venture out on her own. Nonetheless, her ability to survive among the hungries *and* show familiar loyalty to the group of uninfected humans perplexes him: "Parks stares at her for a moment, like she's something written in a language he doesn't speak."[51] Parks does call Melanie "Lassie" at one point, referencing her service to the group as a tracker, but it's clearly meant as a term of endearment.[52] By the end of the novel, after Parks has been infected by a feral child attack, he treats Melanie with the affection of a father, playfully threatening to send her to bed early and telling her if he and his wife *had* had a daughter, she might have looked like Melanie.[53] The responsibility she enjoys because of his confidence and his change in attitude towards her help fashion Melanie into a more self-confident individual.

Of course, the most positive influence on Melanie, and the person who contributes most to her dialectic development into a self-actualized subject, is Justineau, her dedicated teacher. Steele identifies "optimistic teacher-student relationships" as a key strategy to overcome stereotype threat, interactions that discredit negative assumptions through "the authority of potential-affirming adult relationships."[54] While Justineau occasionally thinks of Melanie as "test subject one,"[55] at least while still on the military base, she almost always calls the girl "Melanie," as she refers to *all* the students by their given names. She does call Melanie "sister" once, though, and after the group begins their trek south, she refers to Melanie as "sweetheart."[56] After the group finds a mobile science lab (playfully christened "Rosalind Franklin"[57]), Melanie must spend more and more time away from the uninfected humans, as their supply of "e-blocker"—the chemical that masks the smell of human endocrine sweat[58]—runs low, and her ability to resist her hungry urges diminishes. Parks explains that "the kid" doesn't want Justineau to think of her as "a dangerous animal" but rather as just a kid in her class. Justineau implores, "That *is* how I think of her."[59] Her genuine affection for the girl, manifested on more than one occasion by policy-forbidden physical contact, helps Melanie to see herself as a human girl, a person worthy of praise, attention, and love.

Melanie's Subjective Development

In a decidedly Hegelian way, then, the essential story of *The Girl with All the Gifts* is Melanie's ontological journey to figure out who—and what—she really is. Despite being laid out on a dissecting table as a "specimen" and "test subject" by Caldwell, despite being called all kinds of derisive names by Parks, Melanie still has a personal identity waiting to be discovered and developed. As we've seen, most of her valuable subjective development while still on the military base derives from her positive interactions with her teachers, most relevantly Justineau. Her most beloved teacher recognizes Melanie's subjectivity by regularly looking her in the eye, calling her by name, engaging with her intellectually, and basically just treating her like a fellow human being. Justineau's identity-affirming desire for Melanie, however, must be kept in careful check, as the girl will always represent a real threat to Justineau's physical safety. Indeed, after her teacher rescues her from a night of being strapped immobile in a wheelchair in Hotel Echo, Melanie feels the irresistible human urge to reach out her arms in hopes that Justineau will lift her up, hold her, and allow her whole body to touch her.[60] But Justineau has neglected her e-blocker, and her smell—her "wonderful, terrible smell"—causes Melanie's muscles to stiffen, a moan to escape from her lips, and her mouth to fill with thick saliva.[61] A different desire completely takes over—the atavistic desire to eat her teacher, the *need* to satiate her hunger with the flesh and blood of the other. Melanie consciously struggles against this need, but after the escape from the military base, when Melanie's irrepressible hunger has been awakened by the taste of human blood, she cannot help noticing a change in her perceived identity, a change at the fundamental level of desire. As a result, Melanie is no longer capable of defining or naming herself accurately:

> She's always been a good girl. But she ate pieces of two men, and very probably killed them both. Killed them with her teeth.
> She was hungry, and they were her bread.
> So what is she now?[62]

Melanie fears the hunger inside of her, fears that it has changed her, and her very real fear is that this drive will make her attack Justineau.

Once away from the base and in the wilderness of postapocalyptic England, Melanie encounters a large horde of hungries for the first time, and she takes the time to sit by herself and think about her new "terrible secret."[63] She has realized she is *not* a little girl but rather one of *them*. Not only did the other hungries avoid her as if she weren't even there, but she also finds her "proof," significantly in their very name, in the power of that name to define her identity:

It's the word itself. The name. Hungries.
    The monsters are named for the feeling that filled her when she smelled Miss
Justineau in the cell, or the junker men outside the block. The hungries smell you,
and then they chase you until they eat you. They can't stop themselves.
    Melanie knows exactly how that feels. Which means she's a monster.[64]

Her identity is quickly reduced to a label, a label not affixed on her by the
various humans in her life but the label given to a feeling, an urge, and she
allows that desire—instead of her desire for others—to define her.

    As their journey south towards Beacon progresses, Melanie becomes
increasingly aware of the real world, and she develops a clearer sense of her
identity by observing how she fits into that world. She revises her belief that
she is a hungry, telling her human companions that she is "almost" one of
the hungries—but she is decidedly different because she doesn't *want* to eat
anyone.[65] She recognizes not only that her identity is tied to desire, as everyone's is, but also that she is a fundamentally dualistic creature. "Sometimes
I *need* to eat people," she tells Parks. "I never *want* to."[66] Melanie knows a
battle is waging inside her between the animalistic instincts of the fungal
pathogen—an instinct that drives her towards individualistic behavior—and
the human urges she has developed from her contact with Justineau—which
encourage her to be a part of a community.[67] Justineau tries to comfort a dis-
traught Melanie, explaining how she's not evil because "you're not a hungry,
because you can still think, and they can't."[68] Through Justineau, then, Melanie
sees her rather unique place in the world, but this recognition is soured somewhat when she describes herself, in Caldwell's oft-repeated terms, as "a crucially important specimen."[69]

    After eating her first wild animal—a feral cat—Melanie reflects on her
action with ambivalent horror. The "hunger" drove her to hunt, told her how
to rip into the cat's body, made her eat the flesh raw. But, at the same time,
"another part [of herself] kept itself at a distance from the horrible cruelty
and the horrible messiness."[70] Melanie begins not only to recognize but also
to understand her duality and the need for the "human" portion of her psyche
to maintain control over the "animal" part of her biology, the fungal pathogen
that inhabits her every cell. The more time she spends around the uninfected
humans, especially after they run out of e-blocker, the more she is able to
control her instinctual drive to kill and eat them: "Melanie is amazed that
she's able to be this close without wanting to bite them. She's become used
to it somehow. It's like the part of her that just wants to eat and eat and eat
is locked up in a little box, and she doesn't have to open the box if she doesn't
want to."[71] This confrontation with her conflicted desires in many ways concludes Melanie's journey towards self-conscious identity. As Kojève states,
"For man to be truly human, for him to be essentially and really different
from an animal, his human Desire must actually win out over his animal

Desire."[72] And by the end of the novel, Melanie has more or less mastered the ability to control these two desires, paving the way for her independent, self-conscious subjectivity.

Melanie's discovery of other children like her rocks her self-identity the most. Initially, thanks to Justineau's behavior and influence, she thinks of herself as a human child. Then, based largely on Caldwell and Park's treatment of her, she comes to recognize herself as a specimen and a hungry. By meeting other children like her, however, she begins to reclassify herself as one of the "[c]hildren who were hungries too, and alive, and animated."[73] But she also recognizes that these children are different; they are still in a pre-symbolic state. "I didn't know their names," she tells Justineau. "They probably didn't *have* names. It didn't seem like they could talk."[74] She realizes both her kinship with the other infected children and the source of her difference: "The wild children are just the same as she is, except that they never got to have lessons with Miss Justineau. Nobody ever taught them how to think for themselves, or even how to be people."[75] Melanie had *teachers* in her life, teachers who ushered her into the symbolic order of subjectivity, who taught her to be a person by *treating* her like a person.

At the end of their harrowing journey into the heart of London, Caldwell discovers the truth about the fungal pathogen and the hungries: there are actually *two* kinds of infected humans.[76] The brains of the "newly infected" humans are consumed by the fungal infestation, which "shuts down higher-order thought," enhancing "hunger and the triggers for hunger."[77] However, since Carey's hungries also engage in remembered human behaviors that *don't* serve a function that directly supports the fungus, they may engage in sexual intercourse and even bear children.[78] Thus the second type of hungries in *The Girl with All the Gifts*, the type to which Melanie belongs, is the "second generation" infected, born with the fungus already "spread even throughout the brain" without ever *feeding* on the brain tissue.[79] In other words, as Caldwell explains, first-generation hungries have parasitic fungi; *second*-generation hungries have *symbiotic* fungi, and thus retain their higher-order capabilities.

Armed with Caldwell's research, Melanie decides the best hope for the future of the human race—the *new* human race—is to create the "environmental trigger" needed for the mature fungal sporangium to break open and release millions of spores into the atmosphere.[80] She tricks Parks into helping her, using Rosie's flamethrowers to burn through a dense forest of fungal threads and stems. She later explains to a dying Parks,

> This way is better. Everybody turns into a hungry all at once, and that means they'll all die, which is really sad. But then the children will grow up, and they won't be the old kind of people but they won't be hungries either. They'll be different. Like me, and the rest of the kids in the class.
>
> They'll be the *next* people. The ones who make everything okay again.[81]

Melanie sees the only viable future: a future of natural evolution, a future that will work only when the warring remnants of humanity are gone, the children of the new symbiotic species are safe, and—perhaps most importantly—they have loving teachers to instruct them.

The Girl with All the Gifts represents a new standard for zombie narratives in its semiscientific conception of a plausible zombie infection, its logical deployment of agentic zombie characters, and its focus on positive zombie development and a nonviolent solution to the zombie apocalypse. Furthermore, it represents one of the few apocalyptic narratives—or *any* narrative, for that matter—that features a teacher as a chief protagonist. Like the polarizing character of Morgan (Lennie James) on AMC's *The Walking Dead* (2010–present), Justineau provides us with a new kind of postapocalyptic hero, one invested in education, acceptance, and nurturing affection instead of brutal violence and destructive selfishness. She shows readers the "revelation" of the apocalypse, one that signals a new beginning more than it does a final end. But Carey's novel also makes a compelling argument for those of us living in the *now*, in the pre-apocalyptic world of real life. While teachers in both the public system and higher education may sometimes feel as if their vacant-eyed and smartphone-obsessed students are types of zombies already, they, like Melanie, are merely a new generation of people, developing individuals who stand to benefit from careful attention and self-affirming conditioning. Educators today can learn much from Justineau's pedagogy, because as theorists from Hegel to Steele have demonstrated, words matter, especially those from an authority figure directed to a developing mind. If teachers use their students' proper names, develop positive interpersonal relationships with them, give them challenging work and assignments, and buoy them up with positive and nonjudgmental comments, they can overcome today's "zombie apocalypse" and pave the way for a new generation of smart, capable, and self-actualized individuals.

Notes

1. Derksen and Hick, "Your Zombie and You," 15.

2. See, for example, Daniel Waters' *Generation Dead* (2008), S.G. Browne's *Breathers: A Zombie's Lament* (2009), and Isaac Marion's *Warm Bodies* (2010). Interested readers could also consult Ashley Szanter and Jessica K. Richards' forthcoming essay collection on the romantic zombie.

3. The novel began as a short story titled "Iphigenia in Aulis," which Carey wrote for a 2012 collection of short stories on the theme of "school days," titled *An Apple for the Creature*, for editors Charlaine Harris and Toni L.P. Kelner.

4. At least initially, Carey's zombies closely resemble the mycological monsters featured in Naughty Dog's 2013 hit video game, *The Last of Us* (directed by Bruce Straley and Neil Druckmann; designed by Jacob Minkoff), which are also inspired by the *Cordyceps* fungus.

5. Steele, "Threat in the Air," 614.

6. Carey, *Girl with All the Gifts*, 1.

7. *Ibid.*, 1.

8. Hegel, *Phenomenology of Spirit*, 111.

9. *Ibid.*, 112, 116, 113.

10. Kojève, *Introduction to the Reading of Hegel*, 4.

11. *Ibid.*, 7.

12. Simmons, "This Year's Class Picture," 5.

13. *Ibid.*, 8.

14. *Ibid.*, 12.

15. *Ibid.*, 17.

16. *Ibid.*, 21.

17. Carey, *Girl with All the Gifts*, 3, 47.

18. This "fungal ant" feature appears on the eighth episode of the BBC series *Planet Earth*, "Jungles," which first aired on 8 April 2007, placing the outbreak of *The Girl with All the Gifts* in 2027 and the action of the novel in 2047 (see *Ibid.*, 52–53, where Caldwell establishes this timeline).

19. Carey, *Girl with All the Gifts*, 52–53.

20. *Ibid.*, 55.

21. *Ibid.*, 26.

22. Carey emphasizes Melanie's subjective journey through language when he writes, "Melanie was new herself, once, but that's hard to remember because it was a long time ago. It was before there were any words; there were just things without names, and things without names don't stay in your mind. They fall out, and then they're gone" (*Ibid.*, 1).

23. *Ibid.*, 1. Melanie wants to be called "Pandora" because, as Justineau tells her, that name means "the girl with all the gifts," and the woman from the myth was "clever, and brave, and beautiful, and funny, and everything else you'd want to be" (*Ibid.*, 11).

24. *Ibid.*, 15.

25. *Ibid.*, 11.

26. Steele, "Threat in the Air," 613.

27. *Ibid.*, 613.

28. *Ibid.*, 614.

29. See *Ibid.*, 614

30. Carey, *Girl with All the Gifts*, 25, 36, 68. Lia Habel takes a similar approach with her 2011 novel *Dearly, Departed*, a zombie romance tale that also features agentic revenants.

31. Chapter 28 is an interesting exception. It is divided into five sections, and the narration of each focuses on a different character: Melanie, Parks, Caldwell, Private Kieran Gallager (for the first time), and Justineau.

32. Carey, *Girl with All the Gifts*, 28–29, 28.

33. *Ibid.*, 38.

34. *Ibid.*, 93, 149, 179, 194.

35. *Ibid.*, 157, 227.

36. *Ibid.*, 97–99.

37. *Ibid.*, 224.

38. *Ibid.*, 346, 348.

39. *Ibid.*, 376, 377.

40. *Ibid.*, 2, 5, 44.

41. *Ibid.*, 4, 68, 105.

42. *Ibid.*, 70, 72, 120.

43. *Ibid.*, 73.

44. *Ibid.*, 121, 133.

45. *Ibid.*, 186.

46. *Ibid.*, 188.

47. *Ibid.*, 291.

48. *Ibid.*, 311.

49. Indeed, Hegel identifies "work" as a key requirement of self-consciousness: "Through work, however, the bondsman become conscious of what he truly is…. Work … is desire held in check, fleetingness staved off; in other words, work forms and shapes the thing" (Hegel, *Phenomenology of Spirit*, 118).

50. Steele, "Threat in the Air," 625.

51. Carey, *Girl with All the Gifts*, 229.
52. *Ibid.*, 355.
53. *Ibid.*, 398, 400.
54. *Ibid.*, 624.
55. *Ibid.*, 26.
56. *Ibid.*, 11, 244.
57. *Ibid.*, 261.
58. *Ibid.*, 110.
59. *Ibid.*, 278.
60. *Ibid.*, 62.
61. *Ibid.*, 63–64.
62. *Ibid.*, 123.
63. *Ibid.*, 191.
64. *Ibid.*, 193.
65. *Ibid.*, 229.
66. *Ibid.*, 230.
67. See *Ibid.*
68. *Ibid.*, 244.
69. *Ibid.*
70. *Ibid.*, 296.
71. *Ibid.*, 354–55.
72. Kojève, *Introduction to the Reading of Hegel*, 6.
73. Carey, *Girl with All the Gifts*, 317.
74. *Ibid.*, 318.
75. *Ibid.*, 365.
76. The presence of multiple types of zombies is a growing trend in both cinematic and literary zombies. Inspired perhaps by the necessity to provide players with different foes in zombie-themed video games, many twenty-first-century zombie tales feature two versions of the walking dead, generally a more human-like version and a more animalistic one, as in Isaac Marion's *Warm Bodies* (2010; also the 2013 film, directed by Jonathan Levine) and Rob Thomas' ongoing television adaptation (2015–) of Chris Roberson and Michael Allred's *iZombie* comic series (2010–12).
77. Carey, *Girl with All the Gifts*, 378.
78. *Ibid.*, 378–79.
79. *Ibid.*, 379.
80. *Ibid.*, 398.
81. *Ibid.*, 399.

Desiring Machines
Zombies, Automata and
Cormac McCarthy's The Road

JESSE STOMMEL

The zombie body is a pedagogical body. It teaches us something about who we are. It is a polyvalent body. The zombie is more than just static flesh and sinews. It is raw material that authors and filmmakers draw upon to tell stories about what it is to be human—what it is to be a body in a world where those bodies are imminently threatened. In *The Road* (2008), Cormac McCarthy uses the zombie as a device to put unknown horror at the edges of his postapocalyptic narrative. The book was not marketed as a zombie novel, yet it features roving bands of cannibals in a postapocalypse and even overtly declares itself a zombie narrative early on in the text. McCarthy then improvises at that edge, imagining a world where something like zombies might actually exist and wondering what in our nature as humans could make that world a reality.

*   *   *

We are told that the human is evolving. In their introduction to *The Cyborg Handbook*, Chris Hables Gray, Steven Mentor, and Heidi J. Figueroa-Sarriera write,

> The story of cyborgs is not just a tale told around the glow of the televised fire. There are many actual cyborgs among us in society. Anyone with an artificial organ, limb or supplement (like a pacemaker), anyone reprogrammed to resist disease (immunized) or drugged to think/behave/feel better (psychopharmacology) is technically a cyborg. The range of these intimate human-machine relationships is mind-boggling.[1]

The authors begin by ironically describing their work as just a "*story* of cyborgs" (my emphasis), only to cannibalize this first sentence with their second, in which the cyborg becomes not at all a fiction. By their account, we are all cyborgs, mechanisms more than organisms, desiring machines without the desire.

Our relationship to our cell phones is a poignant example. Because of these "smart" devices, the human body now has the capacity to ring, to vibrate even. It's a rather intimate, even sensual, interaction between human and machine. The cell phone communicates through a subtle stimulation—a tickle of the skin that can't be felt unless the phone is in direct physical contact with the body. And, already, the physicality of some of our most profoundly human moments has been replaced by this other sort of mechanical intimacy.

In *Anti-Oedipus: Capitalism and Schizophrenia*, Gilles Deleuze and Felix Guattari define a machine as "a system of interruption or breaks."[2] So the phrase "desiring machine" suggests that desire is mechanistic, a real, productive force, rather than an imaginary one responding to a *lack*, as Freud would characterize it. They write, "We live today in the age of partial objects, bricks that have been shattered to bits, and leftovers."[3] Desire, in a sense, puts (or attempts to put) these pieces back together, producing what they call a "flow," the series of connections from one desiring machine to another. In this way, automata are machines that merely go through the motions of production, machines that appear connected to other machines but only in the most superficial way. There is *connection* but not *flow*, an empty gesture, like those strange Drinking Birds that perpetually bob their heads in and out of a glass as though (but not actually) drinking the water.

In *Discipline and Punish*, Michel Foucault calls automata "political puppets, small-scale models of power," both "object and target of power."[4] This description correlates with the conventional definition of "automaton," being a self-operating, self-propelled machine. In Foucault's conception, the automaton is not a mindless follower but a habituated one. Jean-Claude Beaune, in "The Classical Age of Automata," describes the world of automata as "a world in which the frontiers and the limits between body and mind, as well as those between nature and culture, and between life and death, have grown so thick, so enduring and so dense that when we look in the mirror each day we confront portraits of the living dead."[5] I would argue, however, that the figure of the automaton differs from the figure of the zombie, in its various incarnations. The automaton regurgitates, opening its mouth to repeat words we've heard or seen before in arrangements we've heard or seen before, but it rarely even registers its own words. The automaton is a *sort* of walking dead, but it might be more accurately described as the endlessly and pointlessly walking *living*. It isn't really dead; it just fails to live in any meaningful way. The automaton represents what we are in danger of becoming in the postmodern age with our increasing reliance on technological gadgets (as human appendages). Our human bodies are becoming vestigial, making way for something increasingly intangible. The zombie, on the other hand, could represent a figurative solution, a powerful opportunity for revolt, a reclaiming of flesh in the wake of rapid technological advancement.[6]

(A brief pause to note: when I speak of embodiment and disembodiment in this piece, particularly when I use the first-person plural to refer to us as collectively human, I must also acknowledge how varied embodiment and experiences of embodiment can be.)

In place of idiosyncratic selves, the characters in McCarthy's *The Road* are left only with automated and habituated action. The father and the boy don't live, not in any real sense. They eat mostly out of habit (with a few notable exceptions), survive out of habit, talk for companionship, and walk with vague intention, clinging to the shopping cart they've gathered their possessions into. But their conversations are empty, grammatically stark. The somewhere they're walking to doesn't really exist. And their dreams of salvation are simulacra, empty copies of a happy future seen only on billboards.[7] McCarthy writes, "They went on. Treading the dead world under like rats on a wheel."[8] In lieu of an actual destination, they walk as though defying death, "treading the dead world under," but they fail to have any measurable effect, circling endlessly, *like rats on a wheel*. To *live* in the world McCarthy imagines is to cling futilely to some semblance of the people we once were.[9] The characters in the book are thus searching for selves that no longer exists—that maybe never existed.

The Road is a zombie novel, in my reading, except the zombies aren't the cannibals that wander the road, or not just the cannibals; the zombies are everyone, everything. The father and the boy. The world itself, the trees, the moss, the trout, all dead but not gone, threatening to rise up—to be reborn from their own ashes. These aren't the zombies we're used to, not the teeth-gnashing, intestine-chomping sort from the films of George A. Romero, but rather a new breed of evolutionary monster, reasserting itself and reclaiming its turf in the aftermath of an apocalypse, the kind of apocalypse that happens without our even registering it. These are melancholic (even sympathetic) zombies, emptied of substance, in much the way McCarthy empties his prose of ornamentation and anything but the crudest of structure.

Early in the book, the boy's mother (later dead or just gone) says to his father, "What in God's name are you talking about? We're not survivors. We're the walking dead in a horror film."[10] The characters in *The Road* are not "survivors" because there was no cataclysmic event for them to survive. McCarthy never offers any clear answer as to why the world has become desolate and empty. Our impulse, as readers, is to assume that there was some specific happening, a nuclear exchange, an asteroid collision, or a superstorm caused by global warming. However, McCarthy makes a very careful choice not to focus on the calamity, the impetus for the story, because it's irrelevant. We don't need to trace the history of our becoming (or unbecoming) to acknowledge and recognize what we've become (or what has been undone). In a similar fashion, very few of the classic zombie films, those contemporary with Romero's *Night of the Living Dead* (1968) and *Dawn of the Dead* (1978), attempt to unequivocally explain the causes of the zombie infestation. This ambiguity allows for (and even encourages) an allegorical reading that suggests that the world of Romero's films and of *The Road* is our world, menaced but fundamentally unchanged.

*   *   *

At one point in the book, the boy asks his father, referring to a set of tracks they've discovered, "Who is it?" The father replies, "I don't know. Who is anybody?"[11] Are we meant to take this question literally, or is it purely rhetorical, suggesting almost flippantly that we are all *no one*? A few important details lead me to believe the former—that this is, in fact, a serious question for McCarthy. When referring to a *body* without a *person* in it (a corpse or a mannequin, for example), we tend to use the pronoun "it." This practice is true even when the personhood of the body is only in doubt (for example, a common phrase like, "Is *it* alive?"). The use of the pronoun "it," then, and the "Who is anybody?" that follows suggest that our personhood *is* in question for McCarthy—that we are becoming bodies without *who*-ness. This suggestion is supported by the lack of proper names throughout the book (of both places and people), just "the man," "the boy," and "the road."[12] In my reading, though, it is less likely that the man and the boy are *nobody* and more likely that they are *anybody*, stand-ins for a new nostalgic human. *The Road* takes place after the apocalypse that can just as easily be imagined as *now*, a postmodern wasteland where a new species of (always already dead) humans is emerging.

Robert Stam offers a rather bleak definition of "postmodernism" in his introduction to the "Politics of Postmodernism" section of *Film and Theory: An Anthology*: "The empty sequentiality of the 'post' corresponds to a preference for prefixes such as *de* or *dis*—*de*centering, *dis*placement—which suggest the demystification of preexisting paradigms. Postmodernism is fond of terms which connote openness, multiplicity, plurality, heterodoxy, contingency, hybridity."[13] It is quite common for postmodernism and its objects to be figured as "empty," something Stam does in his first sentence here, as though our difficulty in grasping the concept derives from its fundamental vacuity. However, I would argue that postmodernism, and specifically the postmodern body, is precisely *not* empty. Rather, its indeterminacy derives from its being hypersaturated with meaning. It's apropos, then, that Stam deviates from the conventions of written English by failing to join the last two items of the list in his second sentence with "and," because postmodernism demands the amorphousness of language, the "open" (a word Stam also uses) and insistent play between one possibility and another, the limitless potential for alternatives and simultaneity.

Daniel Waters plays with this idea in the young-adult novel *Generation Dead* (2008). The zombies in *Generation Dead* are high school students, and, even though they're social outcasts, the teenage zombies "live" mostly ordinary "lives," attending classes, going on dates, wearing plaid skirts, etc. Nonetheless, the fact that they're dead remains a constant source of disgust and bewilderment for the other students, who debate the nature of being dead and being living. The narrator remarks, "Zombie was a word you just didn't say in public anymore."[14] Then, later, one kid says to another, "We are required to refer to them as the *living impaired*, okay? Not dead kid. Not *zombie*, or *worm buffet*, or *accursed hellspawn*, either. Living impaired. Repeat after me. *Living impaired*."[15] Throughout the novel, the zombie comes to represent various disenfranchised persons: the physically handicapped, the socially outcast, women, and homosexuals. As a metaphor, the zombie can come to stand for almost anything, but it does not and cannot stand for nothing.

During the opening credits of Romero's *Land of the Dead* (2005), we hear audio snippets of newscasters as choppy black-and-white newsreel footage flashes on screen. In less than one minute, the film's monsters are called all manner of things but never "zombies": "dead," "recently departed," "unburied human corpses," "they," "them," "it," "these things," and "these creatures." The zombie is not named as a thing, but it is an overfull—not empty—signifier. In *Jennifer's Body* (2009, directed by Karyn Kusama), a film about a girl who becomes a demon after a botched virgin sacrifice, a mother in shock at the death of her son is described as a "zombie mannequin robot statue," the words jammed together in an unhalting burst of syllables. The moment alludes to the way shock, awe, and the abject disrupt our ability to use language. Here, it's the zombie, in particular, for which the character is unable to find the right word.

* * *

The conversations in *The Road* often revolve around language and how words make (or don't make) meaning. The main characters say very little of significance, each exchange littered with the word "okay" repeated over and over to the point of indifference. And it isn't that each instance of the word takes on a different shade of meaning as often happens when we hear the same word repeated. Rather, each "okay" functions in just the opposite way in *The Road*. I find myself more and more disturbed by the word as the story proceeds—disturbed by its increasing lack of meaning.[16] It is a word we use so often in everyday exchanges:

How are you today?
I'm *okay.*

The word functions as a placeholder for all the things we dare not say, a reminder that more is left unsaid, and it's a reminder that language so often fails to communicate. The dialogue in McCarthy's novel is alienating, so rarely constituting an exchange. The gaps at the right-hand side of the page are often more telling than the text, and the characters don't speak with distinct voices, just a series of mono- or duosyllabic gestures toward what only mildly passes for conversation. It becomes quite possible to read the characters of the father and the son as one person, concocting stories and memories to populate an otherwise empty world.[17]

In *The Road,* McCarthy uses a spare modernist style that borders on the Hemingway-esque,[18] and the book riffs on many of the themes that T.S. Eliot addresses in *The Waste Land,* such as memory, nostalgia, communication, relationships, the postapocalypse, time, cultural collapse, etc. However, McCarthy's book is ultimately postmodern in the way it handles these themes and, particularly, in the way it treats issues of the body. The characters in *The Road* are consistently and curiously disembodied, given that survival, finding food, avoiding death are so central to the narrative. We never get physical descriptions of either the father or the boy. Their existences are measured more explicitly by the contents of their shopping cart. In place of physical descriptions, we get references, like this one, to the boy's dwindling frame: "The boy was so thin. He watched him while he slept. Taut face and hollow eyes. A strange beauty."[19] The reference here is not to the boy's body but to his lack of one—to his slow but assured emaciation. Later, McCarthy describes the father and son navigating through the bodies that litter the landscape: "They picked their way among the mummied figures. The black skin stretched upon the bones and their faces split and shrunken on their skulls. Like victims of some ghastly envacuuming."[20]

From the outset of McCarthy's novel, the text is almost devoid of significant punctuation, just the obligatory periods and an occasional apostrophe, although not even these are used with any consistency. The dialogue lacks quotation marks; commas show up here and there but mostly only in fragmented lists. And there are no more than a handful of colons and not a single exclamation mark. So the world McCarthy imagines is empty, empty of people, empty of cities, empty of society, empty of hope, and quite literally empty of grammar—of clear organizing principles for its words. McCarthy uses textured and beautiful words, like "cloven," "sprawled," and "torsional"[21]; however, so often, the words are just lined up in order, one falling atop another in logical sequence but with nothing to break them up into manageable chunks. McCarthy imagines paragraphs as though they're rockslides, burying the reader beneath a rubble of vivid but incessant prose.

Likewise, there are no chapter breaks in *The Road*, making for a flurried but strange reading experience. What we get instead are strangely placed rows of asterisks that transport us abruptly from one scene to another, from place to place, from the concrete to abstraction, from past to present to speculative future. I've read the book from beginning to end several times, and each time, I found myself unable to stop, not because I "couldn't put the book down," so to speak, but because the book doesn't give the reader convenient places to stop. We read *The Road* the way the characters walk the road. One set of events blurs into the next, and, without chapter breaks, McCarthy offers the reader no relief—no sense of satisfaction at the completion of a reading task, however arbitrary. Thus, any interruption of the narrative proves to be an awkward one. This isn't escapist reading; reality, for McCarthy, doesn't break. And this is decidedly not a story of the fantastic, but rather a parable, a story about the world we already live in, a mundane world, in which we are all anonymous.

*   *   *

The following exchange occurs in Romero's *Dawn of the Dead* as the characters stand on a landing overlooking a zombie throng fumbling its way through the mall:

FRANCINE: They're still here.
STEPHEN: They're after us. They know we're still in here.
PETER: They're just after the place. They don't know why; they just remember. Remember that they want to be in here.
FRANCINE: What the hell are they?
PETER: They're us; that's all.[22]

I particularly appreciate the phrase "that's all," and the tone in which it's delivered in the film, a tone of sheer apathy, as though the recognition is hardly a recognition at all, something we know already. We want stuff. We're nothing without it. We conglomerate with groups of others wanting stuff. The mall, where the stuff is kept, is a beacon. And we'll want stuff even after we're dead. Except we already are. It's the stuff that kills us. That's all.

Ironically, in *The Road*, it's also the stuff that keeps us alive, that shelters, that nourishes, that serves as a beacon. Throughout the novel, the man and the boy cling to their shopping cart as though it were a lifeline, even if it's rarely filled with anything more than random odds and ends. And as the man's health fades toward the end of the novel, McCarthy describes him as having to "lean on the cart" to hold himself up,[23] as though it and the stuff in it will literally keep him alive. The stuff in the cart seems, more than anything else, like detritus, but when it's lost at various moments, the characters suffer an immeasurable malaise. On the other hand, when they discover a well-stocked bunker, a "tiny paradise" of truly useful stuff, the father is desperate to leave almost immediately, because "it's dangerous,"[24] even though there's nothing to indicate that the bunker is any more dangerous than the wasteland it shelters them from.

The real reason they leave the bunker is because it doesn't actually exist. "Paradise" never does.[25] Paradise is something advertisers entice us with to get us to buy their products. We live for paradise, but our fixation on a particular brand of unattainable paradise is exactly what annihilates us. McCarthy writes, "He held the boy by the hand and they went along the rows of stenciled cartons. Chile, corn, stew, soup, spaghetti sauce. The richness of a vanished world. Why is this here? the boy said. Is it real?"[26] The man spends most of his time in the bunker cataloguing everything, "[going] meticulously through the stores": "Coffee. Ham. Biscuits," "soap and sponges," "new sweaters and socks."[27] He's shopping, but nothing he finds is real; a "vanished world," which is what McCarthy calls this place, can't be "rich." The bunker and everything in it are simulacra and offer little true fulfillment. The man fills their cart at the bunker, but after they leave, they move on quickly to the next store, a market that they discover in the following scene. They can't seem to get enough. The fact that they leave the bunker suggests that it isn't actual stuff they value but the idea of stuff, just as we (consumers) so often want something and then buy it only to discover that it fails to live up to our expectations—fails to *complete us* as the marketers and advertisers would have us believe.[28]

This sort of futile capitalism, buying for the sake of buying, is parodied in *The Stuff* (1986, directed by Larry Cohen), a horror film in which a blob-like substance bubbles up from the earth and is marketed as a creamy dessert product. The "Stuffies," the film's name for the soulless consumers that eat The Stuff, end up literally hollowed out, their bodies a shell for the goo that controls them from the inside. *Halloween 3: Season of the Witch* (1982, directed by Tommy Lee Wallace) offers a similar though ultimately inferior critique of mass marketing, big business, and capitalist culture. In the film, a mad scientist decides (for no apparent reason) to use enchanted Halloween masks and deadly television commercials to murder America's children so that he can recreate them as mindless, obedient robots. Both films suggest that humans have become mere vectors for the transmission of commercial products, the makers, transporters, sellers, buyers, and consumers of goods. Automata. Zombie-like simulacra. Not as lively as actual zombies.

*   *   *

In my humanities classes, I start a conversation with students about the simulacrum by showing a coveted picture I tote around of a lemon from an Absolut ad. Each year I find myself talking longer and longer. My students stare in bewilderment and sometimes giggle at my fond affection for the image. I ask, "Have you ever seen this lemon?" It glistens with little round beads of moisture, Crayola yellow, with two green leaves sprouting gleefully from the top. It glows, shines even, as though I could check my reflection in it. I want this lemon. I've dug through bin after bin in the produce aisle, searching for it, the perfect lemon, always evading my reach, only to end up staring listlessly, dissatisfied with the hundreds of inferior choices before me. The simulacrum not only stands in for the original but also replaces it, annihilates it. It's not that I don't want other lemons but that all other lemons fail to be lemons in the face of my fantasy of this one almighty lemon.

The characters in *The Road* are haunted by a fantasy of their former life, even the boy, who wasn't alive to experience for himself the world as it was. In scenes that read more menacing than they otherwise would, the father instructs the boy on the horrors of materialism by introducing him to the joys of soda and canned goods. This is the so-called "surviving" they do, in which eating canned pears and peanut butter on biscuits has been elevated to the status of a peak experience.[29] Like the zombies in Romero's *Dawn of the Dead*, the people in *The Road* are consumed by the afterimage of their former lives. They don't know why they wander the desolate landscape aimlessly. They just do. And the hollowest experiences must stand in for the full weight of what they've lost.

McCarthy writes, "The world soon to be largely populated by men who would eat your children in front of your eyes and the cities themselves held by cores of blackened looters who tunneled among the ruins and crawled from the rubble white of tooth and eye carrying charred and anonymous tins of food in nylon nets like shoppers in the commissaries of hell."[30] In lieu of other stuff to eat, they eat each other. And, like animals, they "crawl" and "tunnel," moving on all fours, digging through "rubble" and "ruins," searching for the beings they once were and finding them in "anonymous tins of food" that they flaunt like trophies. This is not evolution. In *The Road*, McCarthy imagines a "[commissary] hell," where the denizens *shop*—for cans, for babies, for limbs, for flesh—all to eat, except it isn't exactly eating they do, because they're never nourished.[31] The *not quite living not quite dead* just munch.

NOTES

1. Hables Gray, Mentor, and Figueroa-Sarriera, *Cyborg Handbook*, 2.
2. Deleuze and Guattari, *Anti-Oedipus*, 36.
3. *Ibid.*, 42.
4. Foucault, *Discipline & Punish*, 136.
5. Beaune, "Classical Age of Automata," 435.
6. In *Copying Machines: Taking Notes for the Automaton*, Catherine Liu offers an expansive account of the evolution of the automaton as a literary and cultural figure. Liu's work is interested in points (and metaphors) of resistance, where humans revolt against their machines. She writes, describing the automaton, "If detachment can be fascinating, the

stupidity of the automaton is also hypnotizing, literally mesmerizing in its idiotic repetition of anthropomorphizing movement" (Liu, *Copying Machines*, xi).

7. Jean Baudrillard describes the simulacrum as a "machine" (*Simulacra and Simulation*, 343), a figuration that recalls Walter Benjamin's argument in "The Work of Art in the Age of Mechanical Reproduction." Copies are made by machines but ultimately become machines themselves. The photographer frames reality, the camera produces a photograph, and the printer reproduces it again and again until eventually the photograph becomes entirely dissociated from the reality that it supposedly resembles. This is when Benjamin would say that the "aura" is lost. Then, other cameras (and by extension other photographers, although they are irrelevant at this point) capture the world in a way that imitates the original photograph, and we attempt to fashion ourselves in a way that imitates this parade of images. And, *voilà*, a culture of the image is born, or what Terry Castle calls the insistent "desire for more compelling illusions" (Castle, *Female Thermometer*, 151). All of this can be traced back not to a specific photographer, not to a specific encounter with the image, but to a specific camera, a specific printer, a means of dissemination, a swarm *not* of people but of images and image-machines. For Baudrillard, this is cause for dismay. It is what he calls "deterrence" (Baudrillard, *Simulacra and Simulation*, 373); now, reality itself is deterred, for the image fragments reality to the point where reality actually begins to dissolve under the weight of the simulacrum—rather, the *illusion* of weight, for the simulacrum has no *actual* weight.

8. McCarthy, *Road*, 273.

9. Early on, the boy uses crayons to paint a "facemask with fangs" (*Ibid.*, 14). Later, the man and boy push their "way out of their den" (*Ibid.*, 99), as though they have become wild animals.

10. *Ibid.*, 55.

11. *Ibid.*, 49.

12. The one character name we do get, "Ely," ends up being fake, and the few mentions of geographical places prove frustrating more than anything, failing to provide clear markers to the location of the events unfolding.

13. Stam, "Politics of Postmodernism," 754.

14. Waters, *Generation Dead*, 2.

15. *Ibid.*, 22.

16. At one point, the father says to his son, "Okay means okay" (McCarthy, *Road*, 165), a second-order moment for McCarthy, commenting on the ability of language to communicate anything beyond the trite and arbitrary, not unlike Gertrude Stein famously writing, "A rose is a rose is a rose is a rose."

17. While this reading might seem to make the whole book an elaborate ruse, there is further evidence in several places. For example, the boy's mother says to the father, "A person who had no one would be well advised to cobble together some passable ghost. Breathe it into being and coax it along with words of love. Offer it each phantom crumb and shield it from harm with your body" (*Ibid.*, 57). And this ("shield it from harm") is exactly what the father does for the boy, his son or, perhaps, just "some passable ghost."

18. This may be understatement. I could quite easily imagine someone mistaking a paragraph from *The Road* for a paragraph from Hemingway's *The Old Man and the Sea* (1951). I suspect that McCarthy is paying homage to Hemingway's work, even though he ultimately upsets any neat and tidy comparison we might make. There is no solace in nature for McCarthy's characters, only a constant reminder of what they've lost.

19. McCarthy, *Road*, 102. There are constant reminders of beauty throughout the book (such as the reference here to the boy's "strange beauty"), both in the small surprises of life that pervade the otherwise desolate world and in the memories that haunt the father (and provide him sustenance) throughout. Even these, though, begin to fade, and turn to nostalgia, the desire for something never really lost at all—something you can't get back because it was never yours in the first place. So McCarthy offers brief moments of the hopefulness many modernists struggle for—the sort of hopefulness that turns the literary work itself into an antidote to the horrors of modern life. I recognize this impulse in McCarthy, but he doesn't allow himself to really indulge it. These moments of real "beauty" (however "strange") are fleeting and always give way to more entropic—more fatalist—forces.

20. *Ibid.*, 191.

21. *Ibid.*, 24, 177, 286.

22. Francine is played by Gaylen Ross; Stephen, by David Emge; and Peter, by Ken Foree.

23. *Ibid.*, 273.

24. *Ibid.*, 150, 148.

25. Baudrillard writes in *America*, "Santa Barbara is a paradise; Disneyland is a paradise; the U.S. is a paradise. Paradise is just paradise. Mournful, monotonous, and superficial though it may be, it is paradise. There is no other" (Baudrillard, *America*, 98).

26. McCarthy, *Road*, 139.

27. *Ibid.*, 142, 144, 147, 148.

28. McCarthy writes, "They passed through towns that warned people away with messages scrawled on the billboards. The billboards had been whited out with thin coats of paint in order to write on them and through the paint could be seen a pale palimpsest of advertisements for goods which no longer existed" (*Ibid.*, 128). It's telling here that coat after coat of paint fails to cover the advertisements on these billboards. These images are so ever-present that they have become burned into our retinas—afterimages, like the jingles and slogans that still haunt me from childhood: "Can't beat it. The feeling you get from a Coca-Cola Classic. Can't beat the feeling. Can't beat the real thing."

29. *Ibid.*, 140–45.

30. *Ibid.*, 181.

31. At one point, the man and the boy come across the remains of "a charred human infant headless and gutted and blackening on the spit" (*Ibid.*, 198). And, elsewhere, we get descriptions of imprisoned amputees with cauterized limbs, suggesting gruesomely that people are being kept alive so that their limbs can be eaten one at a time. It's an ingenious idea, a perfect way to keep the rest of the meat fresh, and the sort of moment that makes the book's appearance on Oprah's Book Club all the more befuddling. McCarthy clearly isn't afraid to muck around with our most sacred taboos.

Afterword:
The Zombie Is Dead
Long Live the Zombie

ROBERT G. WEINER

Ah, the zombie! It seems as though zombies are everywhere these days. In addition to the explosion of zombie films, there are zombie walks, various zombie-related television series, zombie websites and Facebook groups, zombie classes in colleges and universities, zombie candy, zombie conferences, zombie clothing, zombie societies, zombie videogames, zombie guns and ammunition, zombie make-up kits, zombie music, zombie plays, zombie toys, zombie sex fetishes, zombie mash-ups, zombie television advertisements, and zombie children's stories. You can even celebrate Christmas with a zombie Santa and watch Scooby Doo battle zombies on Zombie Island. One writer, Stant Litore, even created a Zombie Bible series. Not bad for a monster that was once considered the lowest creature on the totem pole where werewolves, mummies, mad scientists, and vampires once ruled popular culture. Of course, there are zombie novels, short stories, and long-form series. As this collection from Kyle William Bishop and Angela Tenga shows, although the zombie may not have as long a literary history as, say, the vampire, there is a surprising number of both historical and modern stories featuring every kind of zombie incarnation you can think of.

The Written Dead shows that perhaps the most interesting work being done with zombies today is in the literary realm. I've occasionally taught an honors course titled "Zombie Culture: The Zombie in History, Film, Literature, Sequential Art, and the Popular Imagination." I use Otto Penzler's *Zombies! Zombies! Zombies!* collection, which contains a diverse selection of stories featuring the likes of Edgar Allan Poe, W.B. Seabrook, H.P. Lovecraft, Richard Laymon, Robert Bloch, Joe Lansdale, Richard Matheson, Robert

Howard, and Stephen King. Students are often amused because so many of the stories do not fit with their modern conception of the zombie (in fact, one tale features creatures that seem much more like werewolves than any kind of zombie). Part of the reason behind using a collection that features so many of those old pulp stories is to have students think about the question of what exactly a zombie is. When they think about "the undead," more often than not, someone makes the comment that we as living humans are "the undead" and the zombies and vampires are the "dead who move." This collection asks its readers to ponder this question as well. When pressed on the definition of *zombie,* most would probably respond that it has something to do with the dead rising to eat flesh or those without a soul. Yet there are zombies that don't actually die in the strictest sense (for example, the living zombie and the hater). In the previous pages, you have read about all kinds of zombie narratives and the different zombies that populate them. Regardless of the type of zombie (disenfranchised ghouls, haters, mindless ones, walkers, bathsalt zombies, zombie ants, unmentionables, intelligent zombies who retain a certain amount of consciousness, hungries, reanimates, brain eaters, rotters, infected, walkers, skels, voodoo zombies, and those with Post-Apocalyptic Stress Disorder) into which one is transformed, one's fundamental self has been changed.

While the modern version of the zombie is informed by director George A. Romero's flesh-eating ghouls, the literary zombie has moved beyond Romero into something "posthuman," as many of the contributors to *The Written Dead* have argued. The zombie can be a metaphor for everything from the Vietnam War and racism to the dangers of social media and losing our humanity and ability to converse with one another in an ever-increasing online world (going back to the loss of one's fundamental self). Like Romero, writers like Cormac McCarthy, Robert Kirkman, Michael Swanwick, Stephen Graham Jones, and David Wellington show that it is humans who are truly evil, often treating each other worse than zombies ever could. The zombie acts as an example of humanity's inhumanity.

Sure, Romero changed the way we think of zombies by transforming them into the flesh-eating corporeal dead we know today as opposed to the controlled Voodoo zombie without will or soul. Once at an academic conference, I went to a panel on zombies, and everyone just talked about Romero's influence as though no one else had ever done anything on zombies. I brought up the work of Lucio Fulci, whose zombie films I felt deserved some attention. No one even acknowledged Fulci, and most had no idea who he was. With all due respect to Romero, Fulci is my favorite zombie director. He combined the best of the flesh-eating ghouls with the supernatural elements of the Voodoo zombie (my favorite zombie film is *Zombie* [1979], although *Zombie 3* [1988] features radioactive "fast"-style zombies). At the same conference a few years later, I was told by one scholar that the Voodoo zombie was not even a real zombie since it didn't have the Romero flesh-eating component. Of course, this is just not the case, as the introductory essays in this volume point out (these are found in some of the first zombie films, *White Zombie* [1932, directed by Victor Halperin] and the brilliant *I Walked with a Zombie* [1943, directed by Jacques Tourneur]; in literature, such as Lafcadio Hern's "Country of the Comers-Back" [1889], William Seabrook's *The Magic Island* [1929], and in so many of those pulp stories of the 1930s-1950s; and in pre–Comics Code [1940-early 1950s] comics, such as *Tales from the Crypt*). The supernatural zombie has just as much a place in the zombie canon as any other kind of zombie. I have always found the supernatural/Voodoo zombie compelling. There is something innately creepy about this kind of zombie in both film and literature, and to be controlled by a "zombie master" is just plain evil.

The *Written Dead* is an enlightening and splendidly curated collection of essays covering everything related to the literary zombie from its origins to the present day. You, the reader, will no doubt find a richness here that you can use in your quest to learn about all things zombie. The work of Max Brooks is given its own section, and rightly so, as any analysis of the literary zombie worth "its salt" (pun intended) has to include Brooks' work. I never would have thought of discussing Jack London in conjunction with zombie fiction, but it works. The works of young-adult writer Carrie Ryan are given serious treatment in light of historical Gothic fiction, which shows a maturity beyond the target audience. I have only seen the film *Warm Bodies* (2013, directed by Jonathan Levine) as similar to the Twilight film franchise (2008–12), with zombies substituted for vampires, but, as readers of *The Written Dead* know, Isaac Marion's novel of the same name is much more sophisticated than a casual reading would suggest. And M.R. Carey's *The Girl with All the Gifts* (2014) is one of the most original zombie tales in the last decade. An educator is the hero of the story, which shows that even in the zombie apocalypse, teachers are still important.

Bishop and Tenga's *The Written Dead: The Zombie as a Literary Phenomenon* is the standard academic work on the literary zombie. It will be the go-to text for anyone teaching the zombie in literature and will inform analysis on the zombie for decades to come. What can the historical and present-day zombie teach us about the world we live in? Lots! More importantly, the essays in this collection tell us that the zombie can teach a thing or two about what it means to be human and the importance of being kind to one another.

Filmography

"Always Accountable," *The Walking Dead* (Jeffrey F. January, 2015)

American Sniper (Clint Eastwood, 2015)

The Avengers (Joss Whedon, 2012)

Braindead (Peter Jackson, 1992)

Buffy the Vampire Slayer (Joss Whedon, 1997–2003)

The Cabinet of Dr. Caligari (Robert Weine, 1920)

The Daily Show (Lizz Winstead and Madeleine Smithberg, 1996–)

Dawn of the Dead (George A. Romero, 1978)

Dawn of the Dead (Zack Snyder, 2004)

Day of the Dead (George A. Romero, 1985)

Ex Machina (Alex Garland, 2015)

Halloween III: Season of the Witch (Tommy Lee Wallace, 1982)

Hell of the Living Dead (Bruno Mattei, 1980)

Humans (Chris Fry, 2015–)

I Am Legend (Francis Lawrence, 2007)

I Walked with a Zombie (Jacques Tourneur, 1943)

iZombie (Rob Thomas, 2015–)

Jennifer's Body (Karyn Kusama, 2009)

King of the Zombies (Jean Yarbrough, 1941)

Land of the Dead (George A. Romero, 2005)

The Last Man on Earth (Ubaldo Ragona and Sidney Salkow, 1964)

The Last Man on Earth (Will Forte, 2015–)

The Last of Us (Bruce Straley and Neil Druckmann, 2013)

The Machinist (Brad Anderson, 2004)

Michael Jackson: Thriller (John Landis, 1983)

Night of the Living Dead (George A. Romero, 1968)

Nightmare City (a.k.a. *Incubo Sulla Città Contaminata*) (Umberto Lenzi, 1980)

The Omega Man (Boris Sagal, 1971)

Ouanga (George Terwilliger, 1935)
Rambo: First Blood Part II (George P. Cosmatos, 1985)
Rammbock (Marvin Kren, 2010)
Red Dawn (John Milius, 1984)
Resident Evil (Paul W.S. Anderson, 2002)
Schindler's List (Steven Spielberg, 1993)
Shaun of the Dead (Edgar Wright, 2004)
Slacker (Richard Linklater, 1991)
The Stuff (Larry Cohen, 1985)
28 Days Later (Danny Boyle, 2002)
28 Weeks Later (Juan Carlos Fresnadillo, 2007)
The Walking Dead (Frank Darabont, 2010–)
Warm Bodies (Jonathan Levine, 2013)
White Zombie (Victor Halperin, 1932)
World War Z (Marc Forster, 2013)
The World's End (Edgar Wright, 2013)
Zombie (Lucio Fulci, 1979)
Zombie 3 (Lucio Fulci, 1988)

Bibliography

Ackerman, Spencer. "Army's Disaster Prep Now Includes Tips from the Zombie Apocalypse." *Wired* 4 Apr. 2013.

Adams, John Joseph, ed. *The Living Dead*. San Francisco, Night Shade Books, 2008.

_____. *The Living Dead 2*. San Francisco: Night Shade Books, 2010.

Agamben, Giorgio. *Homo Sacer*. Stanford: Stanford University Press, 1995.

Alderman, Naomi. "The Meaning of Zombies." *Granta*, 20 Nov. 2011. http://granta.com/the-meaning-of-zombies/.

Amusement Securities Corporation Vs. Academy Pictures Distributing Corporation. 618 (New York Supreme Court Appellate Division, 30 June 1936).

Austen, Jane, and Seth Grahame-Smith. *Pride and Prejudice and Zombies*. Philadelphia: Quirk Books, 2009.

Bailey, Dale. "Death and Suffrage." *The Magazine of Fantasy & Science Fiction*, Feb. 2002: 123–60.

Baker, Kelly J. *The Zombies Are Coming!* Bondfire Books, 2013. Kindle ed.

Baldwin, Gayle R. "*World War Z* and the End of Religion as We Know It." *CrossCurrents* 57.3 (2007): 412–25.

Baldwin, James. *Giovanni's Room*. 1956. New York: Vintage, 2014.

Ballou, James. *Long-Term Survival in the Coming Dark Age: Preparing to Live After Society Crumbles*. Boulder: Paladin Press, 2007.

Barker, Clive. "Sex, Death and Starshine." In Jones, *Mammoth Book of Zombies*, 1–42.

Barlow, Jeffrey. "*Feed* Review." *Interface: The Journal of Education, Community and Values*. 10.6 (2010). http://bcis.pacificu.edu/journal/article.php?id=707.

Baudrillard, Jean. *America*. New York: Verso, 1988.

_____. *Simulacra and Simulation*. 1981. Translated by Sheira Faria Glaser. Ann Arbour: University of Michigan Press, 1994.

Bauman, Zygmunt. *The Individualized Society*. Cambridge: Polity, 2008.

_____. *Liquid Life*. Cambridge: Polity, 2005.

_____. *Liquid Modernity*. Cambridge: Polity, 2012.

_____. "The London Riots—On Consumerism Coming Home to Roost." *Social Europe*, 9 Aug. 2011. http://www.socialeurope.eu/2011/08/the-london-riots-on-consumerism-coming-home-to-roost/.

Beaune, Jean-Claude. "The Classical Age of Automata: An Impressionistic Survey from the Sixteenth to the Nineteenth Century." In *Fragments for a History of the Human Body*, edited by Michel Feher, 431–80. Cambridge: MIT Press, 1989.

Beck, Ulrich. *Cosmopolitan Vision*. Cambridge: Polity, 2006.

_____. *A God of One's Own: Religion's Capacity for Peace and Potential for Violence*. Cambridge: Polity, 2010.

_____. *Power in the Global Age: A New Global Political Economy*. Cambridge: Polity, 2005.

_____. *The Reinvention of Politics: Rethinking Modernity in the Global Social Order*. Cambridge: Polity 1997.

_____. *Risk Society: Towards a New Modernity*. Sage Publications, 1992.

Beck, Ulrich, and Edgar Grande. *Cosmopolitan Europe*. Cambridge: Polity, 2007.

Beck, Ulrich, and Elisabeth Beck-Gernsheim. *Individualization: Institutionalized Individualism and Its Social and Political Consequences*. London: Sage, 2002.

Becker, Robin. *Brains: A Zombie Memoir*. New York: HarperCollins Publishers, 2010.

Beckwith, Martha Warren. *Black Roadways: A Study of Jamaican Folk Life*. Chapel Hill: University of North Carolina Press, 1929.

Bell, Alden [Joshua Gaylord]. *The Reapers Are the Angels*. New York: Henry Holt, 2010.

Benjamin, Walter. "The Work of Art in the Age of Mechanical Reproduction." In *Film Theory and Criticism: Introductory Readings*, edited by Leo Braudy and Marshall Cohen, 731–51. Oxford: Oxford University Press, 1999.

Benston, Kimberly W. "I Yam What I Am: The Topos of (Un)Naming in Afro-American Literature." In *Black Literature and Literary Theory*, edited by Henry Louis Gates, Jr., 151–72. New York: Methuen, 1984.

Bickley, Pamela. Introduction to *The Last Man*. In Shelley, vii–xxviii.

Biodrowski, Steve. "Interview: George Romero Documents the Dead." *Cinefantastique Online*, 15 Feb. 2008. http://cinefantastiqueonline.com/2008/02/interview-george-romero-documents-the-dead-part-1/.

Bishop, Kyle William. *American Zombie Gothic: The Rise and Fall (And Rise) of the Walking Dead in Popular Culture*. Jefferson, NC: McFarland, 2010.

_____. "Dead Man *Still* Walking: Explaining the Zombie Renaissance." *Journal of Popular Film and Television* 37.1 (2009): 16–25.

_____. "The Idle Proletariat: *Dawn of the Dead*, Consumer Ideology, and the Loss of Productive Labor." *The Journal of Popular Culture* 43 (2010): 234–48.

_____. "Raising the Dead: Unearthing the Nonliterary Origins of Zombie Cinema." *Journal of Popular Film & Television* 33.4 (2006): 196–205.

_____. "The Sub-Subaltern Monster: Imperialist Hegemony and the Cinematic Voodoo Zombie." *The Journal of American Culture* 31.2 (2008): 141–52.

Boccaccio, Giovanni. *The Decameron*. 1353. Edited and translated by Mark Musa and Peter E. Bondanella. Norton Critical Editions. New York: Norton, 1977.

Boluk, Stephanie, and Wylie Lenz. "Infection, Media, and Capitalism: From Early Modern Plagues to Postmodern Zombies." *The Journal for Early Modern Cultural Studies* 10.2 (2010): 126–47.

_____. "Introduction: Generation Z, the Age of Apocalypse." In Boluk and Lenz, 1–17.

_____., eds. *Generation Zombie: Essays on the Living Dead in Modern Culture*. Jefferson, NC: McFarland, 2011.

Boon, Kevin Alexander. "The Zombie as Other: Mortality and the Monstrous in the Post-Nuclear Age." In Christie and Lauro, 50–60.

Brailer, Max. *Can You Survive the Zombie Apocalypse?* New York: Gallery Books, 2011.

Brandner, Gary. *The Brain Eaters*. New York: Fawcett, 1985.

_____. *Carrion*. New York: Fawcett, 1986.

Briggs, Daniel. "Concluding Thoughts." In Briggs, *English Riots*, 381–400.

_____. "Frustrations, Urban Relations and Temptations: Contextualising the English Riots." In Briggs, *English Riots*, 27–41.

_____. "Introduction." In Briggs, *English Riots*, 9–25.

Briggs, Daniel, ed. *The English Riots of 2011: A Summer of Discontent*. Hook, Hampshire: Waterside Press, 2012.

Brontë, Charlotte. *Jane Eyre*. 1847. New York: Penguin, 2006.

Brooks, Max. "Steve and Fred." In Adams, *The Living Dead 2*, 203–10.

_____. *World War Z: An Oral History of the Zombie War*. New York: Crown Publishing Group, 2006.

_____. *The Zombie Survival Guide: Complete Protection from the Living Dead*. New York: Three Rivers Press, 2003.

Brown, Charles Brockden. *Arthur Mervyn; Or, Memoirs of the Year 1793*. 1799. Edited by Philip Barnard and Stephen Shapiro. Cambridge: Hackett, 2008.

Browne, S. G. *Breathers: A Zombie's Lament*. New York: Broadway, 2009.

Browning, John Edgar. "Survival Horrors, Survival Spaces: Tracing the Modern Zombie (Cine)Myth." *Horror Studies* 2.1 (2011): 41–59.

Bumiller, Elizabeth. "U.S. Lifts Photo Ban on Military Coffins." *New York Times* 7 Dec. 2009.

Cacioppo, John T., Louise C. Hawkley, Elizabeth Crawford, John M. Ernst, Mary H. Burleson, Ray B. Kowalewski, William B. Malarkey, Eve Van Cauter, and Gary G. Berntson," Loneliness and Health: Potential Mechanisms." *Psychosomatic Medicine* 64.3 (2002): 407–17.

Campbell, Ramsey. "Rising Generation." 1975. Jones, *Mammoth Book of Zombies*, 43–48.

Camus, Albert. *The Plague*. Translated by Stuart Gilbert. New York: Vintage, 1991.

Canavan, Anne. "Which Came First, Zombie or the Plague? Colson Whitehead's *Zone One* as Post–9/11 Allegory." In *Representing 9/11: Trauma, Ideology, and Nationalism in Literature, Film, and Television*, edited by Paul Petrovic, 41–52. Lanham, MD: Rowman and Littlefield, 2015.

Canavan, Gerry. "'If the Engine Ever Stops, We'd All Die': *Snowpiercer and* Necrofuturism." In *SF Now*, edited by Mark Bould and Rhys Williams, 41–66. Vashon Island: Paradoxa, 2014.

Cantor, Paul A. "The Apocalyptic Strain in Popular Culture: The American Nightmare Becomes the American Dream." *The Hedgehog Review* 15.2 (2013): 23–33.

Caponegro, Candace. *The Breeze Horror*. New York: Onyk, 1988.

Caputo, Philip. *A Rumor of War*. New York: Henry and Holt Company, 1996.

Carey, M. R. *The Girl with All the Gifts*. New York: Orbit, 2014.

Carroll, Noël. *The Philosophy of Horror or Paradoxes of the Heart*. New York: Routledge, 1990.

Castle, Terry. *The Female Thermometer: 18th-Century Culture and the Invention of the Uncanny*. New York: Oxford University Press, 1995.

Castro, Adam-Troy. "The Anteroom." In Adams, *The Living Dead 2*, 49–56.

Cave, Hugh B. *Legion of the Dead*. Holicong, PA: Wildside, 1979.

Charles, Ron. "'Zone One,' by Colson Whitehead: Zombies Abound." *Washington Post*, October 19, 2011. https://www.washingtonpost.com/entertainment/books/zone-one-by-colson-whitehead-zombies-abound/2011/10/09/gIQAGrMMvL_story.html.

Chetwynd-Hayes, R. "The Ghouls." 1975. In Jones, *Mammoth Book of Zombies*, 63–86.

Christie, Deborah, and Sarah Juliet Lauro, eds. *Better Off Dead: The Evolution of the Zombie as Post-Human*. New York: Fordham University Press, 2011.

Clark, Simon. *Stranger*. New York: Leisure, 2002.

Clute, John, and David Langford. "Zombies." In *The Encyclopedia of Fantasy*, 2nd edition, edited by John Clute and John Grant, 1048. London: Orbit, 1999.

Cohen, Jeffrey Jerome. "Monster Culture (Seven Theses)." In *Monster Theory*, edited by Jeffrey Jerome Cohen, 3–25. Minneapolis: University of Minnesota Press, 1996.

Cohen, Kathleen. "New Study: Social Media as Addictive as Drugs and Alcohol." WIFR. 2 Mar. 2016. http://www.wifr.com/home/headlines/New-Study-Social-Media-as-Addictive-as-Drugs-and-Alcohol-370864881.html.

Cohn, Dorrit. *Transparent Minds: Narrative Modes for Presenting Consciousness in Fiction*. Princeton: Princeton University Press, 1978.

Collins, Margo, and Elson Bond. "'Off the Page and into Your Brains!': New Millennial Zombies and the Scourge of Hopeful Apocalypses." In Christie and Lauro, 187–204.

Conrich, Ian. "An Infectious Population: Zombie Culture and the Modern Montrous." In *The Zombie Apocalypse in Popular Culture*, edited by Laura Hubner, Marcus Leaning, and Paul Manning, 15–25. Basingstoke: Palgrave Macmillan, 2015.

Cooke, Jennifer. *Legacies of Plague in Literature, Theory and Film*. London: Palgrave Macmillan, 2009.

Craige, John Houston. *Black Bagdad*. New York: Minton, Balch, 1933.

Cvek, Sven. "Surviving Utopia in *Zone One*." In *Facing the Crises: Anglophone Literature in the Postmodern World*, edited by Ljubica Matek and Jasna Poljak Rehlicki, 2–14. Cambridge: Cambridge Scholars, 2014.

Dante Alighieri. *Inferno*. Translated by Allen Mandelbaum. New York: Bantam Dell, 1980.

Darwin, Charles. *The Descent of Man, and Selection in Relation to Sex*. In *The Works of Charles*

Darwin, edited by Paul H. Barrett and R.B. Freeman, 9–644. New York: New York University Press, 1989.

Davis, Wade. *Passage of Darkness: The Ethnobiology of the Haitian Zombie.* University of North Carolina Press, 2000.

_____. *The Serpent and the Rainbow.* New York: Simon & Schuster, 1985.

Day, William Patrick. *Vampire Legends in Contemporary American Culture: What Becomes a Legend Most.* Lexington: University Press of Kentucky, 2002.

DeBerry, Jarvis "'The American Sniper's' Preposterous Post-Katrina New Orleans Story." *The Times Picayune* 20 Jan. 2015. http://www.nola.com/entertainment/index.ssf/2015/01/the_american_snipers_preposter.html.

Defoe, Daniel. *A Journal of the Plague Year.* 1722. Edited by Cynthia Wall. London: Penguin Books, 2003.

Dekker, Thomas. "The Wonderfull Yeare." 1603. Transcribed by Risa S. Bear. *Renascence Editions*, 2000. http://www.luminarium.org/renascence-editions/yeare.html.

Deleuze, Gilles, and Felix Guattari. *Anti-Oedipus: Capitalism and Schizophrenia.* Minneapolis: University of Minnesota Press, 1983.

Dena, Christy. "Theorising the Practice of Expressing a Fictional World Across Distinct Media and Environments." Sydney: University of Sydney, 2009.

Dendle, Peter. *The Zombie Movie Encyclopedia.* Jefferson, NC: McFarland, 2001.

Derksen, Craig, and Darren Hudson Hick. "Your Zombie and You: Identity, Emotion, and the Undead." In *Zombie Are Us: Essays on the Humanity of the Walking Dead*, edited by Christopher M. Moreman and Cory James Rushton, 11–23. Jefferson: McFarland, 2011.

Descartes, René. "Meditations on First Philosophy." In *The Philosophical Works of Descartes*, trans. Elizabeth S. Haldane, 1–32. Cambridge: Cambridge University Press, 1911.

Dicce, Domenick. *You're a Vampire—That Sucks! A Survival Guide.* New York: Penguin Publishing Group, 2015.

DiLouie, Craig. *Tooth and Nail.* Portland: Schmidt Haus Books, 2010.

"Disaster." *The Encyclopedia of Science Fiction*, 12 Oct. 2014. http://www.sf-encyclopedia.com/entry/disaster.

Downs, Frederick. *The Killing Zone: My Life in the Vietnam War.* New York: Norton, 2007.

Drezner, Daniel. *Theories of International Politics and Zombies: Revived Edition.* Woodstock, NJ: Princeton University Press, 2014.

Du Bois, W. E. Burghardt. "The Comet." In *Darkwater: Voices from Within the Veil*, 253–73. New York: Harcourt, Brace and Howe, 1920.

Dufour, Éric. *Le Cinéma d'Horreur et Ses Figures.* Paris: Presses Universitaires de France, 2006.

Eburne, Jonathan P. "Zombie Arts and Letter." In *This Year's Work at the Zombie Research Center*, edited by Edward P. Comentale and Aaron Jaffe, 389–415. Bloomington, IN: Indiana University Press, 2014.

Eliot, T.S. *The Waste Land.* In *T.S. Eliot: The Complete Poems and Plays*, 37–55. New York: Harcourt and Brace, 1967.

Ellison, Ralph. *Invisible Man.* 1952. New York: Vintage, 1995.

Emmert, Scott D. "Naturalism and the Short Story Form: Kate Chopin's 'The Story of an Hour.'" In *Scribbling Women and the Short Story Form: Approaches by American and British Women Writers*, edited by Ellen Burton Harrington, 74–85. New York: Peter Lang, 2008.

Engelhardt, Tom. *The End of Victory Culture: Cold War America and the Disillusioning of a Generation.* Amherst: University of Massachusetts Press, 2007.

Fain, Kimberly. "Colson Whitehead: The Postracial Voice in Contemporary Literature." New Books Network, 30 Nov. 2015. http://newbooksnetwork.com/kimberly-fain-colson-whitehead-the-postracial-voice-of-contemporary-literature-rowman-and-littlefield-2015/.

Fassler, Joe. "How Zombies and Superheroes Conquered Highbrow Fiction." *The Atlantic*, 12 Oct. 2011. http://www.theatlantic.com/entertainment/archive/2011/10/how-zombies-and-superheroes-conquered-highbrow-fiction/246847/.

Foucault, Michel. *Discipline & Punish: The Birth of the Prison*. New York: Vintage, 1995.

Frater, Rhiannon. *The First Days: As the World Dies*. 2008. New York: Tom Doherty Associate Book, 2011.

Fratiglioni, Laura, Hui-Xin Wang, and Kjerstin Ericsson. "Influence of Social Network on Occurrence of Dementia: A Community Based Longitudinal Study." *Lancet* (North American Edition) 355.9212 (2000): 1315–19.

Freud, Sigmund. "The Uncanny." In *The Standard Edition of the Complete Psychological Works*, edited and translated by James Strachey, 219–52. London: Hogarth, 1955.

Gehlhar, Mary. *The Fashion Designer Survival Guide, Revised and Expanded Edition: Start and Run Your Own Fashion Business*. New York: Kaplan, 2008.

Geltman, Joani. *A Survival Guide to Parenting Teens: Talking to Your Kids About Sexting, Drinking, Drugs, and Other Things That Freak You Out*. New York: AMACOM, 2014.

Genette, Gérard. *Palimpsests: Literature in the Second Degree*. Translated by Channa Newman & Claude Doubinsky. French Ministry of Culture, 1982.

Gerson, Sharon J., and Steven M Gerson. *Technical Writing: Process and Product*. New York: Pearson, 2000.

Gibson, James William. *Warrior Dreams: Paramilitary Culture in Post-Vietnam America*. New York: Hill and Wang, 1994.

Giddens, Anthony. *The Consequences of Modernity*. Stanford: Stanford University Press, 1990.

_____. *Modernity and Self-Identity: Self and Society in the Late Modern Age*. Cambridge: Polity, 1991.

Giddens, Anthony, and Christopher Pierson. *Conversations with Anthony Giddens: Making Sense of Modernity*. Stanford: Stanford University Press, 1998.

Girard, René. "The Plague in Literature and Myth." *Texas Studies in Literature and Language* 15.5 (1974): 833–50.

Goddard, Richard E. *The Whistling Ancestors*. London: Stanley Smith, 1936.

Gooch, Brad. *Zombie00*. Woodstock: Overlook, 2000.

Grant, Mira. *Blackout*. New York: Orbit, 2012.

_____. *Deadline*. New York: Orbit, 2011.

_____. *Fed*. Orbit Books. 23 May 2012. http://www.orbitbooks.net/2012/05/23/what-if-things-had-ended-differently-fed-by-mira-grant/.

_____. *Feed*. New York: Orbit, 2010.

_____. *Rise: A Newsflesh Collection*. New York: Orbit, 2016.

Gray, Chris Hables, Steven Mentor, and Heidi J. Figueroa-Sarriera. "Cyborgology: Constructing the Knowledge of Cybernetic Organisms." In *The Cyborg Handbook*, edited by Chris Hables Gray, 1–16. New York: Routledge Press, 1995.

Greatshell, Walter. *Xombies*. New York: Berkley, 2004.

Gregory, Daryl. *Raising Stony Mayhall*. New York: Ballatine Books, 2011.

Habel, Lia. *Dearly, Departed*. New York: Del Rey, 2011.

Haining, Peter. Introduction. In Haining, 7–20.

Haining, Peter, ed. *Zombie! Stories of the Walking Dead*. London: W. H. Allen, 1985.

Hall, Stuart. "The Saturday Interview." By Zoe Williams. *The Guardian*, 11 Feb. 2012. http://www.theguardian.com/theguardian/2012/feb/11/saturday-interview-stuart-hall.

Hamm, Sam. "Homecoming." In *Masters of Horror*. Starz, 2 Dec. 2005.

Harper, Steven. "*Night of the Living Dead*: Reappraising an Undead Classic." *Bright Lights Film Journal* 1 Nov. 2005. http://brightlightsfilm.com/night-living-dead-reappraising-undead-classic/#.V55F8pODGko.

_____. "Zombies, Malls, and the Consumerism Debate: George Romero's *Dawn of the Dead*." *Americana: The Journal of American Popular Culture* 1.2 (2002). http://www.americanpopularculture.com/journal/articles/fall_2002/harper.

Harpold, Terry. "The End Begins: John Wyndham's Zombie Cozy." In Boluk and Lenz, *Generation Zombie*, 156–64.

Hearn, Lafcadio. "The Country of Comers-Back." In Haining, 54–70.

_____. *Two Years in the French West Indies*. New York: Harper & Brothers Publishers, 1890.

Heer, Jeet. "Science Fiction's White Boys' Club Strikes Back." *New Republic*, 12 Apr. 2015.

https://newrepublic.com/article/121554/2015-hugo-awards-and-history-science-fiction-culture-wars.

Hegel, G.W. F. *Phenomenology of Spirit*. Translated by A. V. Miller. Oxford: Oxford University Press, 1977.

Hemingway, Ernest. *The Old Man and the Sea*. New York: Scribner, 1951.

Herman, Marc. "Gun Owners Are Obsessed with Zombies." *Salon*. 21 Feb. 2013. http://www.salon.com/2013/02/21/why_are_gun_owners_suddenly_obsessed_with_zombies_partner/.

Herr, Michael. *Dispatches*. New York: Random House, 1991.

Herring, George C. "Vietnam Remembered." *The Journal of American History* 73.1 (June 1986): 152–64.

Hobbs, Frank, and Nicole Stoops. "Demographic Trends in the 20th Century." US Census Bureau, Census 2000 Special Reports, CENSR-4. Washington, D.C.: US Government Printing Office, 33. http://www. census.gov/prod/2002pubs/censr-4.pdf, 2002.

Hoberek, Andrew. "Living with PASD." *Contemporary Literature* 53.2 (2012): 406–13.

Hogle, Jerrold E. "Introduction: The Gothic in Western Culture." In Hogle, 1–20.

_____, ed. *Cambridge Companion to Gothic Fiction*. Cambridge: Cambridge University Press, 2002.

Hood, Gregory. "World War Z." *Counter Currents Publishing*, Jan. 2013. http://www.counter-currents.com/2013/01/world-war-z/.

Hubner, Laura, Marcus Leaning, and Paul Manning, eds. *The Zombie Renaissance in Popular Culture*, 193–207. Basingstoke: Palgrave Macmillan, 2014.

Hurston, Zora Neale. Interview by Mary Margaret McBride. *Mary Margaret McBride Show*. WEAF (WNBC), 25 Jan. 1943.

_____. *Tell My Horse*. New York: J.B. Lippincott, 1938.

Hutcheon, Linda. *A Theory of Adaptation*. New York: Routledge, 2006.

Hutter, G. W. [Garnett Weston]. "Salt Is Not for Slaves." In Haining, *Zombie!*, 39–53.

Hyman, Ira. "Texting Zombies: The Scourge of Text Messaging in Public." *Psychology Today* 2 July 2010. https://www.psychologytoday.com/blog/mental-mishaps/201007/texting-zombies-the-scourge-text-messaging-in-public.

Ignatieff, Michael. "America's Empire Is an Empire Lite." *New York Times* 10 Jan. 2003.

Iser, Wolfgang. "The Reading Process: A Phenomenological Approach." *New Literary History* 3.2 (1972): 279–99.

Jackson, Rosemary. *Fantasy: The Literature of Subversion*. London: Routledge, 1991.

Jacobellis v. Ohio, 378 U.S. 184 (1964).

Jameson, Fredric. *Archaeologies of the Future: The Desire Called Utopia and Other Science Fictions*. London: Verso, 2005.

_____. *Postmodernism: Or, the Cultural Logic of Late Capitalism*. Durham: Duke University Press, 1991.

Jauss, Hans Robert. *Toward an Aesthetic of Reception*. Translated by Timothy Bahti. Minneapolis: University of Minnesota Press, 1982.

Jensen, Jeff. "The Last Man on Earth." *Entertainment Weekly*, ew.com, 25 Feb. 2015.

Johnson, James Weldon. *The Autobiography of an Ex-Colored Man*. 1912. Edited by Jacqueline Goldsby. Norton Critical Editions. New York: Norton, 2015.

Jones, David R. "Why the Democrats Won." *CBS News*. 8 Nov. 2006. http://www.cbsnews.com/news/why-the-democrats-won/.

Jones, Kylene. *The Provident Prepper: A Common-Sense Guide to Preparing for Emergencies*. Springville, UT: Cedar Fort, 2014.

Jones, Stephen. *The Mammoth Book of Zombies*. New York: Carroll & Graf, 1993.

_____. *Zombie Apocalypse!* London: Constable & Robinson Limited, 2010.

"Jungles." *Planet Earth*. Narrated by David Attenborough. BBC, 8 Apr. 2007.

Katz, Steven B. "The Ethic of Expediency: Classical Rhetoric, Technology, and the Holocaust." *College English* 54.3 (1992): 255–75.

Kearny, Creson. "Nuclear War Survival Skills: Updated and Expanded." Cave Junction, OR: Oregon Institute of Science & Medicine, 1999.

Keene, Brian. *The Rising*. 2003. New York: Leisure Books, 2004.

Keetley, Dawn. "Zombie Republic: Property and the Propertyless Multitude in Romero's Dead Films and Kirkman's the *Walking Dead*." *Journal of the Fantastic in the Arts* 25.2–3 (2014): 324–42.

Kielpinski, Gerald, and Brian Gleisberg. *Surviving the Zombie Outbreak: The Official Zombie Survival Field Manual.* Edmonton, AB: Aquarius Publishing, 2011.

Kilpatrick, Nancy. "The Age of Sorrow." In Adams, *The Living Dead*, 332–433.

King, Stephen. *Cell.* New York: Scribner, 2006.

_____. "Home Delivery." In Adams, *The Living Dead*, 236–56.

Kirkman, Robert. "Alone, Together." In Adams, *The Living Dead 2*, 3–16.

Kirkman, Robert, and Jay Bonansinga. *The Walking Dead: The Rise of the Governor.* New York: Thomas Dunne Books, 2011.

Knight, J. *Risen.* New York: Pinnacle, 2004.

Kojève, Alexandre. *Introduction to the Reading of Hegel.* Edited by Allan Bloom. Translated by James H. Nichols, Jr. Ithaca: Cornell University Press, 1980.

Koolhaas, Rem. "Junkspace." *October* 100 (2002): 175–90.

Ksenych, Daniel. "The Other Side of Theory." In Lowder, *The Book of All Flesh*, 166–75. Los Angeles: Eden Studios, 2001.

Kyle, Chris, Scott McEwen, and Jim DeFelice. *American Sniper.* New York: Harper, 2013.

Landon, Brooks. "Is Dead the New Alive?" *American Book Review* 34.2 (2013): 8.

Lane, Fred. *The Concerned Citizen's Guide to Surviving Nuclear, Biological and Chemical Terrorist Attack* Boulder: Paladin Press, 2004.

Lansdale, Joe R. *Dead in the West.* New York: Night Shade, 2005 rpt.

_____. "On the Far Side of the Cadillac Desert with Dead Folks." In Skipp and Spector, 298–342.

LaRose, Nicole. "Zombies in a 'Deep, Dark Ocean of History': Danny Boyle's Infected and John Wyndham's Triffids as Metaphors of Postwar Britain." In Boluk and Lenz, 165–81.

Larsen, Nella. *Passing.* 1929. Edited by Thadious M. Davis. New York: Penguin Classics, 2003.

Lauro, Sarah Juliet, and Deborah Christie. Introduction. In Christie and Lauro, 1–4.

Lauro, Sarah Juliet, and Karen Embry. "A Zombie Manifesto: The Nonhuman Condition in the Era of Advanced Capitalism." *Boundary 2* 35.1 (2008): 85–108.

Lavender, Isiah, III. *Race in American Science Fiction.* Bloomington: Indiana University Press, 2011.

Laymon, Richard. *One Rainy Night.* New York: Dorchester, 2000.

Lebbon, Tim. *Fears Unnamed.* New York: Leisure, 2004.

Lindqvist, John Ajvide. *Handling the Undead.* 2005. Translated by Ebba Segerberg. New York: Thomas Dunne Books, 2009.

Little, Bentley. *The Walking.* New York: Signet, 2000.

Liu, Catherine. *Copying Machines: Taking Notes for the Automaton.* Minneapolis: University of Minnesota Press, 2000.

London, Jack. *The Iron Heel.* London: London Press, 2013.

_____. *The Scarlet Plague.* 1912. Mineola, NY: Dover, 2015.

Loudermilk, A. "Eating 'Dawn' in the Dark: Zombie Desire and Commodified Identity in George A. Romero's *Dawn of the Dead*." *Journal of Consumer Culture* 3 (2003): 83–108.

Lovecraft, H.P. *Herbert West—Reanimator.* Vols. 1–6, in *The Mammoth Book of Zombies*, edited by Stephen Jones, 208–234. New York: Carroll and Graf, 1922.

Lowder, James. *The Book of All Flesh.* Los Angeles: Eden Studios, 2001.

_____. *The Book of Final Flesh.* Los Angeles: Eden Studios, 2003.

_____. *The Book of More Flesh.* Los Angeles: Eden Studios, 2002.

Lundin, Cody. *When All Hell Breaks Loose: Stuff You Need to Survive When Disaster Strikes.* Salt Lake City, UT: Gibbs Smith, 2007.

Maberry, Jonathan. *Patient Zero.* New York: St. Martin Griffin's, 2009.

"Major Describes Moves." *The New York Times* 8 Feb. 1968.

Marcinko, Richard, and John Weisman. *Rogue Warrior.* New York: Pocket Books, 1992.

Marion, Isaac. *Warm Bodies.* New York: Emily Bester Books, 2011.

Mason, Fran. "The Galvanic 'Unhuman': Technology, the Living Dead and the 'Animal Machine' in Literature and Culture." In Hubner, Leaning, and Manning, 193–207.

Matheson, Richard. *I Am Legend*. In *I Am Legend*, 1–159. New York: Tor, 1995.

McCarthy, Cormac. *The Road*. New York: Vintage, 2007.

McFarland, James. "Philosophy of the Living Dead." *Cultural Critique* 90 (2015): 22–63.

McGuire, Seanan. "Writing Faq." *Seanan McGuire*, 2016. http://seananmcguire.com/writefaq.php.

McGurl, Mark. "Zombie Renaissance." *N + 1* 27 (2010): 167–76.

McIntosh, Shawn. "The Evolution of the Zombie: The Monster That Keeps Coming Back." In *Zombie Culture: Autopsies of the Living Dead*, edited by Shawn McIntosh and Mark Leverette, 1–17. London: Scarecrow Press, 2008.

McKinney, Jason. *Memoirs of the Walking Dead: A Story from the Zombie's Point of View*. Charleston, SC: CreateSpace, 2010.

McKinney, Joe. *Dead City*. New York: Pinnacle Books, 2006.

McLuhan, Marshall. *Understanding Media*. New York: McGraw-Hill, 1964.

McNally, David. *Monsters of the Market: Zombies, Vampires and Global Capitalism*. Leiden: Brill, 2011.

Meik, Vivian. "White Zombie." In Haining, *Zombie: Stories of the Walking Dead*, 83–102. Tiptree, Essex: Anchor Brendon, 1985.

Mellick, Carlton, III. *The Steel Breakfast Era*. Portland: Eraserhead, 2003.

Mellier, Denis. *La Littérature Fantastique*. Paris: Seuil, 2000.

Miles, Robert. "The 1790s: The Effulgence of Gothic." In Hogle, 41–62.

Moody, David. *Dog Blood*. New York: Thomas Dunne Books, 2010.

_____. *Hater*. New York: Thomas Dunne Books, 2006.

_____. "Introduction" to "Who We Used to Be." In Adams, *The Living Dead 2*, 315.

_____. *Them or Us*. New York: Thomas Dunne Books, 2012.

_____. "Who We Used to Be." In Adams, *The Living Dead 2*, 315–26.

Moreman, Christopher M., and Cory James Rushton, eds. *Race, Oppression and the Zombie: Essay on Cross-Cultural Appropriations of the Caribbean Tradition*. Jefferson, NC: McFarland, 2011.

Morrison, Toni. *Playing in the Dark: Whiteness and the Literary Imagination*. Cambridge, MA: Harvard University Press, 1992.

_____. "Recitatif." In *The Norton Anthology of American Literature, Volume 2: 1865 to the Present*, edited by Nina Baym and Robert S. Levine, 1403–16. Shorter 8th ed. New York: Norton, 2013.

Mumfrey, W. H. [Grant Murray]. *The Alien Invasion Survival Handbook: A Defense Manual for the Coming Extraterrestrial Apocalypse*. Palm Coast, FL: How Books, 2009.

Nicholson, Scott. *The Harvest*. New York: Pinnacle, 2003.

Niedenthal, Simon. "Un Doux Parfum de Dégoût. L'Avenir du Zombie à l'Ère du Jeu Vidéo Odorant." In *Z Pour Zombies*, edited by Bernard Perron, Antonio Dominguez Leiva, and Samuel Archibal, 203–215. Montréal: Presses de l'Université de Montréal, 2015.

Nutman, Philip. *Wet Work*. New York: Jove, 1993.

Oates, Joyce Carol. *Zombie*. New York: Dutton, 1995.

Paffenroth, Kim. *Dying to Love*. New York: Permuted Press, 2006.

_____. *Gospel of the Living Dead: George Romero's Visions of Hell on Earth*. Waco, TX: Baylor University Press, 2006.

Page, Sean. *Zombie Survival Manual: From the Dawn of Time Onwards (All Variations)*. London: Haynes Publishing UK, 2013.

Palwick, Susan. "Beautiful Stuff." In Adams, *The Living Dead*, 137–47.

Pappademas, Alex, and Colson Whitehead. "When Zombies Attack!" *Grantland*, 24 Oct. 2011. http://grantland.com/features/when-zombies-attack/.

Pendleton, Don. *The Executioner's War Book*. New York: Pinnacle Books, 1977.

Penzler, Otto, ed. *Zombies! Zombies! Zombies!* New York: Vintage, 2011.

Perron, Bernard. "Zombie Escape and Survival Plans: Mapping the Transmedial World of the Dead." In *World Building. Transmedia, Fans, Industries*, edited by Marta Boni and Martin Lefebvre. Forthcoming. Amsterdam: Amsterdam University Press, 2017.

Perry, S. D. *Resident Evil: Umbrella Conspiracy*. 1998. London: Titan Books, 2012.

Pierce, Leonard. "Interview: Max Brooks." *A.V. Club*, 9 July 2010. http://www.avclub.com/article/max-brooks-42941.

Poe, Edgar Allan. "The Masque of the Red Death." In *The Tell-Tale Heart and Other Writings*, 43–49. New York: Bantam, 1982.

Polk, Dylan. "Outbreak Omega Shows Zombie Shooting Going Strong." *Guns and Ammo*. 26 June 2012. http://www.gunsandammo.com/blogs/zombie-nation/nobody-cares-about-zombie-shooting-says-who/.

"Post-Holocaust." *The Encyclopedia of Science Fiction*, 3 Apr. 2015. http://www.sf-encyclopedia.com/entry/post-holocaust.

Pressman, Sarah D., Sheldon Cohen, Gregory E. Miller, Anita Barkin, Bruce S. Rabin, and John J. Treanor. "Loneliness, Social Network Size, and Immune Response to Influenza Vaccination in College Freshmen." *Health Psychology* 24.3 (2005): 297–306.

Protevi, John. *Political Affect: Connecting the Social and the Somatic*. Minneapolis: University of Minnesota Press, 2009.

Pulliam, June. "The Zombie." In *Icons of Horror and the Supernatural. an Encyclopedia of Our Worst Nightmares*, Vol. 1, edited by S. T. Joshi, 723–53. Westport, CT: Greenwood, 2007.

Rabin, Nathan. "I'm Sorry for Coining the Phrase 'Manic Pixie Dream Girl.'" *Salon*. 15 July 2014. http://www.salon.com/2014/07/15/im_sorry_for_coining_the_phrase_manic_pixie_dream_girl/.

Radcliffe, Ann. *The Romance of the Forest*. Oxford: Oxford University Press, 1999.

Raz, Joseph. "The Role of Well-Being," *Philosophical Perspectives* 18.1 (2004): 269–94.

Reagan, Ronald. "Peace: Restoring the Margin of Safety." Veterans of Foreign Wars Convention, Chicago, Illinois. 18 Aug. 1980. *Reagan Library*, n.d. http://www.reagan.utexas.edu/archives/reference/8.18.80.html.

Rhodes, Gary D. *White Zombie: Anatomy of a Horror Film*. Jefferson, NC: McFarland, 2001.

Ritchie, Donald. *Doing Oral History*. Oxford: Oxford University Press, 2014.

Riva, Michele Augusto, Marta Benedetti, and Giancarlo Cesana. "Pandemic Fear and Literature: Observations from Jack London's the *Scarlet Plague*." *Emerging Infectious Diseases* 20.10 (2014). http://wwwnc.cdc.gov/eid/article/20/10/13–0278_article

Romero, George A., and John A. Russo. *Night of the Living Dead*. 1968. *List English*, n.d. http://list-english.ru/pdf/scripts/night-of-the-living-dead.pdf.

Roscoe, Theodore. *A Grave Must Be Deep*. Mercer Island, WA: Starmont House, 1989.

_____. *Z Is for Zombie*. New York: Starmont House, 1989 rpt.

Russell, Jamie. *Book of the Dead: The Complete History of Zombie Cinema*. 2005. Godalming: FAB Press, 2008.

Rutherford, Jennifer. *Zombies*. London: Routledge, 2013.

Ryan, Carrie. *The Dark and Hollow Places*. New York: Random House, 2011.

_____. *The Dead-Tossed Waves*. New York: Random House, 2010.

_____. *The Forest of Hands and Teeth*. New York: Random House, 2009.

St. John, Spenser. *Full Text of "Hayti, Or, the Black Republic," 2nd Ed.* London: Ballantyne Press, 1884.

Saldívar, Ramón. "The Second Elevation of the Novel: Race, Form, and the Postrace Aesthetic in Contemporary Narrative." *Narrative* 21.1 (2013): 1–18.

Schaefer, Christie. "World War Z: Monsters of This Society's Own Making." *World Socialist Web Site*, 25 Oct. 2007. https://www.wsws.org/en/articles/2007/10/mons-o25.html.

Schlozman, Steven. *The Zombie Autopsies: Secret Notebooks from the Apocalypse*. London: Transworld, 2011.

Seabrook, W. B. *The Magic Island*. New York: Harcourt, Brace and Company, 1929.

"Secret U.S. Message to Mullah Omar: 'Every Pillar of the Taliban Regime Will Be Destroyed.'" *The National Security Archive*. 11 Sept. 2011. http://nsarchive.gwu.edu/NSAEBB/NSAEBB358a/.

Selby, Curt. *I, Zombie*. New York: DAW, 1982.

Seltzer, Mark. *Serial Killers: Death and Life in America's Would Culture*. New York: Routledge, 1998.

Seppala, Emma, Timothy Rossomando, and James R. Doty. "Social Connection and Compassion:

Important Predictors of Health and Well-Being." *Social Research: An International Quarterly* 80.2 (2013): 411–30.

Shakespeare, William. *Romeo and Juliet*. Edited by Jill Levenson. Oxford: Oxford University Press, 2000.

Shan, Darren. *Zom-B*. London: Simon & Schuster, 2012.

_____. *Zom-B: Underground*. London: Simon & Schuster, 2013.

Shaw, Valerie. *The Short Story: A Critical Introduction*. London: Routledge, 2013.

Shelley, Mary. *The Last Man*. Ware, UK: Wordsworth Classics, 2004.

Shepard, Lucius. *Green Eyes*. New York: Ace, 1984.

"Show Me the Science." *Handwashing: Clean Hands Save Lives*. Centers for Disease Control and Prevention. 22 Feb. 2016. http://www.cdc.gov/handwashing/show-me-the-science-hand-sanitizer.html.

Simmons, Dan. "This Year's Class Picture." In Adams, *The Living Dead*, 5–22.

Sinclair, May. "The Novels of Dorothy Richardson." *The Egoist*, 5.4 (1908): 57–59.

Skipp, John, and Craig Spector. *Book of the Dead*. New York: Bantam, 1989.

Sloterdijk, Peter. *Rage and Time*. New York: Columbia University Press, 2012.

Slotkin, Richard. *Gunfighter Nation: The Myth of the Frontier in Twentieth Century America*. Norman, OK: University of Oklahoma Press, 1998.

_____. *Regeneration Through Violence: The Mythology of the American Frontier, 1600–1860*. Middletown, CT: Wesleyan University Press, 1973.

Smith, Tara. "Interview with *Warm Bodies* Author Isaac Marion." ScienceBlogswww. 7 Mar. 2013. http://scienceblogs.com/aetiology/2013/03/07/interview-with-warm-bodies-author-isaac-marion/.

Sorensen, Leif. "Against the Post-Apocalyptic: Narrative Closure in Colson Whitehead's *Zone One*." *Contemporary Literature* 55.3 (2014): 559–92.

Southey, Robert. *History of Brazil*. Volume 3. London: Longman, 1819.

Stam, Robert. "The Politics of Postmodernism: Introduction." In *Film and Theory: An Anthology*, edited by Robert Stam and Toby Miller, 753–57. Malden, MA: Blackwell, 2000.

Steele, Claude. "A Threat in the Air: How Stereotypes Shape Intellectual Identity and Performance." *American Psychologist* 52.6 (1997): 613–29.

Stewart, George R. *Earth Abides*. 1949. New York: Ballantine, 2006.

Stewart, James L. "Zombies V. Newsies: Novel Offers Post-Apocalyptic Critique of Journalism." *ASJMC Insights* Spring 2014. http://asjmc.org/publications/insights/spring2014.pdf.

Strong, Jeremy R. "Destruction from Within: The Significance of the Resurgence of Zombies in Film and Fiction." *Critical Issues* May 2013. https://www.inter-disciplinary.net/critical-issues/wp-content/uploads/2013/05/strongapopaper.pdf.

Swanson, Carl Joseph. "'The Only Metaphor Left': Colson Whitehead's *Zone One* and Zombie Narrative Form." *Genre* 47.3 (2014): 379–405.

Swanwick, Michael. "The Dead." In Adams, *The Living Dead*, 98–107.

Teitelbaum, Michael, and Jon Apple. *The Very Hungry Zombie: A Parody*. New York: Skyhorse Publishers, 2012.

Terkel, Studs. *The Good War: An Oral History of World War II*. New York: New Press, 2013.

Thomas, Michael, and Nick Thomas. *Zompoc: How to Survive a Zombie Apocalypse*. London: Swordworks, 2009.

Thompson, Julia. *First Year Teacher's Survival Guide: Ready-to-Use Strategies, Tools & Activities for Meeting the Challenges of Each School Day*. San Francisco: Wiley, 2009.

Todorov, Tzvetan. *The Fantastic: A Structural Approach to a Literary Genre*. New York: Cornell University Press, 1975.

Tremayne, Peter. *Zombie!* New York: St. Martin's, 1981.

Turner, Joan Frances. *Dust*. New York: Ace Books, 2010.

Turse, Nick. *Kill Anything That Moves: The Real American War in Vietnam*. New York: Picador, 2009.

Venables, Toby. "Zombies, a Lost Literary Heritage and the Return of the Repressed." In Hubner, Leaning, and Manning, 208–23.

Wald, Priscilla. *Contagious: Cultures, Carriers, and the Outbreak Narrative*. Durham: Duke University Press, 2008.

Waller, Gregory A. *The Living and the Undead: From Stoker's Dracula to Romero's Dawn of the Dead*. 1986. Urbana: University of Illinois Press, 2010.

Walpole, Horace. *The Castle of Otranto and the Mysterious Mother*. Edited by Frederick S. Frank. Peterborough: Broadview, 2003.

_____. "Preface to the Second Edition." In Walpole, 65–70.

Walsh, Kenneth. "The Battle Cry That Backfired on Howard 'The Scream' Dean." *U.S. News and World Report*, 17 Jan. 2008. http://www.usnews.com/news/articles/2008/01/17/the-battle-cry-that-backfired.

Waters, Daniel. *Generation Dead*. New York: Hyperion, 2008.

Waugh, Patricia. *Metafiction: The Theory and Practice of Self-Conscious Fiction*. New York: Routledge, 1984.

Webb, Kenneth. *Zombie*. Biltmore Theatre, New York City. 10 Feb. 1932.

Weeks, James H. *Among Congo Cannibals*. Philadelphia: J.B. Lipincott Company, 1913.

Wellington, David. "Good People." In Adams, *The Living Dead 2*, 121–34.

_____. *Monster Island: A Zombie Novel*. Philadelphia: Running Press, 2006.

"What College Kids Can Learn from World War Z." *NPR Books*. 10 Sept. 2012. http://www.npr.org/2012/09/07/160758839/what-college-kids-can-learn-from-the-zombie-war.

"When Zombies Attack Lower Manhattan." *NPR.Org*, 20 July 2012. http://www.npr.org/templates/transcript/transcript.php?storyId=157046000

Whitehead, Colson. *Apex Hides the Hurt*. 2006. New York: Anchor, 2007.

_____. *The Intuitionist*. New York: Anchor, 1999.

_____. *John Henry Days*. 2001. New York: Anchor, 2002.

_____. *Sag Harbor*. New York: Doubleday, 2009.

_____. "The Year of Living Postracially." *New York Times*, 3 Nov. 2009. http://www.nytimes.com/2009/11/04/opinion/04whitehead.html.

_____. *Zone One: A Novel*. New York: Doubleday, 2011.

Williams, Evan Calder. *Combined and Uneven Apocalypse*. Winchester: Zero Books, 2011.

Wilson, Daniel. *How to Survive a Robot Uprising: Tips on Defending Yourself Against the Coming Rebellion*. New York: Bloomsbury USA, 2005.

Winlow, Simon, and Steve Hall. "Gone Shopping: Inarticulate Politics in the English Riots of 2011." In Briggs, *English Riots*, 149–67.

Wiseman, John. *SAS Survival Handbook: The Definitive Survival Guide*. London: Harper-Collins Publishers, 2011.

_____. *SAS Urban Survival Handbook: How to Protect Yourself Against Terrorism, Natural Disasters, Fires, Home Invasions, and Everyday Health and Safety Hazards*. London: Skyhorse Publishing Company, 2013.

Wittgenstein, Ludwig. *Philosophical Investigations*. Translated by G. E. M. Anscombe. New York: Macmillan, 1968.

Woerner, Meredith. "The Director of *Warm Bodies and 50/50* Thinks You're the Real Zombie." Io9www. 30 Jan. 2013. http://io9.gizmodo.com/5980243/warm-bodies-director-thinks-youre-the-real-zombie.

Wright, Austin. "The Writer Meets the Critic on the Great Novel / Short Story Divide." *Journal of Modern Literature* 20.1 (1996): 13–19.

Wurth, Kiene Brillenburg. "Posthuman Selves, Assembled Textualities: Remediated Print in the Digital Age." *Between Page and Screen: Remaking Literature Through Cinema and Cyberspace*. Ed. Kiene Brillenburg Wurth. New York: Fordham University Press, 2012.

Zani, Steven, and Kevin Meaux. "Lucio Fulci and the Decaying Definition of Zombie Narratives." In Christie and Lauro, 98–115.

Žižek, Slavoj. "Fantasy as a Political Category: A Lacanian Approach." In *The Žižek Reader*, edited by Elisabeth Wright and Edmond Wright. Oxford: Blackwell, 1999, 87–101.

_____. "Shoplifters of the World Unite." *London Review of Books*, 19 Aug. 2011. http://www.lrb.co.uk/2011/08/19/slavoj-zizek/shoplifters-of-the-world-unite.

"Zombie Nation." *Guns & Ammo*. Outdoor Sportsman Group, n.d. http://www.gunsandammo.com/blogs/zombie-nation/.

About the Contributors

Kyle William **Bishop** is a third-generation professor at Southern Utah University, where he directs the Honors Program and teaches courses in film and screen studies, American literature and culture, and fantasy/horror literature. He has published a variety of articles on popular culture and cinematic adaptation, including two monographs on zombies in popular culture: *American Zombie Gothic* (2010) and *How Zombies Conquered Popular Culture* (2015).

Arnold T. **Blumberg** is a zombie scholar and expert known as "Doctor of the Dead." He is coauthor of *Zombiemania: 80 Movies to Die For* and appears in the feature documentaries *Doc of the Dead, The Walkers Among Us,* and *The 50 Best Horror Movies You've Never Seen.* He has contributed chapters to *Triumph of the Walking Dead; Braaaiiinnnsss! From Academics to Zombies,* and *The Undead and Theology* (which was nominated for a Stoker award).

Kevin Alexander **Boon** teaches writing, film, and literature for Penn State Mont Alto. He is the author or editor of eleven books, including *Script Culture and the American Screenplay* (20008), the novel *Absolute Zero* (1999), and a number of books on Kurt Vonnegut, F. Scott Fitzgerald, Ernest Hemingway, Virginia Woolf, and other writers. He was nominated for a Pushcart Prize in 2011 for his short story "The Angels of Marie Fontaine."

Steven **Holmes** is a lecturer at the University of Hawai'i at Mānoa. His research interests include genre theory, particularly contemporary fantasy and science fiction, rhetorical theory, Shakespeare studies, visual culture, and the digital humanities. His work has appeared in *War Gothic in Literature and Culture, Gender and Sexuality in Contemporary Popular Fantasy,* and *Beyond the Frontier: Innovations in First Year Composition.*

Laura **Hubner** is a senior lecturer in film at the University of Winchester, UK. She is working on a monograph, *Fairytale and Gothic Horror* (forthcoming), and is author of *The Films of Ingmar Bergman* (2007), editor of *Valuing Films* (2011), and coeditor of *Framing Film* (2012) and *The Zombie Renaissance in Popular Culture* (2014).

Dawn **Keetley** is a professor of English and teaches horror/gothic literature, film, and television at Lehigh University in Bethlehem, Pennsylvania. She has published on AMC's *The Walking Dead* in the *Journal of the Fantastic in the Arts* and the *Journal of Popular Television*, is the editor of "*We're All Infected*" (2014), and the coeditor of a second collection on *The Walking Dead*, "*There's Us and the Dead*" (forthcoming).

Marcus **Leaning** is a senior fellow in the School of Media and Film at the University of Winchester. In 2011, together with colleagues from the school, he organized the Zombosium, a symposium on zombies. The Zombosium attracted international attention, and he regularly speaks to the press on the topic of zombies. Together with Paul Manning and Laura Hubner, he coedited *The Zombie Renaissance in Popular Culture* (2014).

Wylie **Lenz** is an assistant professor of English at Florida Polytechnic University in Lakeland, Florida. He received an MFA in creative writing and a Ph.D. in English from the University of Florida. His research interests include American literature and popular culture. He is coeditor (with Stephanie Boluk) of *Generation Zombie* (2011), and a forthcoming collection on representations of poverty in popular culture.

Bernard **Perron** is a professor of film and game studies at Université de Montréal. He has coedited *The Video Game Theory Reader 1* (2003), *The Video Game Theory Reader 2* (2009), *The Routledge Companion to Video Games Studies* (2014), *The Archives* (2014), *Z pour Zombies* (2015), *Video Games and the Mind* (2016), and *Horror Video Games* (2009). He has also written *Silent Hill* (2012) in the Landmark Video Games book series.

W. Scott **Poole** is a professor of history at the College of Charleston, as well as an author and historian. His work includes *In the Mountains of Madness* (2016). He is also the author of *Monsters in America*, which won that John Cawelti Award from the Popular Culture Association in 2011. He is working on a manuscript about World War I and the origins of horror in film, literature, and the arts.

Cory James **Rushton** is an associate professor in the Department of English at St. Francis Xavier University (Nova Scotia, Canada). He has coedited collections on the zombie, medieval romance, medieval sexuality, and Thomas Malory's *Morte Darthur*. He has published on texts ranging from Irish zombie films to Chaucer's *Troilus and Criseyde* to Terry Pratchett.

Kelli **Shermeyer** is a doctoral candidate in English at the University of Virginia and a theater director, producer, and dramaturg. She is interested in several areas: representations of violence; texts about war, catastrophe, and apocalypse; site-specific performance projects; and the fantastic in art and literature. She also teaches courses on modern and contemporary literature, political theater, and the zombie as a literary and cultural phenomenon.

Jesse **Stommel** is a documentary filmmaker who teaches courses about digital pedagogy, film, horror, and new media. He is the executive director of the Division of Teaching and Learning Technologies at University of Mary Washington. He is also cofounder of *Digital Pedagogy Lab* and *Hybrid Pedagogy: a digital journal of learning, teaching, and technology*. He experiments relentlessly with learning interfaces, both digital and analog, and works to emphasize new forms of collaboration.

Angela **Tenga** teaches courses on literature, popular culture, and history at the Florida Institute of Technology. She has published two articles on AMC's *The Walking Dead*, and is coeditor with Dawn Keetley of *Plant Horror* (2017). She earned her doctoral degree from Purdue University, and her research interests include monster studies, representations of criminality and violence, early English literature, and the renewal of the medieval in modern popular culture.

Robert G. **Weiner** is a popular culture librarian at Texas Tech University. He teaches honors classes related to popular culture, including one about zombies. He is the editor/coeditor of *From the Arthouse to the Grindhouse*, *Cinema Inferno*, *Graphic Novels and Comics in the Classroom*, *Marvel Comics into Film*, and *Marvel Graphic Novels: An Annotated Guide.* He has also published a wide array of articles and book chapters related to film, music, comics, and popular culture.

Index

GR 581 .W75 2017